Lecture Notes in Computer Science 4868

Commenced Publication in 1973
Founding and Former Series Editors:
Gerhard Goos, Juris Hartmanis, and Jan van Leeuwen

Christian Peter   Russell Beale (Eds.)

Affect and Emotion in Human-Computer Interaction

From Theory to Applications

Springer

Volume Editors

Christian Peter
Fraunhofer Institute for Computer Graphics
Joachim-Jungius-Str. 11, 18059 Rostock, Germany
E-mail: christian.peter@igd-r.fraunhofer.de

Russell Beale
University of Birmingham, School of Computer Science
Edgbaston, Birmingham, B15 2TT, UK
E-mail: r.beale@cs.bham.ac.uk

Library of Congress Control Number: 2008933384

CR Subject Classification (1998): H.5, I.2.7, I.4.8, I.5

LNCS Sublibrary: SL 3 – Information Systems and Application, incl. Internet/Web and HCI

ISSN   0302-9743
ISBN-10   3-540-85098-8 Springer Berlin Heidelberg New York
ISBN-13   978-3-540-85098-4 Springer Berlin Heidelberg New York

Springer is a part of Springer Science+Business Media

springer.com

© Springer-Verlag Berlin Heidelberg 2008
Printed in Germany

Typesetting: Camera-ready by author, data conversion by Scientific Publishing Services, Chennai, India
Printed on acid-free paper   SPIN: 12445844   06/3180   5 4 3 2 1 0

Preface

Interacting with computers is ever changing; the activities computers are used for, the domains they are used in, the people who use them, and the way that they are used have been constantly evolving. But over the past few years an additional dimension has been added to this interaction, which considers the utility and effectiveness of incorporating emotion into the interface. Over ten years ago, Rosalind Picard coined the phrase "affective computing" for computing that relates to, arises from, or deliberately influences emotion or other affective phenomena[1]. Since then, numerous researchers all over the world have devoted themselves to studying the role affect and emotion play in our interactions with technology. The affective computing community is growing rapidly. A number of workshops, symposia, and even conferences make emotion in HCI their subject. This book actually developed out of some of those events. When Springer approached us to compile a book on the subject, we were just organizing the third workshop on emotion in HCI at the British HCI Group's annual conference, held in the UK. While the workshop had numerous contributions from the traditionally very active British and European community, we also received contributions from overseas.

We decided early on not to make this merely a book about the workshops, but to broaden it: this book is intended to give a wider overview on the developments in the field. We hence decided to also issue an open call for contributions. We aimed for a balanced report with as wide a spectrum of research presented as possible, addressing the topics

- Theoretical foundations (e.g., emotion representations, ethical and legal issues)
- Emotion and affect as input (e.g., sensor systems, multimodal sensor networks, sensor fusion, data enhancement and analysis)
- Emotion and affect as output (e.g., desktop applications and agents, Web-based services and applications, presence and smart environments, mobile applications, robots)
- User experience studies, usability, and design issues
- Community reports (e.g., on related research networks, national and international research programs, or standardization efforts)

This list evolved out of our experiences at the workshops, reflecting the topics people were most interested in. Looking at the contributions and comparing them with the list above, many of our experiences at the workshops are confirmed, namely that people show an interest for many aspects of this young discipline as well as awareness of its challenges and risks. There is somewhat of a bias towards applications and studies, rather fewer on sensing, and actually none on ethics (although at each workshop all participants agree this is a very important subject!). The community section was also mainly ignored, which might be interpreted as the affective computing research

---

[1] Picard, R.W. (1997). Affective Computing. M.I.T. Press, Cambridge, MA.

landscape being fairly fragmented at present—but this scattering of work reflects the fact that this area is a relatively young, fast-moving field.

We got numerous high-quality submissions covering most of the themes, which made it very difficult for us to decide on which should be included in the book and which not. All papers were extensively refereed, and revised by the authors, and if we had accepted all submissions that were suggested for inclusion by the scientific committee members, the book would nearly be twice as big as it is now. So we had to decide against many very good papers, from known and (as yet) unknown authors.

Finally, based on the accepted contributions, we restructured the book as follows:

- *Theoretical Considerations:* with contributions raising awareness on typical pitfalls and shortcomings of currently common approaches, suggesting new views, and working on well-known problems or open issues
- *Sensing Emotions:* namely, on speech-related issues and multimodal data fusion
- *User Experience and Design:* with interesting studies and suggestions on how to motivate and make use of affect and emotion in real-world applications
- *Affective Applications:* the largest section, showcasing a wide range of projects across diverse domains

We hope this fine selection of the state of the art will make its contribution to providing solid foundations for this fast-growing research field, making it less fragmented, and giving up-to-date orientation on the developments in the domain.

We would like to thank all members of the Scientific Committee for their valuable assistance, feedback, and suggestions, and all authors who took the time to write about their fascinating ideas, projects, and results. Thanks also to the Springer team, for giving us the opportunity to compile this volume as well as for their highly professional support. And finally: thanks to you for considering this book worth reading!

June 2008   Christian Peter
                                                                            Russell Beale

Organization

Scientific Committee

Elisabeth Andre	Augsburg University, Germany
Ruth Aylett	Heriot-Watt University Edinburgh, UK
Nick Campbell	ATR, Japan
Lola Cañamero	University of Hertfordshire, UK
Pabini Gabriel-Petit	Spirit Softworks, USA
Roland Göcke	Seeing Machines & Australian National University, Australia
Kristina Höök	KTH/SICS, Sweden
Nicola Millard	British Telecom plc, UK
Ana Paiva	Instituto Superior Técnico, Purtugal
Karina Oertel	Fraunhofer IGD Rostock, Germany
Marc Schröder	DFKI, Germany
Jianhua Tao	Chinese Academy of Sciences, China
John Waterworth	Umeå University, Sweden
Robert Ward	University of Huddersfield, UK
Ian Wilson	neon.AI, Japan

Table of Contents

Affective Applications

The Role of Affect and Emotion in HCI

Russell Beale[1] and Christian Peter[2]

[1] Advanced Interaction Group, School of Computer Science, University of Birmingham,
Edgbaston, Birmingham, B15 2TT, UK
R.Beale@cs.bham.ac.uk
[2] Fraunhofer Institute for Computer Graphics, J. Jungius Str. 11,
18059 Rostock, Germany
christian.peter@igd-r.fraunhofer.de

Abstract. Affect and emotion play an important role in our everyday lives: they are present whatever we do, wherever we are, wherever we go, without us being aware of them for much of the time. When it comes to interaction, be it with humans, technology, or humans via technology, we suddenly become more aware of emotion, either by seeing the other's emotional expression, or by not getting an emotional response while anticipating it. Given this, it seems only sensible to commit to affect and emotion in human-computer interaction, to investigate the underlying principles, to study the role they play, to develop methods to quantify them, and to finally build applications that make use of them. In this introductory chapter we discuss and give short accounts on present developments in the field, covering theoretical issues, user experience and design aspects, sensing issues, and report on some affective applications that have been developed.

Keywords: Affect, Emotion, Human-Computer Interaction, Case Studies, Theory, Design, Affect Detection.

1 Introduction

When one talks of giving emotions to computer systems, it is hard not to imagine the science fiction futures embodied in books and film, that of computers becoming self-aware sentient machines that then suffer the same dreams of self-importance or even megalomania that afflict their human creators. These systems tend to go bad and try to take over the world, and have to be brought back down to size by a hero who engages in some daring-do and in doing so reasserts the values of being properly human. However, the reality is that most researchers in the field are not trying to produce this future, real or imagined. Adding emotion into computers is not about making new forms of artificially intelligent, human-like systems – as Rosalind Picard wrote more than ten years ago:

"Computers do not need affective abilities for the fanciful goal of becoming humanoids, they need them for a meeker and more practical goal: to function with intelligence and sensitivity towards humans" ([1], p. 247).

C. Peter and R. Beale (Eds.): Affect and Emotion in HCI, LNCS 4868, pp. 1–11, 2008.
© Springer-Verlag Berlin Heidelberg 2008

In our everyday interactions with other humans, we encounter emotional responses all the time, whether it be others' emotions, or our reactions to their activities. These emotions influence all parties' responses and approaches to interacting with each other; they pervade every aspect of interchanges between people so deeply that we are often only consciously aware of extreme ones in such exchanges – of anger, rage, upset, sudden love, and so on. But the influence of emotion is deeper than this – it affects our attention, our perceptions, our memory and decision-making abilities. It also makes us somewhat uncomfortable when emotion is absent – the cold, dead feeling when there is just a machine to deal with, or when dealing with people who are behaving like machines – call centres, complaint lines, and so on. Even then, emotion is not completely absent – these approaches raise all sorts of emotions within us, and we react in different ways to those that we may normally do, often in ways that are ultimately less productive for us. A personal example demonstrates this most effectively – and most examples tend to be personal, since that is exactly what emotions are. One of us recently started getting emails from a recruitment company, telling us how interested he would be in the abilities of this candidate they had found for us. Well, he wasn't interested, and rang them to politely ask to be removed from their email lists. After a brief apology, he was assured that he had been so removed, and thought nothing more about it, until the next week, when he was offered the services of a wonderful candidate with great Java skills. It was late in the day after a stressful meeting, and, for whatever reason, it made him furious. Now, the rational, unemotional thing to do would have been to waste no more time, and delete it – or mark it as junk, so that the junk filter would continue to delete these in future. But because he was peeved, he scrolled to the bottom of the email, found the contact number of the recruitment consultant, and rang him, berating him for his IT department's inefficiency, and making him promise to see to it personally that he wouldn't be disturbed again. He put the phone down, feeling absurdly, childishly pleased, and mildly embarrassed at the same time at the conversation he had just had. Why did he do it? There are certainly several aspects playing a role but what is sure is that emotion played a very big part here. The emotions were strong, motivating, effective at spurring him to action – but also transient, and possibly unproductive in terms of the action that ensued. The point is we react according to both our logical, rational selves and to the deep elements that respond to emotional stimulus. And the situation is deeper than just us as humans having emotions. Reeves and Nass [2] investigated a number of scenarios that demonstrated that we treat computers as if they were social actors – i.e. as if they had emotions, feelings and intelligence too, even if we know that we are dealing with just a computer. Given this, it seems only sensible to try and utilize this to make our dealings with machines smoother, simpler, and more appropriate, and if they are to act in a more appropriate way, then they need to exhibit the emotional responses that we ascribe to them anyway. Furthermore, it seems to us that, as digital systems become ever more prevalent and ubiquitous, there will be ever-increasing need for us to interact with computer systems. With human relationships, emotion starts to surface after the initial acquaintance, as one gets to know more about the other party in the interaction – indeed, this is part of the getting to know them; what makes them tick, what makes them happy, sad, angry, and so on are all elements of the progressive disclosure that we engage in as we develop from acquaintances towards colleagues and possibly further into friendship. So it should be for these protracted, ongoing relationships that we are now building with our computer systems, for it is becoming rarer to find one-time interactions, and much more common to find areas in which we have much longer term involvement. These interactions may be sporadic and disjointed, but they span increasing amounts of time: just consider the increasing frequency with which people order groceries online, buy airline tickets and use the online checking facility, or drive everywhere with their satellite navigation system giving them directions. This increasing trend for extended, repeated relationships with technology suggests that we need to consider further aspects of interaction than have traditionally been covered, especially those that relate to longer-term relationships, and hence emotion has become a very interesting area for many. This is not to argue that all interactions should be emotionally-mediated, or even that long-term ones need be so – we find it hard to envisage the benefits of an emotional airline booking system, whether it was detecting our emotions, or displaying some of its own. However, we do see some benefit of developing a stronger, more personal relationship with an in-car navigation system, which could both learn the sorts of routes preferred to drive and so offer more than the choice of shortest or fastest – and one that nagged us if we were to drive too fast, especially if it was late at night and we seemed tired, or stressed, may eventually convey some significant benefits.

The present book provides an account of the latest work on variety of aspects related to affect and emotion in human-technology interaction. It covers theoretical issues, user experience and design aspects, sensing issues, and reports on some affective applications that have been developed.

The first five papers deal with general **Theoretical Considerations.** We start with a paper from Leysia Palen and Susanne Bødker, *Don't get emotional!* (Chapter 2). While this sounds a little provocative in a book on affect and emotion, Palen and Bødker are indeed right: they warn us that while the community is currently very euphoric about what has been done and what seems to be possible with the technologies at hand, we should be careful not to watch out for emotions everywhere and anytime. We should not put the focus onto emotion for all our endeavours, but rather keep it on the interaction and overall experience, and how it should be conceptualized in the particular context, *including* affective aspects. Palen and Bødker state that "emotion is so large an idea that it can be descriptive of all kinds of interaction and non-interaction, meaning that it is fundamental to these things, and so therefore it is not powerful to us as analysts of human computer interaction. We need instead ... to rely on more pointed understandings of what interaction means in different contexts and at different units of analysis, and give those experiences their proper notice and place." This article reminds us that affect and emotion are just parts of a bigger, very complex whole which needs to be conceptualized anew for each considered scenario. In fact, affect and emotion can, in many cases, be considered as "just" additional contextual information for the system. If we keep this in mind when designing affective systems or applications, the chances increase for our products being accepted as useful and meaningful. If not, if we put all our efforts in the emotion part and pass over the traditional design aspects, it is likely that our system will not attract much positive attention. If you are a designer and have proudly demonstrated your affective product to ordinary people, you might have experienced that heartsinking feedback from them: but what is it good for? We certainly have. And in the course of discussion it often works out that the main value of the application is *not* the affective bit, but the bigger idea behind it. The affective component just adds functionality that makes the product friendly, nice, attentive, … more likable. And that's what affective computing should be all about: making systems more pleasant for the user, and the interaction with it a positive experience. The examples in the Applications section of this book provide good evidence for this. There are times when the affective component is stronger than this, however: for some applications, the incorporation of emotion produces a much stronger experience for the user, and this may trigger some significant change – an alteration in mood, or even in long-term behaviours. A functionally similar system without the emotional contribution may not be sufficiently engaging to demonstrate that effect.

William Bainbridge contributes an essay on personality and its influence on and importance for affective interaction (*Computational Affective Sociology* - Chapter 3). He encourages us to draw on the rich and well grounded knowledge of social sciences, suggesting that use of sociological methods will benefit the design of interactive software. He is in a sense in line with Palen & Bødker, arguing that personality is just another facet in the colourful picture of human-computer interaction. Just as Palen and Bødker declare that knowledge on affect and emotion itself is meaningless for a system without knowledge on context and the interaction involved, Bainbridge adds that knowledge of the user, here specifically the personality traits, is an important aspect for systems to analyze and make use of emotion-related information. In fact one wonders how interaction designers could do so long without considering these aspects. Or, put the other way, it becomes clearer now why so many people can't get on with the one product but with others, while other people experience it exactly the other way around. Consider the Big Five personality model [3] favoured in Bainbridge's article. Its five dimensions (Neuroticism, Extraversion, Openness, Agreeableness, Conscientiousness) clearly specify aspects of a user's behaviour pattern, the user experience and attitude towards the product and interaction with it. Neuroticism deals with the user's experience of emotions, i.e. if the user is emotionally stable or tends to experience negative emotions more easily. Extraversion marks the tendency of being active and open for (inter-personal) interactions. Taking this further and considering Reeves' and Nass' remarks on computers as social actors [2], extraversion would indicate a person's tendency to actively engage with a system or to wait for being invited to interactions by it. Openness adds to this a person's curiosity and openness for new ideas and experiences. For interactions, it reveals if a user is inclined to explore a system's capabilities and new interactions out of curiosity, or if the system is expected to stick to traditionally known interaction patterns. Agreeableness is about a person tending to be cooperative and trustful, or sceptical and hostile; for designing interactions this is of particular importance since gaining the trust and cooperation of the user are often keys for successful interactions. Conscientiousness finally describes the tendency to act diligently and planned versus superficially and spontaneously. This might be interesting for designing personalized agents or other supportive applications. These five dimensions, even in their raw form, provide some interesting concepts with which to analyse problems and interactions, and to guide the design of solutions to them, depending on the people they are meant to interact with and the impression that they are trying to convey.

The fourth chapter, *Comparing Two Emotion Models for Deriving Affective States from Physiological Data* by Lichtenstein et al. also elaborates on research results from other domains and their applicability in the HCI context. Their focus is on applicability of emotion models which have their roots in psychology. Those models are often applied to study affect or emotion without thorough reflections in the HCI domain. That the choice of the right model is a delicate issue has been addressed before by others [4, 5, 6], as has the question if models from psychology can be used without alterations in HCI [e.g. 7]. Lichtenstein et al. now provide a study comparing the two emotion models mostly used in HCI, the Basic Emotion model [8] and the dimensional approach of valence and arousal [9]. The aim of their study was to investigate on the models' suitability for self-assessment of emotions as well as for deriving affective states from physiological readings. Their results can be used to negotiate between the advocates for the one or the other model: according to Lichtenstein et al., the Basic Emotion model is better suited for assigning pre-selected states to physiological patterns while the dimensional approach has been found to be more accurate for self-assessments. On the other hand, the participants of their study found it more difficult to assess their affective state using Lang's [10] self-assessment manikins (SAM) used for valence and arousal measures, compared to pictures and descriptive words for Ekman's basic emotions. How these findings affect each other (i.e. how accurate are results which are based on a model assessed as difficult to use, and how useful are results based on pre-selected states) is also briefly discussed by Lichtenstein et al., but remains open as for now.

Chapter 5, *Consideration of Multiple Components of Emotions in Human-Technology Interaction* builds on another model to describe emotions. Mahlke and Minge use Scherer's appraisal approach [11] to analyze emotions in a multi-component fashion. According to Scherer's component process model, emotional states can be seen as being composed of states of five components: cognitive appraisal, physiological activation, motor expression, behaviour intentions, and subjective feeling. Mahlke and Minge now make use of these five components to better distinguish between the effects each of them has on the overall emotional experience. While this approach faces new challenges in accessing the particular information, we think it opens a new perspective for better understanding and exploiting emotion information in interactive systems.

Taking this section's papers that discuss psychological emotion theories, we can see that their application to interactive systems analysis and design raise as many questions as they give answers – there seems to be no one right model, but a range of approaches that all contribute different facets to our understanding. Indeed, one of the other open questions in the field is whether there needs to be an expansion or alternative modelling paradigm for human-computer emotional modelling – in other words, are there key differences between human emotions and human-computer emotions?

The last contribution to the Theoretical Considerations draws our attention to the audio channel. Tajadura-Jiménez and Västfjäll give account on the so far quite rare research on the influence of sound on affect and introduce results of a study they performed. In *Auditory-Induced Emotion: A Neglected Channel for Communication in Human-Computer Interaction* (Chapter 6) they suggest that acoustic stimuli can be used to influence a user's emotional state in a gentle, almost unnoticeable manner. Since humans can and often do perceive sounds without turning their attention to them, this channel seems to be designated for stimulating a certain mood or emotional state (just think of the different music styles people pick for different activities). To make use of auditory induced emotion, Tajadura-Jiménez and Västfjäll suggest considering four aspects of affective reactions to sound which they call the physical, psychological, spatial, and cross-modal determinants. Physical aspects refer to qualitative characteristics of a sound, e.g. intensity and frequency. While it seems obvious that a loud sound is more unpleasant the louder it gets, it is interesting to learn that certain frequency bands are experienced differently as pleasant or unpleasant depending on the intensity of the signal. The psychological determinants which deal with the subjective judgment of a sound are more difficult to assess. There are differences in perceiving artificial sounds (e.g. the fan in a laptop computer) and natural sounds (e.g. a dog barking, birdsong, or footsteps). Additionally, natural sounds can be divided further as to their affective evaluations, depending on their sources and our emotional associations with them. It also seems clear that the emotional evaluation of a sound should be strongly dependant on the context the user is in. The full sound of a car engine might be enjoyable to hear for the young driver, but not enjoyable for the person just crossing the road. The sound of footsteps might be relieving for someone who found himself locked in a museum, but scary for someone who thought to be alone at home. So again, context and emotion seem to be very closely related to each other. For the spatial dimension, Tajadura-Jiménez and Västfjäll show that spatial information is important for emotional assessment of auditory information and that the subjective sense of presence will increase with the spatial resolution of the sound. From this it can be concluded that the degree of immersiveness into a task or activity can be influenced by spatial characteristics of sound used. Finally, the cross-modal determinant is about how an affective evaluation of information from one channel (e.g. sound) interferes with the affective evaluation of information from other channels, like sight or touch. For instance, there is evidence for the perception of visual information being influenced by affective sounds. This underlines the importance of the audio channel when it comes to effectively conveying affective or emotional information.

Vogt et al. also deal with the audio channel as they open the **Sensing** section with an overview and guidelines on how to address the technical challenges of extracting emotion information from speech in the HCI context (Chapter 7: *Automatic Recognition of Emotions from Speech*). They begin with more general theoretical and practical considerations of emotion recognition in speech and point out that all results reported in scientific papers so far are only of limited value for real-world application designers, due to a number of restrictions. First, most of them work on acted data – even acted by trained actors with often exaggerated, single emotions. This makes the corpus less valuable for real-world application designers since in real life emotions are usually quite shallow and might overlap with each other (known as "blended" or "mixed emotions"). Second, reported results are often not comparable due to different underlying corpora and/or the different application fields they have been designed for, so their results can only provide for interesting considerations for building one's own dedicated corpus. Last but not least there are high requirements on speed, robustness and accuracy of real-time emotion recognition algorithms, since failure of one of these might result in the application being not acceptable to users. But Vogt et al. also raise hope. They suggest that it does not always need to be the best algorithm available, that not all speech features need to be considered, and that one could indeed try to work with one of the standard (i.e. staged) corpora to train one's classifiers, and one can get satisfying results nonetheless. It all depends on the requirements of the application and the context. Emotion recognition in general tends not to be perfect – not by machines, nor by humans. And as we have learned before, emotion information is just one piece of the bigger picture, so it should be sufficient for emotion recognition to provide just hints on this ever-changing element of the context.

The two other articles in the Sensing section report on approaches to increase accuracy of emotion recognition by merging results from different modalities. Castellano et al. (*Emotion recognition through multiple modalities* – Chapter 8) merge information from facial expressions, body gestures and speech. They report on two approaches to this. While in the first they perform modality specific classifications and merge the results, in the second they put the features of all modalities in one large feature set and work with these merged data. They found that by merging multiple modalities, recognition rates can increase by up to thirty percent compared to classification results of single modalities. Comparing the two approaches, they observed that merging data at the feature level yields slightly better results than merging them at the decision level, at least for their specific setup.

While Castellano et al. use acted data and put restrictions on subjects' clothing, faces, and the background, the focus of McIntyre and Göcke's Chapter 9 is on emotion detection in real-world, natural settings. In *The Composite Sensing of Affect* they remark that affective expressions are very dynamic, versatile, and specific for each individual and are influenced by the context the person is in (as we already have learned). McIntyre and Göcke suggest dealing with those challenges by providing semantic clues based on background information (e.g. social, cultural, context) for reasoning about affective content in the collected sensor data. To support this process, they propose a generic model for affective communication accompanied by a domain-specific ontology, which offers a way to include context information into affective reasoning.

To sum up the sensing section, we have learned that, with the current state of the art, it is still not possible to accurately infer the whole range of affective states in real-time, in real-world settings. The main reasons for this are: first, that the corpora available to train emotion classifiers are not of sufficient quality for use in general real-world applications; second, the quality of the sensing devices is still at laboratory level, requiring well-controlled environments to provide good measurements; and third, the sheer complexity of the real world with its effect on affect and emotion in the human exposed to it. We have also learned that, because of this, we might be better off restricting ourselves to detect just a few states which can be distinguished quickly and reliably with robust algorithms, instead of trying to identify a variety of states with high uncertainties and long processing times. A common theme emerges: don't be too ambitious trying to always identify an emotion - your system will (or at least should) work as well without emotion updates every few seconds. The affective applications portrayed in this book are good examples of this.

The **User Experience and Design** section starts with an investigation in design and its influence on people's emotional experiences (Chapter 10: *Emotional Experience and Interaction Design*). Just as Don Norman and Andrew Ortony have described [12, 13], Lim et al. work out that emotions can indeed be designed, and support this with experimental results. In their study, they examine product quality based on Norman's three levels of emotional response (visceral, behavioural, reflective), by use of semantic differentials. They found that the interaction-related features of a product can significantly influence the emotional experience. They also found that functional as well as interaction qualities of a product are directly linked to emotional experiences, leading to the conclusion that emotion can't be considered independent from functionality and interaction, but result from these. This is a strong hint to designers that emotions need to be consciously designed into products and systems, since people seem to perceive emotions and their effects even if they are not explicitly present.

Walker & Prytherch's Chapter 11: *How is it for you?* motivate us to make use of psychologist's insights in behaviour theory and consider users' response to our designs as a result of the mental processes of perception, cognition, and emotion. They even suggest that design, by shaping users' experiences, can influence users' behaviour which can be exploited to motivate the user. Highly motivated users will respond more interactively to a system, which in turn will result in a better user involvement and understanding of the product. Since motivated users might be more prepared and willing to cope with usability problems, Walker & Prytherch argue for extending our perception of usability to include user motivation.

Porat and Tractinsky contribute a model to study the influence of design characteristics on user' affect and emotion in Chapter 12 *(Affect as a Mediator between Web-Store Design and Consumers' Attitudes towards the Store)*. They propose to apply Mehrabian & Russell's environmental psychology model [14] and add to it HCI design aspects. The Mehrabian-Russell model of environmental influence is well suited here since it nicely allows to apply HCI design variables as "environmental parameters" influencing peoples' emotional states, leading to an "approach/avoidance response" which in the given context corresponds to staying with or leaving that particular web site or, more generally, using or rejecting a product or service. Porat and Tractinsky offer nine propositions regarding antecedents and consequences of emotion, specifically in the context of e-commerce, most of which apply also to other products and services.

While Porat & Tractinsky focus on e-retail applications, Harbich & Hassenzahl emphasize the need of positive affective experiences to improve the overall quality of products for the workplace. In Chapter 13: *Beyond Task Completion in the Workplace* they argue that traditional usability measures should be expanded by non-utilitarian aspects. Their e^4 (for execute, engage, evolve, expand) model of user experience is especially targeted at workplace products which often suffer from the inconvenience of *having* to be used, instead of *wanting* to be used as e-stores, games or social network sites are. Particularly for these products, it is essential that their value does not draw solely on the functional, utilitarian aspects, but also on hedonistic qualities which are perceived by the user independently of the actual task to be performed. The e^4 approach is behaviour oriented, with its four components complementing each other. The Execute component considers traditional aspects related to accomplishing a task like effectiveness and efficiency. The Engage component is about motivating the user to use the product, ideally enjoying it and looking forward to use it in the future, regardless of its efficiency. An example for this is a user who prefers one text processor over another, despite the fact that composing and formatting the text might actually take longer with it. The Evolve component considers the desire of humans to explore, manipulate and adjust their environment to their ideas. The design of a product should invite exploration of its functionality and offer ways to do so in an unobtrusive manner. With the text processor example, this could be the program offering alternative or advanced editing or formatting options related to the user's context (with the user's affective state being part of that context). The fourth component, Expand, can be considered as the icing on the cake, sweetening and intensifying the effect of the other three components. If users have the opportunity to develop new working methods or usage scenarios with existing products, they feel much more involved in the whole working process, giving them the feeling of their creativity being appreciated, which will in turn make them more engaged and motivate them to evolve further approaches. A text processor offering possibilities to, for example, create document templates or dedicated plug-ins would be an example here.

The final chapter in this section explores in detail how users respond to displays of emotion from affective agents (*Simulated Emotion in Affective Embodied Agents* – Chapter 14). Creed and Beale review the research in this space, highlighting a lack of comparative studies between emotional and unemotional agents and hence a lack of definitive results to demonstrate what effects are due to emotion and what to other causes. They also highlight that emotions are developed over time, and so longer-term studies are needed in order to properly develop an understanding of this. They note that in human-human interaction, people we like and trust exert a much stronger influence on us, and examine whether this is true for human-affective agent interaction too. Would it be the case that agents that are emotionally expressive and empathetic be more able to exert an influence on users and make more significant changes to their behaviour than unemotional ones? They test this through an experiment that first checks whether users can recognize the emotions represented by the agent, and then tested user perceptions of the emotionally expressive agent as well, finding that it was more likeable and caring. This experiment forms the basis of a future longitudinal experiment into behaviour change, attempting to improve people's eating habits over a long course of interaction. This work ties in to the tenants of Walker & Prytherch, explored earlier, in that emotionally engaged users are more likely to be affected than those less engaged.

The **Affective Applications** section presents a series of contributions on systems that utilize affective components to achieve some significant interaction effect. These cover a range of domains, from call centres to gaming to car driving. In Chapter 15: *Affective Human-Robotic Interaction* Jones and Deeming look at the future for affective entertainment in the home through the development of a robotic dog that can recognize emotional states of its owner through acoustic cues in the owner's speech, and perform appropriate actions – for example, if the owner is perceived as being happy, the dog makes a playful bark and wags its tail. This makes it appear more emotionally intelligent and 'alive'. Trying to work with the mood of call centre employees is the focus of Millard and Hole's research (Chapter 16: *In the Moodie: Using 'Affective Widgets' to Help Contact Centre Advisors Fight Stress*). They create animated, affective widgets called Moodies that can be released to wander over the screen as a way of combating stress in advisors. These widgets allow the advisors to use humour to alleviate tension and stress by allowing the moodie to stomp about on the screen. By producing a visual record of their internal emotional turmoil, they are also able to indicate this to their colleagues and so get support from them as well.

In Chapter 17: *Feasibility of Personalized Affective Video Summaries* Money and Agius look at a very different application: they use physiological measurements of emotional response, and ascertain that users have significant, measurable affective responses to different video segments. This allows them to identify emotionally significant changes in video streams and opens the way for a personalized video summary that is based on key moments in the video that generate an emotional response in the viewer. This differs from the more usual approach of analysing the semantic content of the video. Jones and Sutherland (*Acoustic Emotion Recognition for Affective Computer Gaming* – Chapter 18) also use recognition of user emotion (in speech), but they take their recognized emotions and map them onto a character in a computer game, changing the characteristics of that avatar. In order to undertake some energetic activity, the character is more likely to succeed if it is imbued with upbeat, lively emotions – conversely, if the task requires slow, careful movement and planning, then downbeat, quiet emotions make it more likely that it can be successful. This game was evaluated with users, who found that it made the game more engaging, though the input of emotional state through talking to the game made some users uncomfortable. These two applications, one using detailed physiological measurements, and the other a simpler voice recognition approach, do demonstrate the wide range of potential input approaches that can be used.

Loviscach & Oswald present a system that uses either sensor input or the state of a computer game to determine probable emotional state, and then uses this information to select and play appropriate music (Chapter 19: *In the Mood: Tagging Music with Affects*). The user tags some music as it is entered into the system, which is used as the basis for an automatic tagging of the rest of the music library based on feature extraction and pattern matching with the tagged items. This has some similarities to the work by Voong & Beale [15] on tagging music with colour to represent emotion, though the playback mechanisms in their work are explicitly user defined, not calculated.

Chapter 20 presents the final paper in this section, by Jones and Jonsson (*Using Paralinguistic Cues in Speech to Recognise Emotions in Older Car Drivers*), and considers the detection of emotion in car drivers, in particular older ones, and demonstrates that it is possible to create a system that can recognize and track the emotional state of the driver. This information can then be used to modify the car's navigational voice so as to respond more appropriately to the driver. This system therefore has the potential to de-stress and relax a tense driver, or to make them happier about the conditions, which increases their concentration and hence makes them safer. Emotional systems have clearly moved on from just being interesting add-ons: this demonstrates that they have an active role to play in safety critical situations as well.

Looking at the papers collectively in this volume, we can draw some general conclusions. Firstly, the case for considering affect in interaction design seems to have been successfully made, and won – affect exists within systems whether we design it there or not, and leveraging it appropriately can lead to more engaged users who are more committed to the systems and more affected by their influences. Secondly, the field is complex: trying to develop independent scientific metrics for emotional measures often requires controlled laboratory-style setups, in which users may not behave as naturally, and in which the complex interplay of different elements that is critical to the overall effect is lost. Conversely, other more holistic experiments demonstrate something useful but potentially domain-specific, and obtaining generalisable results is hard. We have also seen, however, that if we consider emotion as a component in an interaction, our often coarse and imprecise measurements can provide sufficiently useful data for us to be able to make a significant impact on the quality of the interaction: we do not need perfection in detection or understanding in order to make a useful difference. But the major lesson is that there is a large amount of work that remains to be done before we can claim to understand, model, design and use emotion effectively in interactive systems.

References

1. Picard, R.W.: Affective Computing. MIT Press, Cambridge (1997)
2. Reeves, B., Nass, C.: The Media Equation: How People Treat Computers, Television, and New Media Like Real People and Places. The Center for the Study of Language and Information Publications (1996)
3. Wiggins, J.S. (ed.): The five-factor model of personality: Theoretical perspectives. Guilford, New York (1996)
4. Russell, J.A.: How shall an emotion be called? In: Plutchik, R., Conte, H. (eds.) Circumplex Models of Personality and Emotion, pp. 205–220. APA, Washington (1997)
5. Douglas-Cowie, E., et al.: HUMAINE deliverable D5g: Mid Term Report on DatabaseExemplarProgress(2006),
   http://emotion-research.net/deliverables/D5g%20final.pdf
6. Schröder, M., Devillers, L., Karpouzis, K., Martin, J.-C., Pelachaud, C., Peter, C., Pirker, H., Schuller, B., Tao, J., Wilson, I.: What should a generic emotion markup language be able to represent? In: Paiva, A., Prada, R., Picard, R.W. (eds.) ACII 2007. LNCS, vol. 4738, pp. 440–451. Springer, Heidelberg (2007)
7. Peter, C., Herbon, A.: Emotion Representation and Physiology Assignments in Digital Systems. Interacting With Computers 18(2), 139–170 (2006)
8. Ekman, P.: An argument for basic emotions. Cognition and Emotion 6 (3/4) (1992)
9. Russell, J.A.: A Circumplex Model of Affect. Journal of Personality and Social Psychology 39, 1161–1178 (1980)
10. Lang, P.J.: Behavioral treatment and bio-behavioral assessment: computer applications. In: Sidowski, J.B., Johnson, J.H., Williams, T.A. (eds.) Technology in Mental Health Care Delivery Systems, pp. 119–137. Ablex, Norwood (1980)
11. Scherer, K.R.: On the nature and function of emotion: A component process approach. In: Scherer, K.R., Ekman, P. (eds.) Approaches to emotion, pp. 293–317. Erlbaum, Hillsdale (1984)
12. Norman, D., Ortony, A.: Designers and Users: Two perspectives on emotion and design. In: Proc. of the Symposium on Foundations of Interaction Design at the Interaction Design Institute, Ivrea, Italy (2003)
13. Norman, A.D.: Emotional Design: Why We Love (Or Hate) Everyday Things. Basic Books (2005)
14. Mehrabian, A., Russell, J.A.: An approach to Environmental Psychology. MIT Press, Cambridge (1974)
15. Voong, M., Beale, R.: Music organisation using colour synaesthesia. In: CHI 2007 extended abstracts on Human factors in computing systems, pp. 1869–1874. ACM, San Jose (2007)

Don't Get Emotional

Leysia Palen[1] and Susanne Bødker[2]

[1] University of Colorado,
Boulder, Colorado, USA
palen@colorado.edu
[2] University of Århus,
Århus, Denmark
bodker@daimi.au.dk

Abstract. The topic of *emotion* in computing is enjoying recent and growing attention. Such attention is problematic because, we argue, foregrounding *emotion* marks it as a subcomponent of interaction, which has the surprising consequence of reducing the importance of emotion's function. Emotion has come into vogue in reaction to the emphasis put on *work*, on *efficiency* and *productivity* in human computer interaction for so long. We discuss how this dichotomy is not in itself very fruitful in changing human-computer interaction. We offer this article as a voice in an ongoing discussion about where we are heading, and which directions this discussion could take.

Keywords: Human-computer interaction, efficiency, emotion.

1 Introduction

Emotion is a new, hot topic in human-computer interaction. This attention leverages creativity and inspires ideas while moving away from inaccurately spare notions of *interaction*. However, at the same time, we are concerned that the attention to *emotion* is a reaction to the misplaced attention on *efficiency* and *productivity* for so long. We feel that the focus on *emotion* could have limited traction, and that it introduces new problems to our critical understanding of computer-mediated interactivity.

Consider how, for example, not very long ago, a concern about the viability of ambient displays in ubiquitous computing were that they did not always offer users an opportunity to responsively interact about the information such systems passively—and emotionally—conveyed. These systems are often quite lovely in their communication about the states of things: the installation of LiveWire used a string dangling from the ceiling that moved and danced in response to local Ethernet traffic (the work of Natalie Jeremijenko as described in [20]). AmbientROOM illustrated how information like the amount of email backlog and the degree of activity of others could be conveyed through variation of light and the playing of birdsong [11]. These were engaging designs, but they challenged us to ask if conveyance of information alone and in this form was enough, and if a response was needed for some kind of interactive completion. With all the cache that *emotion* currently has, we might now embrace without much question the aesthetic and experience such systems offer.

C. Peter and R. Beale (Eds.): Affect and Emotion in HCI, LNCS 4868, pp. 12–22, 2008.

It also was not long ago when the human-computer interaction community dismissed usability outcomes that amounted to claims such as, "Our users thought that was cool!" or "It made them feel happy." Where was the substance in that kind of assessment, many wondered. Now, with *emotion* having come into vogue, we might judge these remarks to be newly appropriate indications of a system's viability and suitability.

Re-interpreting these claims that many suspected were important, but could not validate on the terms we had historically come to expect in the field of human-computer interaction, is a worthy objective. Defining what emotions are and envisioning what we might do with them in human-computer interaction, is far from trivial. However, existing side-by-side with these benefits is a danger. By foregrounding *emotion, we place* it as a *feature* of interaction, a sub-component of a greater whole, and perhaps to the exclusion of other features of interaction. We submit that it is more powerful to simply consider emotion as a fundamental quality of interaction; in other words, to the extent that there are different, discernable features of interaction, emotion underlies all of them. Marking emotion has the surprising consequence of trivializing its function, and, in some cases, problematizes how we then address emotion in design and critique.

We further submit that *emotion* has come into vogue as a dichotomic reaction to the troublesome emphasis put on *efficiency* and *productivity* in human computer interaction for so long. This focus on *emotion* could be just as problematic.

And so, with our tongue-in-cheek title, we turn the otherwise unpleasant directive on its head by claiming that emotion is far too important and integral to treat as something distinct in interaction. We use this paper to argue why we should temper the attention given to emotion, explore alternatives, and consider the challenges brought on by this current focus in human-computer interaction (HCI).

2   The Pendulum Swings: From Efficiency to Emotion

Information and communications technology (ICT) inhabits many if not most aspects of life in many societies. The primary site of ICT use is no longer the workplace, nor is it even localized to a particular realm. In addition, the infrastructural state-of-the-art has reached a threshold of sophistication that allows for its appropriation to a number of settings and occasions. These conditions are two of the bases for our community's collective turn to *emotion*.

As a research community, we have moved from the work domain as the primary object of concern and destination for development, and into the domains of home (e.g. [8,19]), assisted living (e.g. [9, 1]), the community (e.g. [6, 16]), even the bedroom [4, 2], and so on. The places for new forms of computer-mediated interaction call upon attributes of human life that could once more easily be analytically and intellectually excluded when addressing matters of work—including matters that we broadly call *emotion*. Within the context of the workplace, we found that themes of *efficiency* and *productivity* offered the kind of rationality much of society likes to imagine work and the workplace as having. And technologically, simply making digital connection possible—and efficient and productive—was a first-order goal in support of day-to-day business operations to enable such networking feats as printing, file sharing, and emailing.

As ICT became more sophisticated, cheap and portable, it began to move outside the workplace, where it increasingly became adapted to more situations and occasions where efficiency and productivity were most obviously not the only goals—or even goals at all. It is here we encounter the problem of distinctions: It is notable that the "rest of life" is hard to conveniently and singularly name in the way *work* seems to be—and that we seem to want to do this in our research. As HCI researchers, we see our work on technology as having some attachments to places (if not spaces) and "worlds" and "realms." The very need to make distinctions about the sites of use indicates that we attribute meaning to them that are somehow important to our ICT interests.

Furthermore, the realm outside of *work* is clearly so complex that it eludes naming. In fact, it largely seems defined by negations: "everything but work," or "non-work," and maybe irrational, ineffective, inefficient and so on [5]. If work is the site of efficiency and rationality, then the "rest of life" might also then be something else. That *work* should be effective, while emotions belong to the "rest of life" mirrors ideas that evoke the most old-fashioned Tayloristic conceptions of industrial work, at the same time that work today takes many other forms. Secondly, home/family life seems equally over-idealized, given, for example, Hochschild's [10] discussions of how some American parents try to escape the time trap of home with its complex and aggravating scheduling requirements by spending more hours at work.

These underlying assumptions crop up in the problem of naming and attribution of activities in our own professional scholarly world, where many of us wrestle with what to call and how to describe academic workshops, papers, our research. *Home* offers as convenient (though probably just as inaccurate) a term as *work* in referring to a place or state where much of life occurs. *Leisure* is often understood in contrast to *work* as well, but this choice of term fails to hold because *work* serves not only to refer to employment, but also to describe a general state of action that is broader than employment, too. So *home* serves to be a contrast to "work-as-employment," but *home* is most certainly not the same as *leisure*; home is the place for yet other kinds of work.

It is here, then, where *emotion* has its opening, in reaction to the shift away from HCI's extended attention to *efficiency* and *work*. Many might not see this reaction as a problem, and indeed, there are clear benefits to organizing a stream of research around *emotion*. But we feel that *emotion* should not be a destination, but instead a waypoint to fuller and integrated notions of interaction. By making *emotion* a *feature* of interaction rather than a *purpose* of interaction, we box it in. We continue to pose the problem of understanding ICT development, design, use and evaluation vis-à-vis our starting place—*work*—making our attention a point of contrast, rather than an acknowledgement—in hindsight—that all computer-mediated interaction, regardless of its place of activity, is, in fact, emotional. A challenge, then, is to move beyond these impossible distinctions of *work* and *everything else* that, in part, underpin false contrasts, and the possibility that the targets of our attention—including *emotion*—be given shape by them.

3 Tempest in a Teapot

We consider a few of the perspectives that have informed the attention to *emotion*, as well as some alternative perspectives that differently address some of the same matters. Following the cognitivist frame represented by Norman's teapot [14]—which we figuratively (and apologetically) borrow for our subtitle to illustrate the fervor the topic of *emotion* has reached—we describe Boehner, DePaula, Dourish, Senger's [3] work that represents the interactionist frame.

With his book, *Emotional Design* [14], Don Norman offered an outline for how HCI might deal with *emotion*. Pointing out that design is emotional was an important step that helped bring additional attention to existing ideas of affective computing [18], and we believe, like many others, that this issue is deserving of further attention.

First, however, we will look at *how* Norman deals with interaction in relation to *emotion*. He discusses at length his collection of teapots, and in particular, his favorite teapot. In this discussion, moves he discussions of emotion beyond primary emotions of, for example, fear, and beyond the immediacy of affect and arousal. Norman connects emotions to experiences and things, and he points out how in addition to relating to things cognitively, human beings relate to them emotionally.

As the emotional response to digital artifacts started to become an acceptable topic of the science and design of HCI, we saw the rise of another view: that emotion is not an isolated experience resident in the head of a single person; it is instead an interactional and social experience. Boehner et al. [3] point out how Norman is constrained to the cognitivist paradigm, which means that he sees emotions as add-ons to cognition.

Boehner et al. [3] tackle the topic of *emotion* from a social and interactionist point of view, arguing that meaning in emotion is generated by the interaction of people, and that emotion is understood and often modified by interaction with others—rather than an internally-generated experience. Whereas Norman focuses on the single human being and her relation to things, Boehner et al. focus on the relationships between human beings, in a framework that does not easily address, for example, personal history— a further issue we believe is important to consider.

Accordingly Norman's perspective on *emotion* in HCI as an add-on to cognition has many limitations: it ignores how emotions are created in interaction among human beings, how these emotions arise from many types of human needs, some of which are created outside the object of emotion itself. And it ignores how emotions are created in historical processes where experiences are not only created but also recreated through anticipation and recounting. Norman really seems to be thinking about single-user experiences with the machine and information that the machine presents.

Boehner et al.'s interactional framing is problematic because it puts emotion in the foreground as a feature of interaction, whereas we believe it is more helpful to think of all interaction as emotional—even when it is allegedly unemotional, it is still defined by emotion through, once again, negation (as in an attempt to remove, or hide, or "keep in check"). So in some ways, Boehner et al. make too little of emotion by making too much of it, and ignore richer ways of understanding emotions than the ones that are directly tied to the interactional situation.

4 An Anecdote: Crisis at Midnight

We now turn to one of our own recent experiences that help illustrate how the cognitivist, interactionist, and—then—experientialist perspectives might interpret a series of computer-mediated events, and the recounting of those events.

Susanne remembers:

> Not long ago, I went to friends' for dinner. It was quite a long drive, and on the way there I remember thinking—do I need gas? No, no, I would probably make it.
>
> On the way back, at almost midnight, I decided to stop for fuel anyway. Off the highway and into the nearest town I went. At the major road crossing was a gas station. It was quite deserted, but I was pleased to see it. I pulled up, took out my credit card and went out to punch in my pin-code and open the gas tank. "Please insert the card"—I did—a pause— "This card cannot be read." I tried to turn the card, but that did not help. Who cares?, I thought, I've got more cards! I inserted another card, and the same happened. Now I started to worry—what had happened to my credit cards? Did I have cash? No. Could I make it home without extra gas? Oh misery!
>
> I decided to move the car to the pump behind me as a last attempt to identify if it was the card or the pump causing the trouble. And I still negotiated with myself whether I could make it home. Somehow the new gas pump did not share the problem—it read my card, and asked for the pin-code. What a delight! There was no problem with my cards, and I would not be stranded on the freeway in the middle of the night! I fuelled the car while another car pulled up across the aisle. An elderly couple—who given the way they talked, were on a date, they weren't married—got out and the woman offered to use her card. That was not accepted by the machine either, and they started to futz about "doing things right." At that point, I had gotten my fuel, and I felt that I could help out by telling them that I had problems too. Somehow, the man's card worked. So in the end, it probably wasn't because I moved the car that the problem resolved; rather it seemed due to some sort of periodic error in the payment system.

Based on Susanne's experience (and the couple's lack of it), she "read" the situation differently than the couple. They thought it was their mistake, whereas she had ruled that out when it happened to her. Susanne explains that she has had earlier dramatic problems of credit cards not working, and those experiences triggered a host of emotions. This type of analysis could probably be made using Norman's understanding of emotion. However, these emotions were not made better with the risk of being stuck along on the freeway, a level of analysis that is not quite included in Norman's thinking. This new experience changed her emotional state and compelled her to help the poor people at the other gas pump. This "interactional emotion" could also be investigated from the perspective presented by Boehner et al., but neither would their framework consider Susanne's past history. The question for us is how these emerging and historical bits of the emotional situation get addressed.

4.1 Experiential Perspectives

The experiential approach—an emerging approach in HCI—offers some assistance in focusing on more than primary emotions. Furthermore, it helps with analytical concepts to unfold the larger process of experience and emotion. Cockton [7] writes:

> Quality in use and fit to context are qualities of user experience during interaction. Outcomes and lasting impacts endure beyond interaction. The determinants of interaction quality thus can rarely lie within interactions themselves, but instead they lie in the lasting value of enduring outcomes (p. 166).

Cockton points out how some aspects of emotions, values or experiences last beyond the origination. Our example similarly points out that past experience at many levels (including previous credit card pin-code problems and earlier rainy nights on empty freeways) frames emotions in the situation, as do the specific interactions with the gas pumps and with other people also present in the situation. How do we address these wider issues?

McCarthy and Wright [13] address the matter of *experience*, which differs from *emotion*—though perhaps not *emotion* broadly construed—with a perspective that is useful to our discussion. They outline 6 elements of experience: *anticipating, connecting, interpreting, reflecting, appropriating, recounting.* If we consider Norman's writing [14] from the perspective of experiential processes, he recounts his personal story with the teapot without seeming to consider that, for example, anticipation and recounting are part of the emotional moment, and that, therefore, his emotions with the teapot have personal, historical and temporal dimensions. In addition, recounting is inherently social, though perhaps not quite in the manner outlined by Boehner et al. There is a personal experience that triggers emotions, but the experience and emotions also reach outside the direct encounter between people; that is, there is a need to have an audience—or an idea of an audience—to recount the story to, even if that audience is uncertain or anonymous or even without guarantee. The experience of blogging about one's life without knowing if any or many are reading is a now commonplace illustration of this point. The tragic shooting event at Virginia Tech in 2007 offers a serious and particular instance. The widespread on-line memorialization of the event on Facebook and other on-line sites was a part of both individual and social processing—or sensemaking—of the event. Personal expressions of grief were as much about helping oneself as they were about expressing solidarity with a vast and largely unknown audience [17].

Understood this way, emotion becomes an element of both the personal and social; it is experience-based and can leave lasting effects. Furthermore, emotion is not only a matter of recalling particular past events, it is as much a matter of anticipating how one might feel in the future, and of re-interpreting those experiences and communicating them to others.

5 Beyond Emotion

From our perspective, the useful effect of these experiential perspectives is that they provide ways of discussing interaction, with its emotions, affective actions, etc. in ways that reach out of the direct encounter between the human being and the computer, as processes over time, where researchers can be allowed to focus on emotional phenomena other than only those reactionary emotions given rise by beautiful teapots and frustrating gas pumps.

5.1 Putting Emotion Back into the Background

Our example illustrates how emotion is not, after all, detached from efficiency and safety, security and all those more ordinary concerns of HCI. Emotion is also not only "good;" just as Norman offers that "attractive things work better" [14] we know that emotion includes fear, terror, anxiety etc. that are often counterproductive to efficiency[1].

Susanne's interaction with the system and with the couple and their interaction with the system were fuelled by a larger set of emotional interpretations that had everything to do with the experience at the gas pump. In our example, the potential trouble in the space of interaction came from many levels—and potential units of analysis—including typing in and receiving feedback about the pin-code; pushing the right buttons on the gas pump; being stranded on the freeway; interpreting the couple's experience and their interpretation of events, including their personal relationship and possible embarrassment about the status of their credit cards; and so on.

When *emotion* is the foregrounded object of design and analysis, the burden at some point or another sits on bounding units of analysis for emotion's consideration. If emotion is a cognitive activity, and an interactive one, and an experiential one, then the obligation to honestly consider its relational contexts becomes impossible. Perhaps we are earnestly working toward a poorly framed target? Or put differently, framing human-computer interaction as emotional as well as efficient has not made it any clearer how the field should adjust its focus or methodology. Again this dilemma has historical parallels: When Mumford and others [12] presented socio-technical design as an alternative to traditional machine thinking in information systems and organizational design, the problem was exactly that while their thinking shifted the design focus away from the machine and efficiency and to the "emotional man," they had a problem of analyzing and designing for this new frame. This problem yielded odd analytical comparisons. For example, in questionnaires designed to analyze a workplace, they made workers rate both how clean the bathrooms were and how much influence that had on the detailed planning of their work—and clean toilets are almost Norman's teapot qualities ("attractive things work better")!

---

[1] This is indeed a well-known reason why Taylorism had to be substituted/supplemented with other forms of production: Workers were simply more productive when they "felt better." This has been achieved through socio-technical improvement of the production [12], by making workers an item of concern (the Hawthorne effect) or through more radical ways of giving up industrial production all together.

5.2   Looking Ahead

Our point is not that we ignore *emotion*, but rather that we need to think more criti-
cally about how the community uses fashionable trends like *emotion* to productive
ends, and even how we conceptualize *interaction* in the first place. Such conceptuali-
zations have critical outcomes.

Perhaps we can help ourselves understand what it is we get with the focus on emotion by looking beyond and anticipating what some instances of the next "wave" will
be in HCI. Emotion is a segue to this next wave, as a negation of work and efficiency,
but perhaps other concepts highlight different attributes of interaction. Some of these
might be later thought of as fashions or trends, or maybe they will endure. Perhaps
only what we can do now is try on for size a "negation of the negation" in dialectical
terms: something that emerges in reaction to the limits of *efficiency* and *emotion,* or
both, and be something "third" [5].

Such an exercise might anticipate the limits we will encounter with *emotion.* How
does it differ when we think about, for example, *play, relaxation, laziness, sentimentality, inefficient togetherness*—all themselves additional conceptual contrasts to *productivity* and *efficiency?* And what about *solitude,* a contrast to or negation of the
current focus on emotion? Much research has, at one time or another, put these ideas
into the foreground; the question is, should they be there still now? Is it emotion that
should be foregrounded, or other states of being and human activity that emotion,
instead, helps realize?

We focus here on the idea of *solitude* in relation to *emotion. Solitude* is an almost
inevitable fashionable topic in HCI. Disconnectedness, privacy, and access are known
needs of our digital society, certainly, although much of our use of the state of the art
dismantles understandings around being alone and being together. Furthermore, we
believe *solitude* is a predictable contrast to some essential matters we face when we
focus on *emotion,* and yet clearly differs from what *efficiency* offers as a contrast.
Efficiency-emotion plays at the rational-irrational tension. *Emotion* emphasizes the
fascination that we (mostly) collectively have about the power of digital connection.
Though we are not ignorant of its problems and compromises, these are the heady
days of ICT development and use, where ICT has penetrated the everyday—the
irrational, messy, mundane everyday—but is still fairly "visible" and not quite taken-
for-granted. We are still discovering the ways we might leverage digital connection
anytime and anywhere. This itself is an emotional experience, as the interaction with
digital devices and with each other sometimes shatters boundaries (including boundaries other than spatial and temporal ones) that constrained our previous experiences.
ICT itself is an impetus for emotional response, as was the rocket to the moon, and
the television, and the printing press, and the car, and so on (and continue to be, as we
think of some of these memories with wistfulness, or a retroactively applied sense of
doom, or relief, or whatever one's experiences might bring to these points in time).

So whatever our emotional reaction to ICT, we are also naturally fascinated by the
power of digital connection and the social connections that result. These forms of
social connections are rich and meaningful in spite of constraints, even those imposed
by ascii text (eg., SMS or text messaging), and so we rightly attribute the richness of

interactions to are our emotions. And now, through deliberate design, we hope to further facilitate the expression of these emotions in our connectedness with things and with people through things.

That brings us to what it is the community is ultimately trying to do through our calling out of *emotion* for design and analytical purposes—trying to bring computer-mediated interaction to its fullest fidelity in support of this pervasive connection. *Emotion,* then, is on par with *connectedness*, which is why it is more powerful to think about emotion *as* interaction, rather than a feature of interaction. It is also the basis for our proposal that *solitude* will be an imminent conceptual turn for innovation. That concept is, of course, already percolating in terms of complaints among people at large in reaction to the interruptive quality of their lives. However, we propose that *solitude* will be explored as a countermove to the some of the issues that are at the core of our current discussion around *emotion*.

Take, for example, mobile telephony. Mobile phones offer connection to others. Its early appeal to many new users first rested on meeting perceived needs of safety, though the benefits to convenience and interpersonal connection very quickly became clear and valued [15]. Eventually, as the means to these personal connections, the mobile phone came to embody them. Some age groups especially want to tailor and customize their phones, signaling an emotional connection with the device itself. We note that here, where the desire to have emotional connection with others translates into an emotional connection with the phone device, is where the cognitivist and interactionist frames work in complement. But as soon as these telephonic connections were possible, we began to see a backlash to this pervasive availability and the affect on our other lived experiences. With the possibility of all this digital connection came the recognition (or reinforcement of existing belief) that disconnection is also important and valuable. Disconnection offers "emotional release" from others—the pleasure of *solitude*.

Emotion is so large an idea that it can be descriptive of all kinds of interaction and non-interaction, meaning that it is fundamental to these things, and so therefore it is not powerful to us as analysts of human computer interaction. We need instead—or at the very least, in addition—to rely on either more pointed understandings of what interaction is at different units of analysis, or on the composites of emotion and circumstance that give rise to constructs such as *solitude*, *play*, *sentimentality*, and so on, in human life.

6 Closing Remarks

We would be remiss if we did not communicate our support for all things irrational. Our interest in reframing and expanding our understanding of interaction in this paper still argues for a place for emotion in HCI, though perhaps it is now time that this place should be more explicitly considered. We have pointed out how history in some ways seems to repeat itself with respect to *emotion* and *efficiency*. While there is certainly more to be learned from this past, as well as from other elements of the discussion around *emotion* than what we have brought here, we hope that our consideration of how *emotion* relates to *interaction*—and what happens when we conceptualize *emotion* as a waypoint rather than as a destination—supports progress in this innovative area. We are hopeful that HCI research will benefit from the pursuits and interests represented in this volume on *emotion*.

Acknowledgments. We thank our human-computer interaction colleagues at the University of Aarhus for many conversations that supported the development of these ideas. We thank Olav Bertelsen, Sarah Vieweg, Christian Peter, and anonymous reviewers for their helpful feedback. Work was supported in part by National Science Foundation grant CAREER IIS-0546315, but does not represent the views of NSF. Furthermore, this work was supported by the Centre for New Ways of Working, the Centre for Pervasive Healthcare, and the Centre for Palpable Computing, all at the University of Aarhus.

References

1. Ballegaard, S.A., Bunde-Pedersen, J., Bardram, J.E.: Where to, Roberta?: reflecting on the role of technology in assisted living. In: Mørch, A., Morgan, K., Bratteteig, T., Ghosh, G., Svanaes, D. (eds.) Proceedings of the 4th Nordic Conference on Human-Computer Interaction: Changing Roles, Oslo, Norway, October 14–18, 2006. NordiCHI 2006, vol. 189, pp. 373–376. ACM Press, New York (2006)
2. Bertelsen, O.W., Petersen, M.G.: Erotic Life as a New Frontier in HCI. In: Ramduny-Ellis, D., Rachovides, D. (eds): Proceedings of the 21st British Computer Society HCI Group Conference, vol. 2, pp. 7–10 (2007)
3. Boehner, K., DePaula, R., Dourish, P., Sengers, P.: Affect: from information to interaction. In: Bertelsen, O.W., Bouvin, N.O., Krogh, P.G., Kyng, M. (eds.) Proceedings of the 4th Decennial Conference on Critical Computing: between Sense and Sensibility, Aarhus, Denmark, August 20–24, 2005, pp. 59–68. ACM Press, New York (2007)
4. Brewer, J., Kaye, J., Williams, A., Wyche, S.: Sexual interactions: why we should talk about sex in HCI. In: CHI 2006 Extended Abstracts on Human Factors in Computing Systems, Montréal, Québec, Canada, April 22–27, 2006, pp. 1695–1698. ACM Press, New York (2006)
5. Bødker, S.: When second wave HCI meets third wave challenges. In: Mørch, A., Morgan, K., Bratteteig, T., Ghosh, G., Svanaes, D. (eds.) Proceedings of the 4th Nordic Conference on Human-Computer interaction: Changing Roles, Oslo, Norway, October 14–18, 2006, vol. 189, pp. 1–8. ACM Press, New York (2006)
6. Carroll, J.M.: Community computing as human-computer interaction. Behaviour and Information Technology 20(5), 307–314 (2001)
7. Cockton, G.: Designing worth is worth designing. In: Mørch, A., Morgan, K., Bratteteig, T., Ghosh, G., Svanaes, D. (eds.) Proceedings of the 4th Nordic Conference on Human-Computer interaction: Changing Roles, Oslo, Norway, October 14–18, 2006, vol. 189, pp. 165–174. ACM Press, New York (2006)
8. Edwards, W.K., Grinter, R.E.: At Home with Ubiquitous Computing: Seven Challenges. In: Abowd, G.D., Brumitt, B., Shafer, S. (eds.) UbiComp 2001. LNCS, vol. 2201, pp. 256–272. Springer, Heidelberg (2001)
9. Hirsch, T., Forlizzi, J., Hyder, E., Goetz, J., Kurtz, C., Stroback, J.: The ELDer project: social, emotional, and environmental factors in the design of eldercare technologies. In: Proceedings of the 2000 Conference on Universal Usability, Arlington, Virginia, USA, November 16–17, 2000, pp. 72–79. ACM Press, New York (2000)

10. Hochschild, A.R.: The Time Bind: When Work Becomes Home and Home Becomes Work. Metropolitan Books (1997)
11. Ishii, H., Wisneski, C., Brave, S., Dahley, A., Gorbet, M., Ullmer, B., Yarin, P.: AmbientROOM: integrating ambient media with architectural space. In: CHI 1998 Conference Summary on Human Factors in Computing Systems, Los Angeles, April 18–23, 1998, pp. 173–174. ACM Press, New York (1998)
12. Land, F., Hawgood, J., Mumford, E.: A Participative Approach to Forward Planning and Systems Change, Information Systems Methodologies. LNCS, vol. 65, pp. 39–61. Springer, Heidelberg (1978)
13. McCarthy, J., Wright, P.: Technology As Experience. MIT Press, Cambridge (2004)
14. Norman, D.: Emotional Design: Why we love (or hate) everyday things. Basic Books, New York (2004)
15. Palen, L., Salzman, M., Youngs, E.: Discovery and Integration of Mobile Communications in Everyday Life. Personal and Ubiquitous Computing Journal 5(2), 109–122 (2001)
16. Palen, L., Liu, S.B.: Citizen Communications in Crisis: Anticipating a Future of ICT-Supported Participation. In: Proceedings of the ACM Conference on Human Factors in Computing Systems 2007, pp. 727–736. ACM Press, New York (2007)
17. Palen, L., Vieweg, S., Sutton, J., Liu, S., Hughes, A.: Crisis Informatics: Studying Crisis in a Networked World. In: Proceedings of the Third Annual Conference on E-Social Science, Ann Arbor, MI, USA, October 7–9 (2007),
http://ess.si.umich.edu/papers/paper172.pdf
18. Picard, R.W.: Affective Computing. MIT Press, Cambridge (1997)
19. Petersen, M.G.: Remarkable computing: the challenge of designing for the home. In: CHI 2004 Extended Abstracts on Human Factors in Computing Systems, Vienna, Austria, April 24–29, 2004, pp. 1445–1448. ACM Press, New York (2004)
20. Weiser, M., Seely Brown, J.: Designing Calm Technology Xerox PARC (1995),
http://sandbox.xerox.com/hypertext/weiser/calmtech/calmtech.htm

Computational Affective Sociology

William Sims Bainbridge

National Science Foundation*,
4201 Wilson Blvd., Arlington, Virginia 22230 USA
wbainbri@nsf.gov

Abstract. An alternative tradition concerning emotion in human-centered computing is based on sociological conceptions of personality and the emotional meanings of decisions. This essay summarizes work in this area, beginning with the classic Big 5 personality dimensions and the semantic differential, then illustrates recent work with two projects that developed software research tools. The first builds on the semantic differential to measure an individual's self-esteem across several dimensions, and the second assesses the subject's reactions to 2,000 common events in terms of 20 emotions.

Keywords: Affective computing, human values, personality capture, semantic differential, sociology.

1 Introduction

The primary tradition in affective computing is represented by Picard's work [1-3], but other traditions also exist, and this is a good time to begin to integrate them with it. In particular, much work has gone into computer-assisted research on the dimensions of human personality, and recently we have begun to see a range of potential applications of this research in human-centered computing. In this context, the concept may be defined thus: *Personality is the constellation of relatively stable propensities to feel and act in certain ways in response to a range of stimuli, that distinguishes one individual human being from another.*

Several fields of social and behavioral science have something to say about the topic. Personality psychology is the twin of social psychology, as personality greatly determines how an individual will behave in social interaction, and social interaction shapes the individual [4]. However, many social psychologists are sociologists rather than psychologists, and they use terminology such as identity, ideology, attitudes, preferences, or values that in one or another way overlap the concept of personality. Two things these perspectives have in common are a strong linkage between emotions and behavior, and a tendency to link emotion with cognition, especially through such feeling-laden cognitions as self-image and self-esteem. Clearly, personality is an interdisciplinary topic, and applying it to affective computing compounds the complexity

---

* Any opinion, finding, and conclusions or recommendations expressed in this material are those of the author and do not necessarily reflect the views of the National Science Foundation.

C. Peter and R. Beale (Eds.): Affect and Emotion in HCI, LNCS 4868, pp. 23–34, 2008.

of the cross-disciplinary connections. My own research goal entails developing comprehensive methods for measuring and ultimately emulating individual human personalities in fine detail, what I call "personality capture" [5].

A landmark in the convergence of affective computing with artificial intelligence and personality capture was a 1993 workshop on *Artificial Social Intelligence* (ASI), sponsored by the National Science Foundation and held at the National Center for Supercomputing Applications [6]. ASI is the application of machine intelligence techniques to social phenomena. The workshop report noted Robert H. Frank's analysis of emotion as a tool of game-like interaction [7, 8], highlighted *affect control theory*, and advocated using AI to represent the thinking of an individual person [9].

This essay springs from an effort to build a library of software to administer approximately 100,000 questionnaire items for high-resolution personality capture [10-12]. It illustrates that a variety of ways must be found to bridge between the social or behavioral sciences and the computer or information sciences, in order to provide the affect necessary for realistic personality capture and emulation.

2 Personality Psychology and Sociology

Computer science is not well linked to personality psychology, as suggested by a 2007 article in *Communications of the ACM* titled "Does Personality Matter?" [13] advocating organizing employees in terms of personality, but using the Myers-Briggs Type Indicator (MBTI) considered highly inferior by modern psychologists [14]. A far better starting point than the MBTI would be the "Big 5" personality dimensions that are central to personality psychology and emphasize affect [15]: Neuroticism (anxiety, angry hostility, depression), Extraversion (warmth, gregariousness, assertiveness), Openness to Experience (fantasy, aesthetics, feelings), Agreeableness (trust, straightforwardness, altruism), Conscientiousness (competence, order, dutifulness). Already, a few researchers have begun designing virtual humans on the basis of this personality model [16, 17], or a simplified version of it [18], but the relevance of sociology is not yet fully appreciated.

The Big 5 dimensions are social as well as emotional. Anger, interpersonal warmth, altruism, and a sense of duty all involve feelings about how to relate to other people. Openness to Experience specifically means a willingness to experience new feelings in new settings, including with new people. Personality capture cannot be limited just to the Big 5, but must include many dozens of "small" measures as well. Also, slightly different versions of the Big 5 exist.

Lewis R. Goldberg [19, 20] created a collection of fully 2,036 personality items, validated many of them against standard measures whose use is limited by copyright, and placed them in the public domain. A leading Big 5 researcher, Goldberg offers 100 Big 5 items, 20 measuring each of the five dimensions. Each item is a phrase describing a characteristic a person might have. The respondent rates each item in terms of how accurately it describes him or her, using a 5-point scale from 1 to 5. Here are Goldberg's Big 5, along with affective characteristics from the dimension's list of twenty items. The second example for each dimension is scored negatively:

Extraversion: Feel comfortable around people; Bottle up my feelings
Agreeableness: Feel others' emotions; Feel little concern for others

Conscientiousness: Love order and regularity; Find it difficult to get down to work
Emotional Stability (opposite of Neuroticism): Seldom get mad; Get overwhelmed
  by emotions
Imagination (comparable to Openness to Experience): Love to think up new ways of
  doing things; Try to avoid complex people.

To explore the logistics of personality capture, I ported Goldberg's 2,036 items
into a pocket computer. A portable device allows the person to answer in convenient
moments during the day, and facilitates administering very long questionnaires. Subject A was comfortable rating how well one item described him about every five seconds, so the entire 2,036 took about 3 hours. Then the respondent went through the
list again, rating each as he would wish himself to be in the future. This took another
3 hours, and provided a contrast between the person as he currently views himself
versus the ideal he would wish to achieve, his self-image versus values.

The primary goal of personality archiving is simply to get the individual's data into
the information system. However, secondary goals can help motivate the person to do
the work necessary for archiving, such as providing him or her with insights about
fundamental desires, social characteristics, and strategies for action. For example,
Table 1 shows how the subject scored on the Big 5.

Table 1. Five Personality Dimensions of One Individual

	Yourself as you generally are now	Yourself as you wish to be in the future	Difference
Extraversion	2.6	4.1	1.6
Agreeableness	2.2	3.2	1.0
Conscientiousness	3.4	4.6	1.2
Emotional Stability	2.8	4.1	1.4
Imagination	4.5	4.9	0.4

A high score means the respondent feels he has the characteristic (yourself as you
generally are now) or wants it (yourself as you wish to be in the future). The difference shows how much the respondent needs to gain the characteristic, according to
his own personal wants. This particular research subject wants to be more extraverted,
and more emotionally stable, but is less interested in becoming more agreeable in
dealings with other people.

Of course personality is not just a person's self-image and values; it is also reflected in what other people feel about us. Table 2 summarizes responses from two
sisters who were asked to rate each other as well as themselves, on Goldberg's 100
Big 5 items. Note how the two siblings rate on Extraversion. Subject B rates herself at
2.7 on the scale from 1 to 5, whereas her sister rates her higher at 3.5. In contrast, both
agree that Subject C should be rated around 2.0 or 2.1. Both research subjects rate the
other higher on Agreeableness than the other rates herself, and indeed they rate each
other higher than they rate themselves. Subject C rates Subject B higher on Conscientiousness than Subject B rates herself. Each rates the other higher on Intellect or
Imagination than the rater rates herself.

Table 2. Five Personality Dimensions of Two Siblings

	Subject B Rated By:		Subject C Rated By:	
	self	sibling	self	sibling
Extraversion	2.7	3.5	2.1	2.0
Agreeableness	2.9	3.5	3.1	3.7
Conscientiousness	3.1	3.9	2.9	2.7
Emotional Stability	3.7	3.5	3.0	2.9
Imagination	3.5	4.7	4.4	4.0

The fact that one person's description of another may not perfectly match the individual's own self-description does not invalidate the approach. Rather, the two kinds of data reflect different aspects of the person, and thus combined provide a more complete description. It should be kept in mind that the Goldberg items concern perceptions of the individual. Very different measures would be used to capture attitudes, beliefs, preferences, observable behavior, and meanings.

3 Affective Semantics

Sociology tends to conceptualize emotion in terms of the meanings people use to make decisions and those chains of decisions that constitute planning. This orientation can be integrated with computer and information science in many ways, but immediately we can see a connection to decision-support systems and rule-based approaches in artificial intelligence. For example, one of the most influential classics was the 1897 book, *Suicide*, by the French pioneer sociologist Emile Durkheim [21]. Rather than conceptualizing the affective component of suicide psychologically as depression or despair, Durkheim argued it could often be the result of *anomie*, which is meaninglessness, normlessness, or the state of being without effective rules for living. Whereas Durkheim believed society was a unit and provided a coherent system of meaning for all its inhabitants, later sociologists used questionnaire survey research to uncover the many subcultures in society that could have somewhat different systems of meaning, and the socio-economic variables that could cross-cut each other and thus produce a wide range of individual differences.

More than half a century after Durkheim, Talcott Parsons and a group of colleagues at Harvard published *Toward a Theory of Action*, synthesizing the work since Durkheim and packaging its ideas in a comprehensive categorization scheme [22, 23]. Notably, they argued that anything people respond to can be described in terms of five dimensions called pattern variables, the first of which was *affectivity versus affective neutrality*. That is, a crucial aspect of people's responses to things, people, and actions is whether they elicit strong feelings or not. In a separate analysis, the book also distinguishes *cognition*, *cathexis*, and *evaluation*. These are three distinguishable but intertwined functions of the human mind: 1) how a person understands something, 2) how the person feels about it, and 3) how the person decides which of several actions to perform in response to it. Taken from personality psychology, the concept of cathexis refers to the investment of emotional energy in something. Thus, classical sociology always connected feelings with the things the person feels about, rather than addressing them as purely internal physiological states.

A particularly fruitful research tool, called the *semantic differential*, can be included in questionnaires to assess the affective meanings people attach to things. Developed and extended to international comparisons by a team headed by Charles E. Osgood [24, 25, 26]. It consists of a set of questionnaire items asking the respondent to rate a particular stimulus, such as "computers." Each item is a pair of antonyms with a rating scale between, such as: BAD -3 -2 -1 0 +1 +2 +3 GOOD. A respondent who felt computers were moderately good might circle the number +2, for example. A respondent who felt they were very, very bad, would circle -3. Osgood initially used dozens of items, each employing a pair of words having roughly opposite meaning, then used statistical techniques like factor analysis to identify the key dimensions of meaning reflected in data from thousands of research subjects.

Three primary dimensions emerged: evaluation (e.g. good-bad), potency (e.g. strong-weak), and activity (e.g. active-passive). Because there is a certain amount of noise in any questionnaire data, each dimension would be measured by several items, whose scores would be combined for analysis.

The three dimensions represent three different real factors that were vital for the evolution of human decision-making in prehistoric times. Walking through the jungle, you suddenly encounter an animal. Quickly, you must decide what to do. Is it good or bad, for example an antelope or a tiger? You see that it is feline. Is it powerful or weak, a tiger or a kitten? You see that it is a big tiger. Is it active or passive, running or sleeping? Appropriate responses include whether to move rapidly or stealthily, either toward or away from the animal, or simply to ignore it. A wrong choice can be very costly, but a choice must be made decisively. Therefore it is energized by the feelings we associate with different emotions, hopefully appropriate to the situation.

The most important dimension is evaluation, and it continues to play a central role in sociological theories [27]. Douglas Massey [28], in his presidential address to the American Sociological Association, argued that the crucial step in the development of human evolution from our primate ancestors was the cognitive elaboration of emotion, permitted by an increase in the size and complexity of our brains and the related development of language, which he suggests were driven by the increasing size of social groups. Massey conceptualizes norms and values in terms of the interaction between emotions in the brain and social structures outside the person, and in terms of connections between emotions and memories of specific objects, places, experiences, actions, and thoughts.

Sociologist David Heise [29, 30, 31, 32] has been especially prominent in affective sociology and semantic differential work over the years, contributed substantially to the Artificial Social Intelligence report, and has done much to bridge the gap between the sociology of emotions and computer science. His affect control theory concerns how people use available cultural standards as baselines against which to calibrate their own feelings, and he has employed web-based questionnaire methods to collect semantic differential ratings of vast numbers of concepts in several societies [33].

Importantly, Heise has suggested a kind of affective generative grammar, in which it is possible to predict the evaluation, potency and activity scores of a whole sentence on the basis of the scores of individual words, with the aim of using this information to program rule-based artificial intelligence agents to mimic human emotional responses

[34, 35]. For example, if you know a given culture's semantic differential ratings for "tired," "mother," scold," and "child," you can accurately predict how the culture rates, "The tired mother scolded her child." I have been mindful of Heise's work not primarily because he participated in the Artificial Social Intelligence workshop, nor because he published his seminal paper with Schneider in the same issue of *Mathematical Sociology* where I published one on using neural networks to model human racial prejudice [36], but because he consistently showed over the years how development of a very large number of well-calibrated questionnaire items was necessary for the creation of really effective AI avatars of particular people.

4 The *Self* Program

An example is the *Self* program, published on a CD in connection with a methodological essay [39]. Following classic questionnaire-development methods, including a pilot study with 512 respondents, I programmed a personality capture software system that presents the user with 1,600 adjectives that could describe a person, arranged in 20 groups of 80 items. Each group consists of 40 antonym pairs in a particular topic area, but separated to evaluate whether the person connects them in the expected manner. Each adjective is followed by two questions: "How BAD or GOOD is this quality? How LITTLE or MUCH do you yourself have this quality?" To discourage respondents from associating these two dimensions with each other, a pair of user interface modules presented them orthogonally, as shown in Figure 1.

The cross input method, shown at the top of Figure 1, encouraged careful answering but requires three mouse clicks for every two bytes of data: (1) select the GOOD-BAD rating, (2) select the LITTLE-MUCH rating, and (3) click "OK" to register the ratings and move on to the next adjective in the group. The "block" method in the lower part of Figure 1 requires only one click for two measurements. Each of the sixty-four squares represents one possible pair of measurements, and the numbers appear when the mouse hovers over that square.

I programmed the software to generate many kinds of reports, including a brief description of each of the twenty groups, such as the following concerning the affective dimension of the personality of Subject D: "What is your self-image in the general area of 'feelings' qualities? What are your moods, in general, and your emotional ups and downs? Your self-image has 15 of the qualities in this group: jubilant, enthusiastic, sentimental, anxious, cheerful, joyful, cowardly, nervous, apprehensive, satisfied, tense, blissful, cool, optimistic and longing. The opposites of these qualities are: suicidal, unenthusiastic, unsentimental, composed, stern, sad, fearless, sedate, unruffled, frustrated, tranquil, sorrowful, warm, pessimistic and delighted. On average you judge your 15 feelings qualities to be 5.1 on the scale from bad=1 to good=8. Roughly speaking, you feel these qualities are slightly good. Your self-esteem is measured by the correlation between rating qualities good and saying that you have them. With respect to 'feelings' qualities, your self-esteem is 0.38. That is, you have moderate self-esteem. You rated all 40 pairs of opposites. The average difference in your rating of the antonyms in each pair was 1.7 on the 8-point Little to Much scale. This is a very small difference. Apparently your characteristics in this area are weak or ambiguous. On the 8-point Bad to Good scale, the average difference in your rating of the antonyms in each pair was 3.4. Your values are rather clear, but not striking, when it comes to 'feelings' qualities."

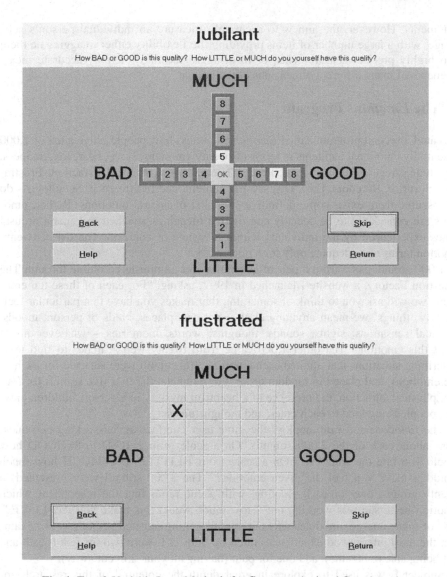

Fig. 1. Two 2-Variable Input Methods for Computer Assisted Questionnaire

For many groups of adjectives – such as those describing physical, mental or social characteristics – the correlation between having a quality and judging that it is good is properly described as *self-esteem*. This research subject was consistent in evaluating pairs of antonyms, but I designed the software to point out such inconsistencies so the person could ponder them. Pilot research has suggested, as Heise would have predicted, that people tend to agree about which qualities are good or bad, but tend to rate themselves quite variously in terms of how much they have the characteristics.

From the standpoint of traditional semantic differential research, it might seem overkill to have 1,600 adjectives, each with two rating scales, for a total of 3,200 judgments. However, the aim is to accurately measure an individual person's self-image, with a large number of items providing the flexibility either to aggregate them into highly precise measurements, or to disaggregate into tolerably accurate measurements of many different dimensions of the person.

5   The *Emotions* Program

I created a second program called *Emotions* to assess how people judge a list of 2,000 potentially emotional incidents in terms of twenty emotions: Love, Fear, Joy, Sadness, Gratitude, Anger, Pleasure, Pain, Pride, Shame, Desire, Hate, Satisfaction, Frustration, Surprise, Boredom, Lust, Disgust, Excitement, and Indifference. Sociologists do not assume there exists some definitive short list of natural emotions. Rather, emotions are considered to be socially constructed meanings attached to general arousal states experienced by the individual within a variety of contexts. The list of twenty emotion terms was adequate only for a pilot study.

1,000 stimuli came from a pair of questionnaires administered online through The Question Factory, a website I launched in 1997, asking: "For each of these ten emotions, we will ask you to think of something that makes you have that particular feeling. By 'things' we mean anything at all – actions, places, kinds of person, moods, physical sensations, sights, sounds, thoughts, words, memories – whatever might elicit this emotion." The other 1,000 came from twenty web searches to find texts describing situations that elicited each emotion. 100 stimuli were selected for each of the emotions, and placed in random order. For example, the first five stimuli for *love* are: physical attraction, the presence of a beautiful mystery in a person, children playing, people being kind to each other, and thoughtfulness.

The *Emotions* software employs the same user interface as *Self*, asking two questions about each of the 2,000 stimuli: "On a scale from 1=BAD to 8=GOOD how would you rate the stimulus?" On a scale from 1-LITTLE to 8=MUCH how much would it make you feel the given emotion?" The 2,000 stimuli were presented in twenty groups, one for each emotion, with a cue reminding the respondent which emotion he or she was working on: "How much would this make you feel LOVE?" One of many analysis modules sifts out stimuli getting selected responses. For example, the most intense bad experiences rated by Subject E were two for fear (death and not being able to breathe), and one for pain (having all your skin cut away).

Subject E was used to explore in great depth the potential of this research approach. First, he answered the 4,000 questions in *Emotions* twice, with a two-year gap between, to examine the issue of stability over time. His emotional views had polarized over the two years, implying this approach could have diagnostic value. A new program was written for a pocket computer, so Subject E could rate each of the 2,000 stimuli in terms of all 20 emotions, rather than just the one emotion it was believed to elicit. My interface simply presented each stimulus by each emotion separately, with a single rating scale, stepping through at one tap per measurement. The resulting 40,000 measures can be analyzed in many ways, but one obvious step was to factor analyze the data to see how the respondent conceptualizes the twenty emotions. The data turned out to have primarily three dimensions in it, one collecting positive emotions, the second collecting negative emotions, and the third collecting four emotions that describe the energetic character of the stimulus: excitement, surprise, indifference, and boredom.

The bad-good question asked about the evaluation dimension of the semantic differential, and the pocket PC program asked the respondent to rate each stimulus in terms of additional weak-strong and passive-active scales, to capture the potency and activity dimensions. In fact, this particular respondent did not distinguish between potency and activity, combining them mentally in what I am here calling an energetic dimension. Figure 2 graphs the twenty emotions in terms of the average evaluation at the two points in time versus the average of the potency and activity scales (energetic), based on correlations with how much the 2,000 stimuli would elicit each emotion in this individual.

The map for another person would be both similar and different. Many members of many cultures would distinguish potency from activity, but Subject E does not. Interestingly, he considers most positive emotions to be more energetic than most negative emotions. Fear is the only exception. This is consistent with the prevalent American ideology that people can actively achieve good things for themselves, but if they remain passive they may become victims to bad things. Note that some emotions generally considered similar occupy almost exactly the same spots on the map, anger and hate, satisfaction and joy.

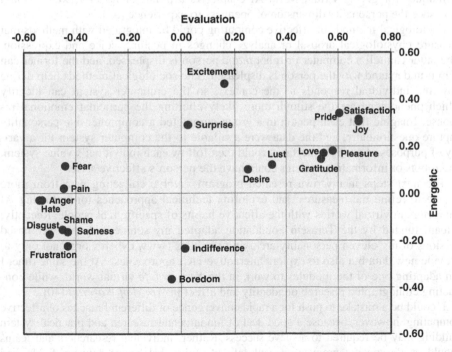

Fig. 2. Map of Twenty Emotions as Implicitly Defined by One Individual

6 Conclusion: Future Directions and Applications

Humans have implicit theories of personality, and one interpretation of the Big 5 is that they are dimensions of evaluation built into human language, reflecting shared folk theories. Computers do not yet possess this taken-for-granted human knowledge, but future AIs and personalized computer systems will need it. Context-aware mobile computing, adaptive interfaces, and personalized information retrieval systems will work best if they incorporate models of the users' values, preferences, and feelings.

Already, for example, simulated people and animals in computer games like *World of Warcraft* depict emotions like anger and fear, as they attack or flee. AI warriors in this game become enraged after suffering damage, and this "rage" makes their own attacks more powerful. In his influential book *Synthetic Worlds*, Edward Castronova argues that the greatest potential for advances exists in the area of artificial intelligence: "Improvements in game AI allow the computer-driven entities we encounter in synthetic worlds to get better at meeting our emotional needs" [38].

The popular "software toy," *The Sims*, incorporated a five-dimensional model of personality from its very inception, and the user could make his or her character: neat or messy, outgoing or reclusive, grouchy or nice, playful or serious, and active or passive. The first three of these look like the Big 5 dimensions of conscientiousness, extraversion, and agreeableness, and the last is exactly the activity dimension of the semantic differential. Recently, Kathryn Merrick and Mary Lou Maher have explored techniques for giving virtual world AI characters a thirst for novelty, which would introduce the personality dimension of openness to experience [39].

Sociological methods of affective computing could be integrated with methods that measure physiological arousal or analyze changes in posture, voice and expression. The latter can tell a computer or robot *that* a person is displeased, and the former can help it understand *why* the person is displeased. The sociological methods help define how the individual responds to the context, so the computer system can identify which phenomena are the stimuli more likely eliciting the particular emotional response. Imagine that each person in a group completed a comprehensive personality capture questionnaire, and the data were available to the computer system for a variety of purposes. Adaptive interfaces could then follow each individual's value system, and robots or information systems could have the person's affective style.

The next steps in my own research program involve collecting data from more people to refine the measures, and exploring technical approaches for endowing AI characters in virtual worlds with the affective habits of specific real people. Recently, a team funded by the Terasem Foundation adapted my source code for web-based versions of my eleven personality-archiving modules (www.cyberev.org), not only to provide new data but also to explore alternative HCI approaches. At the same time, I am adapting one of the modules to work in the *Second Life* virtual world, while conducting ethnographic research on identity and affect in *World of Warcraft* [40].

It could be a mistake to push for a rapid convergence of different branches of affective computing, however, because a good deal of fundamental research and practical system building may be required to achieve success. Rather, individual researchers and teams should tackle specific projects on well-defined topics that bridge between fields, and multidisciplinary conferences or workshops should brainstorm about the wider issues. To bring affective sociology and affective computing together is a worthy long-term goal.

References

1. Picard, R.W.: Affective Computing. MIT Press, Cambridge (1997)
2. Cohen, I., Huang, T.S., Chen, L.S.: Affective Computing. In: Bainbridge, W.S. (ed.) Encyclopedia of Human-Computer Interaction, Berkshire, Great Barrington, Massachusetts, pp. 7–10 (2004)
3. el Kaliouby, R., Picard, R., Baron-Cohen, S.: Affective Computing and Autism. In: Bainbridge, W.S., Roco, M.C. (eds.) Progress in Convergence, pp. 228–248. New York Academy of Sciences, New York (2006)
4. Zajonc, R.B.: Emotions. In: Gilbert, D.T., Fiske, S.T., Lindzey, G. (eds.) The Handbook of Social Psychology, pp. 591–632. McGraw-Hill, Boston (1998)
5. Bainbridge, W.S.: Personality Capture. In: Bainbridge, W.S. (ed.) Encyclopedia of Human-Computer Interaction, Berkshire, Great Barrington, Massachusetts, pp. 546–551 (2004)
6. Bainbridge, W.S., Brent, E.E., Carley, K., Heise, D.R., Macy, M.W., Markovsky, B., Skvoretz, J.: Artificial Social Intelligence. Annual Review of Sociology 20, 407–436 (1994)
7. Frank, R.H.: Passions within Reason, Norton, New York (1988)
8. Frank, R.H.: The Strategic Role of the Emotions. Rationality and Society 5, 160–184 (1993)
9. Brent, E.E., Glazier, J., Jamtgaard, K., Wetzel, E., Hall, P.M., Dalecki, M., Bah, A.: Erving: A Program to Teach Sociological Reasoning from the Dramaturgical Perspective. Teaching Sociology 17, 38–48 (1989)
10. Bainbridge, W.S.: Survey Research: A Computer-assisted Introduction, Wadsworth, Belmont, California (1989)
11. Bainbridge, W.S.: Massive Questionnaires for Personality Capture. Social Science Computer Review 21, 267–280 (2003)
12. Bainbridge, W.S.: Cognitive Technologies. In: Bainbridge, W.S., Roco, M.C. (eds.) Managing Nano-Bio-Info-Cogno Innovations: Converging Technologies in Society, pp. 203–226. Springer, Berlin (2006)
13. Da Cunha, A.D., Greathead, D.: Does Personality Matter? An Analysis of Code-Review Ability. Communications of the ACM 50, 109–112 (2007)
14. McRae, R.R., Costa, P.T.: Reinterpreting the Myers-Briggs Type Indicator From the Perspective of the Five-Factor Model of Personality. Journal of Personality 57, 17–40 (1989)
15. McRae, R.R., Costa, P.T.: Toward a New Generation of Personality Theories: Theoretical Context for the Five-Factor Model. In: Wiggins, J.S. (ed.) The Five-Factor Model of Personality: Theoretical Approaches, Guilford, New York, pp. 51–87 (1996)
16. Kshirsagar, S., Magnenat-Thalmann, N.: A Multilayer Personality Model. In: ACM Symp. on Smart Graphics, Hawthorne, NY (2002)
17. Arya, A., Di Paola, S.: Multispace Behavioral Model for Face-Based Affective Social Agents. EURASIP Journal on Image and Video Processing (2007)
18. Su, W.-P., Pham, B., Wardhani, A.: Personality and Emotion-Based High-Level Control of Affective Story Characters. IEEE Trans. Visualization and Computer Graphics 13, 281–293 (2007)
19. Goldberg, L.R.: The Structure of Phenotypic Personality Traits. American Psychologist 48, 26–34 (1993)
20. Goldberg, L.R.: A Broad-bandwidth, Public Domain, Personality Inventory Measuring the Lower-level Facets of Several Five-factor Models. In: Mervielde, I., Deary, I., De Fruyt, F., Ostendorf, F. (eds.) Personality Psychology in Europe, vol. 7, pp. 7–28. Tilburg University Press, Tilburg (1999)
21. Durkheim, E.: Suicide. Free Press, New York (1897)

22. Parsons, T., Shils, E.A. (eds.): Toward a General Theory of Action. Harvard University Press, Cambridge (1951)
23. Parsons, T.: Some Comments on the States of the General Theory of Action. American Sociological Review 18, 618–631 (1953)
24. Osgood, C.E., Suci, G.J., Tannenbaum, P.H.: The Measurement of Meaning. University of Illinois Press, Urbana (1957)
25. Osgood, C.E., May, W.H., Myron, M.S.: Cross-Cultural Universals of Affective Meaning. University of Illinois Press, Urbana (1975)
26. Bainbridge, W.S.: Semantic Differential. In: Asher, R.E., Simpson, J.M.Y. (eds.) The Encyclopedia of Language and Linguistics, pp. 3800–3801. Pergamon, Oxford (1994)
27. Lawler, E.J.: An Affect Theory of Social Exchange. American Journal of Sociology 107, 321–352 (2001)
28. Massey, D.S.: A Brief History of Human Society: The Origin and Role of Emotion in Social Life: 2001 Presidential Address. American Sociological Review 67, 1–29 (2002)
29. Heise, D.R.: The Semantic Differential and Attitude Research. In: Summers, G.F. (ed.) Attitude Measurement. Rand McNally, Chicago, pp. 235–253 (1970)
30. Heise, D.R.: Controlling Affective Experience Interpersonally. Social Psychology Quarterly 62, 4–16 (1999)
31. Morgan, R.L., Heise, D.R.: Structure of Emotions. Social Psychology Quarterly 51, 19–31 (1988)
32. Heise, D.R., Calhan, C.: Emotion Norms in Interpersonal Events. Social Psychology Quarterly 58, 223–240 (1995)
33. Heise, D.R.: Project Magellan. Electronic Journal of Sociology 5 (2001), http://www.sociology.org/content/vol005.003/mag.html
34. Schneider, A., Heise, D.R.: Simulating Symbolic Interaction. Journal of Mathematical Sociology 20, 271–287 (1995)
35. Heise, D.R.: Enculturing Agents With Expressive Role Behavior. In: Payr, S., Trappl, R. (eds.) Agent Culture, pp. 127–142. Lawrence Erlbaum Associates, Florence (2004)
36. Bainbridge, W.S.: Minimum Intelligent Neural Device: A Tool for Social Simulation. Mathematical Sociology 20, 179–192 (1995)
37. Bainbridge, W.S.: Validity of Web-based Surveys. In: Burton, O.V. (ed.) Computing in the Social Sciences and Humanities, pp. 51–66. University of Illinois Press, Urbana (2002)
38. Castronova, E.: Synthetic Worlds: The Business and Culture of Online Games, p. 93. University of Chicago Press, Chicago (2005)
39. Merrick, K., Maher, M.L.: Motivated Reinforcement Learning for Non-player Characters in Persistent Computer Game Worlds. In: Proceedings of the 2006 ACM SIGCHI international conference on Advances in computer entertainment technology, Hollywood, California (2006)
40. Bainbridge, W.S.: The Scientific Potential of Virtual Worlds. Science 317, 472–476 (2007)

Comparing Two Emotion Models for Deriving Affective States from Physiological Data

Antje Lichtenstein[1], Astrid Oehme[2], Stefan Kupschick[2], and Thomas Jürgensohn[2]

[1] Technische Universität Berlin, Institut für Psychologie und Arbeitswissenschaft
Fachgebiet Mensch-Maschine-Systeme, Franklinstr. 28-29, 10587 Berlin, Germany
`Antje.Lichtenstein@zmms.tu-berlin.de`
[2] HFC Human-Factors-Consult GmbH,
Köpenickerstraße 325, 12555 Berlin, Germany
`{astrid.oehme,stefan.kupschick,`
`thomas.juergensohn}@human-factors-consult.de`

Abstract. This paper describes an experiment on emotion measurement and classification based on different physiological parameters, which was conducted in the context of a European project on ambient intelligent mobile devices. Emotion induction material consisted of five four-minute video films that induced two positive and three negative emotions. The experimental design gave consideration to both, the basic and the dimensional model of the structure of emotion. Statistical analyses were conducted for films and for self-assessed emotional state and in addition, supervised machine learning technique was utilized. Recognition rates reached up to 72% for a specific emotion (one out of five) and up to 82% for an underlying dimension (one out of two).

Keywords: Emotion classification, dimensional model of affect, basic emotions, ambient intelligence, psychophysiology.

1 Introduction

The European Integrated Project e-SENSE[1] (Capturing Ambient Intelligence for Mobile Communications through Wireless Sensor Networks) aims at enabling Ambient Intelligence in "Beyond 3G Systems" using wireless sensor networks (WSN) for providing context-rich information to applications and services. Dey [1] describes context as '*any information that can be used to characterize the situation of an entity.*' With entity, he refers to a '*person, place, or object that is considered relevant to the interaction between a user and an application, including the user and applications themselves.*' According to his definition, a system that is context aware provides relevant information (and/or) services to the user. The relevancy of the information naturally depends on the user's task.

---

[1] www.e-SENSE.org; e-SENSE is an Integrated Project (IP) supported by the European 6th Framework Programme. The study is a result of a collaboration between Human-Factors-Consult HFC, Berlin and the University of Surrey UniS, Guildford.

C. Peter and R. Beale (Eds.): Affect and Emotion in HCI, LNCS 4868, pp. 35–50, 2008.
© Springer-Verlag Berlin Heidelberg 2008

Context-awareness enables applications and systems to obtain additional information in a situation and therewith to correspond in a richer, more human-like manner with the user. Thus, the user-system interaction is enhanced and the user is able to interact with the application in a more natural and pleasant way.

Within e-SENSE three application spaces and themes have been defined that depict the usage of the e-SENSE concept in various situations. These aim at personal life (Personal application space), the community of professional users (Community application space), and industrial applications (Industrial application space). Especially the Personal application space focuses on the measurement of the users' affective states. Based on emotions, intelligent, i.e. context-aware applications will respond meaningfully, e.g., by offering information, comforting the user or even helping to relive excitement during previously undertaken activities (c.f. [2]).

Fig. 1. Danger Warning Scenario selected from e-SENSE D1.2.1 ([2] p.13)

Figure 1 depicts one of the envisioned scenarios aiming at personal security. The collection of voice, breathing rate, heart rate, noise, and position is symbolized. The woman depicted is riding a public transport vehicle all by herself when a dangerous person enters and begins to approach her. Fear is inferred from Body-Sensor-Network data and an alert is triggered to inform security staff members at the next stop [2].

The experiment reported in the following is a first step on processing captured context information. Emotional states are triggered with short audio-visual stimuli and collected via body sensors.

2 Empirical Literature on Physiological Emotion Measurement

In order to form a theoretical base for research on assessing emotions through contextual and especially physiological data, a literature review on previous psycho-physiological studies concerned with emotional states in particular was conducted. Special attention was given to theoretical models of the structure of emotion that were utilized, since in order to develop an algorithm for emotionally intelligent applications one has to commit to an underlying framework of what exactly emotions are, i.e. what is to be inferred from the data. Previous studies on the physiological assessment of emotions have mainly used two different emotion models.

Several authors (e.g., [3, 4, 5, 6, 7, 8]) based their experimental set-ups on the basic emotion theory, which assumes the existence of a certain number of universal emotions, that can be distinguished clearly from one another [9]. These are: anger, disgust, fear, happiness, sadness and surprise. Even though results were often controversial between those studies, some physiological correlates of emotions could be identified more frequently than others: increase of heart rate, skin conductance level and systolic blood pressure has been associated with fear (e.g. [7]), while an increase of heart rate, systolic and diastolic blood pressure has been associated with anger (e.g., [6]). Sadness has been found to sometimes lead to an increase (e.g., [11]) and sometimes to a decrease (e.g., [7]) of heart rate. Palomba et al. [12] could not find a significant heart rate difference to the measured baseline at all.

A second approach to structure emotions is the dimensional one. Authors that have based their empirical studies on this theoretical assumption (e.g., [13, 14, 15, 16]) have used two or three dimensions (1. valence, 2. arousal, 3. dominance) to define the emotional states induced in their subjects. The theory goes back mainly to work done by Russell and Feldman Barrett (e.g., [17, 18, 19]). Using this approach physiological parameters are not correlated to certain emotional states, but instead to the underlying dimensions. In most of these studies, valence was found to correlate positively with heart rate while arousal correlated positively with skin conductance level. Herbon et al. [20] additionally measured pupil diameter and found it to be a rather strong indicator of the valence of an emotion with small values for negative emotions and larger values for positive emotions. The assessment of facial muscle activity has resulted in the identification of two muscles (zygomatic and corrugator EMG) which correlate with the dimension of valence.

The question of which of the two approaches is more suitable to be used in emotion measurement studies has not been answered yet. Ritz et al. [21] showed in an experiment on different respiration parameters that both, the dimensional and the basic emotion model can be valuable to explain assessed data. They found that arousal and valence alone could not explain vagal excitation differences between two positive emotions. This indicates either the necessity of adding another dimension to differentiate between two particular emotions – which does not have to be essential to differentiate between others – or the added value of additionally taking into account the basic emotion model for data analysis. Feldman Barrett [22] suggested that the applicability of one of the two models might differ individually.

Another way to describe emotions is the appraisal based approach with Klaus Scherer's component process model being the one mostly used in the HCI context. Mahlke & Minge's contribution to this book [23] is dedicated to this approach and elaborates on its prospects for affective computing research.

Most of the above mentioned studies have used photographs to induce positive or negative emotions in their subjects. This strategy is troublesome in as far as emotions induced are usually not very intense. The project, however requires the measurement of intense emotions in everyday life, since only meaningful messages are to be sent by the e-SENSE applications, e.g., in fearful situations when an alert for the security staff is triggered. This ensures the reduction of false alarms and generally enhances the perceived significance of the system. A continuous stream of triggered mood icons could negatively impact the acceptance and therewith usage in a more private context as well.

More suitable in the e-SENSE context, Herbon et al. [20] and also Mahlke & Minge [23] used interactive computer-scenarios of some minute's length to ensure that the emotional response would be strong enough to reliably measure physiological changes. However, interactive scenarios are hard to control and therefore result in a non-estimable amount of error-variance, which is to be kept at a minimum in this first phase of the e-SENSE project. The current study therefore used 4-minute-film clips to a) present a stimulus long enough to induce a strong emotional response and b) standardize the experimental situation.

3 Experiment

Both theoretical models presented in Chapter 2 coexist and are currently used in psycho-physiological studies. However, their results cannot be compared. Developers of emotionally intelligent systems have to decide which model to base their systems on and can then only use data from respective studies. Results of studies based on the competing model are useless and dispensable. One objective of the experiment was therefore to compare the two approaches as to their suitability to form the basis for emotion measurement studies and identify the one approach that researchers should commit to in the future to avoid inflationary and parallel research without use. Findings on correlations of physiological measures with emotions were to be used to implement emotionally intelligent applications in the e-SENSE project. Following general practice in psychological methodology, an experimental design was chosen in order to support the classification approach by collecting data with minimal noiseration, i.e., to control interfering variables, that are unavoidable in field studies as much as possible. This procedure firstly enables the actual detection of effects if there are any and secondly avoids the measurement of effects that are possibly not replicable because they are based on variable-variations not definable in the field.

If this fundamental research step will be successful, further measures will be taken to gradually adapt the classification algorithms to the field.

3.1 Participants, Procedure and Materials

The test sample consisted of 40 subjects (27 male), recruited from the Center for Communication Systems Research CCSR and Surrey's School of Management, who voluntarily took part in the experiment and were not rewarded. Mean age was 30.1 with an age range from 22 to 54. The sample was multi-cultured with representatives from 16 different countries participating.

The experiment was performed at the I-Lab of the University of Surrey, England over a period of five days. Subjects sat in a separated 3.2mx4.5m windowless test room in 2m distance of a 2.4mx1.35m screen (projector solution: 1920x1080 pixels). Stereo sound was provided by two front speakers. The investigators observed the trial via a glass pane from a separate room. Microphones ensured that test-leaders and subjects could talk to each-other in case of any problems.

Subjects were equipped with the HealthLab System (Koralewski Industrie-Elektronik oHG) for physiological measurement, which included a chest belt for respiration measurement, ECG electrodes, EDA electrodes (on the palm of the subject's left hand),

EMG electrodes for facial muscle measurement and a wristband for measurement of skin temperature. The procedure was explained to them and it was made clear that they were to watch short films and afterwards state how they had felt in doing so.

The basic emotion model and the dimensional model imply two different methods of collecting statements about the actual emotional state of a person: According to the basic emotion model, a person who is experiencing an emotion is expected to be able to choose one emotion out of the six universal ones that represents her actual feeling best. In the experiment subjects were prompted with evaluated pictures of people making angry, disgusted, fearful, happy, sad or surprised faces after an emotion induction phase. The corresponding emotion word was written underneath each picture and subjects were asked to pick one. If test-subjects had trouble choosing one of the pictures/words simply because they did not feel like one of them, they were asked to say so and in addition state if they either felt a different emotion (then name it) or if they did not experience an emotion at all.

The dimensional approach implies a very different rating method, which is based on the assumption that emotions can be described by their degrees of valence and arousal. Lang [24] introduced rating scales for these dimensions which consist of pictures of manikins, called SAM for Self Assessment Manikin (see Figure 2).

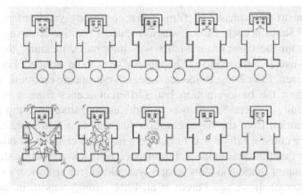

Fig. 2. SAM-Scales for valence (top), arousal (bottom)

In the experiment after each emotion induction phase subjects were prompted with each of the scales separately and then indicated their respective level by saying the letter that was written underneath either each manikin or in between two manikins.

The emotion induction material consisted of five films of a mean duration of approximately 4.15 minutes. The main requirement of the material was to give consideration to both approaches of modeling emotions, since both models were to be compared to one another and constructing material based on only one of the approaches might have had the effect of decreasing the goodness of fit of the other approach. The films were to induce emotions in all four quadrants of the coordinate system shown in Figure 3. In addition, they had to represent one of the six basic emotions anger, disgust, fear, happiness, sadness or surprise.

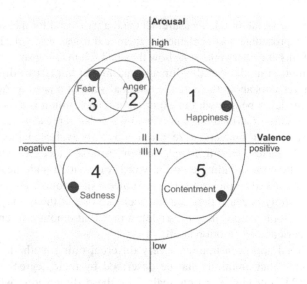

Fig. 3. Films in all four quadrants of the coordinate system

During the construction phase, all films were constantly validated and adjusted in three trials of 5–7 subjects each. *Film 1* was to induce a positive-arousing emotion. The target emotion from the basic emotion list was happiness, meaning that an emotion similar to what is usually referred to as "happiness" was to be induced. For this purpose, a cartoon was chosen. *Film 2* was to induce a negative-arousing emotion, with the target emotion anger from the basic emotion list. Different scenes from a political drama movie were carefully chosen. *Film 3* was to induce a negative-arousing emotion also, but the target emotion from the basic emotion list was fear. Different scenes from a horror movie were chosen. *Film 4* was to induce a negative-calming emotion. The target basic emotion for this film was sadness. It consisted of black-and-white slides, to which special music in minor mode and slow tempo was added (for empirical evidence on the emotional character of music see Peretz et al. [25]. *Film 5* was to induce a positive-calming emotion. There is no basic emotion which can be considered to be located in the fourth quadrant, which is why no target emotion from the basic emotion list could be set for this film. An emotion like content was kept in mind while the film was con-structed. Again, special music was utilized.

At the end of the experiment, subjects were asked to fill out a brief questionnaire on their experience using the two different rating methods. Preference, difficulty and advantages of the rating scales were assessed.

3.2 Data Capture

Data was recorded via Bluetooth on a laptop. There were separate data records for each film and person, which contained the data of all sensors. In the following sec-tion, the utilised physiological measures and derived parameters are described.

Electrocardiogram (ECG): An important parameter which can be extracted from the ECG is heart rate variability (HRV), which is calculated by analyzing the time series of beat-to-beat intervals. Heart rate is the average number of heart beats per minute. Different studies indicated fairly strong correlations with valence [26, 27]. Differences between adjacent beat-to-beat intervals that are larger then 50 msec are measured with pNN-50. As mental stress increases, HRV decreases and thus, pNN-50 should decrease as well. A frequency domain analysis was performed to investigate effects of the sympathetic and parasympathetic nervous system.

The LF/HF ratio (high frequency to low frequency) seems to be the most promising parameter from the frequency domain analysis, as it describes the relation between the activating (sympathetic) and deactivating (parasympathetic) influence of the autonomic nervous system [28]. Larger values indicate an increased activity level.

Breathing rate data has been collected via a chest strap and passed a similar preprocessing as the heart rate data. After baseline and shock removal the peaks of single breaths were detected. Breathing rate was measured as number of breaths per minute. If the amplitude met certain criteria, the inspiration was marked as deep breath. As the number of deep breaths increases in calm situations, a negative correlation with arousal is assumed.

Electrodermal activity (EDA) is a measure of the potential difference between two areas of the skin and is often associated with levels of emotional arousal [29]. At large, electrodermal activity consists of two components. The tonic component is a low frequency baseline conductivity level, the phasic is of higher frequency. Especially for EDA highly significant correlations with valence and arousal have been observed [13]. Arousal has been hypothesized to be a drive state or a non-specific energizer of behavior, something that describes the intensity of an experience. The EDA-median of the raw signal provides an impression about the average level of the electrodermal activity. Statistically meaningful tonic parameters are: EDA-changes (total number of turning points of the low-pass filtered signal) and EDA-increase (percentage of increasing data of the low-pass filtered data curve). Selected phasic parameters are: EDA-responses (total number of short term variations of the signal with amplitudes larger than 3 kOhm and a duration of the decrease of 0.5–5 sec [30]) and EDA-slope (average slope of a response).

The *electromyogram* (EMG) measures electrical potentials generated by the muscles in activation and rest. Zygomatic EMG (corners of the mouth) and corrugator EMG (eyebrows) were used in this study. Very strong correlations with the valence dimension are described in [13]. The following parameters were extracted: EMG-reactions (total number of typical contractions of the respective muscle), EMG-activity (percentage of the data in which any activity is measured) and EMG-sd (standard deviation of the signal). Higher values indicate stronger muscle activity.

Skin temperature was measured on the wrist. It evolves inversely proportional to skin resistance. Two parameters were extracted from the signal: TEMP-mean (mean value of the smoothed signal) and TEMP-increase (gradient of the linear regression function of the signal).

This vast number of parameters was reduced after preliminary computations to the nine most promising ones that were then included in further analyses. Results are reported in the following chapter.

4 Data Analysis and Results

4.1 Subjective Ratings and Physiological Reactions

Pearson correlations of the physiological parameters and the two dimensions valence and arousal were calculated. Table 1 summarizes the results of this analysis. While changes in ECG and EMG parameters are mainly associated with changes in valence, EDA measures correlate with arousal only.

Table 1. Correlation analysis results (* = p<.05, ** = p<.01)

		Valence	Arousal
ECG	HR	-.248**	-
BR	BR	.142*	.152*
	deep breaths	-	-
EDA	Median	-	-.330**
	Increase	-	-.149*
	Responses	-	-
EMG	corr. SD	-.162*	-.162*
	zyg. Act %	.315**	-
Temperature	Increase	-	-

For analyses of basic emotion ratings, repeated measures ANOVA's were conducted. While the experimental set-up was originally a within-subjects design, analyses had to be conducted in a between-subjects design because hardly any subjects felt every one of the six emotions on the list[2], but instead usually four or five different ones. However, results were corrected for test subject number in order not to bias effect sizes. Results are reported parameter-wise.

Heart rate varied significantly with the basic emotion subjects reported to have experienced ($F_{(5, 635)}$=3.8, p<.01, part. Eta^2=.119) and pair-wise comparison revealed group differences between happy and sad. *Breathing rate* varied significantly ($F_{(5, 635)}$=4.0, p<.01, part. Eta^2=.125), which was due to differences between happy and sad also. The *number of deep breaths* did not show a significant effect for basic emotion rating. While analyses did not reveal significant variations for *EDA-increases, EDA-responses* varied significantly ($F_{(5, 635)}$=3.0, p<.05, part. Eta^2=.097), mainly due to group differences between happy and sad again. *EDA-median* varied significantly ($F_{(5, 635)}$=3.5, p<.01, part. Eta^2=.106) and differentiated between afraid and angry, afraid and sad, happy and sad, and sad and surprise. Both, *corrugator* and *zygomatic EMG* varied significantly with values of $F_{(5, 635)}$=3.6, p<.01, part. Eta^2=.112 and $F_{(5, 635)}$=5.8, p<.01, part. Eta^2=.170, respectively. While corrugator EMG mainly differed between happy and sad, zygomatic EMG significance was additionally due to group differences between a) happy and angry and b) happy and disgusted. *Temperature* parameters did not reach significance in this ANOVA.

---

[2] Boredom and Contentment were additionally stated by a number of subjects, even though they were not on the list. They are included in classification analyses later in this chapter.

4.2 Films and Physiological Reactions

After having analyzed subjective emotion data, repeated-measures ANOVAs were conducted for the respective physiological parameters with the within-subjects factor film. The following section reports these results parameter-wise.

Heart Rate varied significantly with less than 1% error probability with the stimulus films presented ($F_{(4,156)}$=9.207, part. Eta^2=.191) Subsequently, Bonferroni-adjusted mean-comparisons for pairs of films were calculated when the overall effect of film in the ANOVA reached p<.05 significance. We found significant differences between fear and anger, fear and sadness, anger and contentment, anger and happiness, as well as sadness and happiness. Both, *breathing rate* with $F_{(4,156)}$=10.742 (p<.01, part. Eta^2=.216) and *number of deep breaths* with $F_{(4,156)}$=2.819 (p<.05, part. Eta^2=.191) varied significantly between films. Breathing rate means were different for fear and happiness, anger and sadness, contentment and happiness, as well as sadness and happiness. Means of deep breaths differed significantly for fear and sadness. The overall *EDA-median* revealed a significant effect of the factor film with $F_{(4,152)}$= 16.091 (p<.01, part. Eta^2=.297). Subsequent single comparisons revealed significant mean differences for fear and anger, fear and contentment, fear and sadness, anger and happiness, contentment and happiness, sadness and happiness. The tonic EDA-parameter *EDA-increase* varied between the stimuli with less than 1% error probability ($F_{(4,152)}$=4.166,), due to differences for fear and contentment as well as contentment and happiness. The factor film reached p<.01 significance for *EDA-responses* ($F_{(4,152)}$=4.936, part. Eta^2=.112), due to sadness and happiness differences. The *corrugator-EMG* varied significantly between films with $F_{(4,156)}$=6.312, p<.01, part. Eta^2=.139, due to differences for anger and sadness, contentment and happiness, sadness and happiness. *Zygomatic-EMG* varied significantly ($F_{(4,156)}$=17.629, p<.01, part. Eta^2=.311) for all comparisons with happiness. The increase of *temperature* was significantly different between films with $F_{(4,156)}$=5,881, p<.01, part. Eta^2=.131. This effect is due to several significant mean differences as depicted in Table 2, which summarizes the significant results found in single Bonferroni-adjusted comparisons between film means for each parameter.

Table 2. Results of film-wise comparisons

	No 1 (Happiness)	No 2 (Anger)	No 3 (Fear)	No 4 (Sadness)	No 5 (Contentment)
Happiness		HR EDA-median ZEMG	BR ZEMG	HR BR EDA-median EDA-response CEMG-SD ZEMG-activity	BR EDA-median EDA-increase CEMG-SD ZEMG Temp-increase
Anger			HR EDA-median	BR CEMG	HR Temp-increase
Fear				HR EDA-median	EDA-median EDA-increase Temp-increase

4.3 Classification

Mood-detection algorithms are a complementary approach to statistical analyses and aims at assigning the physiological data to a specific emotion in order to achieve a reliable prediction of a certain emotion. We used a Support Vector Machine (SVM) classifier to categorize the specified emotions [30]. SVM is a supervised learning method which minimizes the classification error and maximizes the margin between the classes by constructing a multidimensional hyperplane. Only a few data points from every class are needed for the construction: the so called "support vectors". To split the classes as clearly as possible, a so called "soft margin" is used, which maximizes the distance to the nearest clearly split examples by using a slack variable measuring the degree of misclassification of a special datum. The training data for the SVM consisted of the extracted parameters for every film and subject and the known class memberships (either the films or the subject's rating). Leave-one-out cross-validation was used to process the classification results, i.e., for each subject a separate SVM was trained with the data of all remaining participants and subsequently tested with the respective subject's data. Thus, the classification rate for one parameter set is the mean value of all trained SVMs.

4.3.1 Film-Based Analysis

The film-based approach assumes that the chosen movie induces a specific emotion. Following the dimensional model, two classifiers were trained, one for 'valence' and one for 'arousal'. Data was assigned to a high or low level of the specific dimension based on the coordinate of the movie in the model (cp., Figure 3). As expected, detection rate increased with the number of considered parameters and reached about 82 % for 'arousal' and 72 % for 'valence' with 5 parameters each (see Figure 4). The most useful parameters for 'arousal' were breathing rate, EDA-increase, TEMP-increase and corrugator-EMG sd. 'Valence' was predicted best with the parameters zygomatic-EMG activity, corrugator-EMG sd, deep breaths and EDA-increase.

In a second step, a SVM was trained following the basic-emotion model, based on what was intended to be stimulated by the presented movies. With this approach, subjective ratings do not matter. Data of a participant who rated herself as 'calm', for example, while watching a 'scary' movie is still considered 'scared'. Rates can be increased by about 50%, if a specific parameter set is used for every basic emotion. However, classification is no longer mutually exclusive. For the use in a common parameter set, heart rate seems to be essential. Further important parameters are zygomatic-EMG activity and TEMP-increase. For the specific sets almost every single one of the parameters plays an important role for a unique basic emotion. So, taking 5 parameters and identical parameter sets for every film, data was correctly classified in about 47 % of the cases, classification rates increases to about 72 % using the specific parameter sets (happiness: 72.5%, fear: 60%, sadness: 60%, anger: 57.5%, contentment: 52.5%). Thus, for the basic emotion approach many different parameters have to be monitored simultaneously to achieve satisfactory results.

4.3.2 Rating-Based Analysis

Taking into account, that every individual is able to estimate her own emotional state, training data based on a subject's self assessment should lead to fine results also.

Following the film-based approach, two SVMs were trained for the dimensional and one was trained for the basic emotion model. Normalized self ratings were divided into two dimensions (arousal and valence) each with two groups (high and low). In contrast to the film-based dimensional analysis, here valence was predicted slightly better than arousal. However, the percentage of correct estimations of arousal was about 10% lower (see Figure 4). Predictive parameters for arousal were EDA-increase, breathing rate and EDA-reactions. Valence was predicted best with heart rate and EDA reactions.

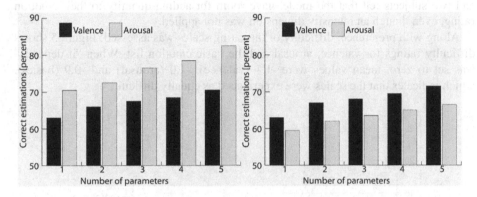

Fig. 4. Comparison of film based (left) and rating based (right) dimensional classification

For the basic-emotion approach, subjects had to choose between different emotion categories, which differed in number from the presented films. Additional basic emotions were 'boredom' and 'surprise' as well as 'contentment' for the sake of comparability. Numbers of chosen basic emotions were not uniformly distributed. This and the larger number of classes (8 vs. 5) resulted in inferior classification rates (about 30%) in comparison to the film-based analysis. Even utilizing specific instead of identical parameter sets did not lead to better results (boredom: 50%, surprise: 42.5%, fear: 35.4%, disgust: 33.3%, contentment: 30%, sadness: 28.3, happiness: 26.6%, anger: 25%). Most frequently used parameters were EDA-increase, breathing rate, deep breaths, zygomatic-EMG activity and TEMP-increase.

4.4 Rating Experience

When asked whether they preferred one of the two rating methods, i.e. the dimensional or the basic emotion approach, 18 subjects stated that they preferred using the basic emotions and 22 stated that they preferred using the dimensional scale. Advantages were identified through content-analysis of written choice-explanations.

Eight subjects chose the basic emotion model for its intuitiveness, seven for its clearness. A sample statement from one of the subjects describing this issue was: "It's more close to the fact, very clear." Three subjects stated that they liked the facial photographs more than the manikins from the dimensional rating scale and three subjects described that the basic emotion approach because it takes into account the multi-factoriality of emotions ("Emotions are too complex to be expressed just by the combination of positive/negative and excitement."). Two subjects preferred the basic emotion scale because it gave them the opportunity to verbalize a totally different emotion, which was not on the list. However, this is not an advantage of this particular approach, but instead simply of the scale as it was used in this study.

Eleven subjects chose the dimensional emotion model for its accuracy. A sample statement was: "[It] can more accurately represent emotions by using different parameters to define the emotional condition." Seven subjects liked the infinity ("This [note: SAM] has a broader range."), two preferred the manikins over the real faces and two subjects felt that the model gave room for adding quantity to their emotion rating, even though an intensity dimension was not applied.

Along with preference, difficulty of the rating scales was assessed. Figure 5 shows difficulty ratings for valence, arousal and the basic emotion list. When "it depends" was set to zero, mean values were -1.1 (valence), -1.0 (arousal) and -0.9 (basics), which indicates that the scales were experienced as equally difficult.

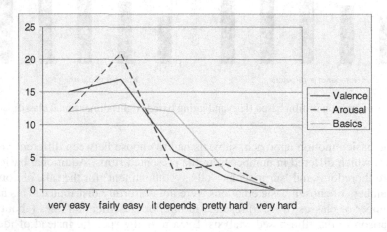

Fig. 5. Difficulty ratings for the dimensional scales and the basic emotion list

5   Discussion

5.1   Subjective Ratings and Physiological Reactions

An important question to be answered was which of the two approaches to structure emotion can best explain variance in physiological reactions while watching short films of emotional content. Correlation data and ANOVA results attained from the analyses of subjective emotion ratings can be compared as to their degree of statistically explained variance[3] (Table 3). It can clearly be observed, that ratings based on the basic emotion model account for far more variance than ratings based on the dimensional model are able to. This indicates that the six-point-basic emotion scale assessed different and/or additional information about the emotional state of a subject

---

[3] Derived from squared correlation coefficients and partial eta^2-values.

Table 3. Comparisons of explained variance for the to emotion models

Parameter	Dimensional Model	Basic Emotion Model
Heart Rate	6%	12%
Breathing Rate	4%	13%
Number of deep breaths	0%	5%
EDA-median	11%	11%
EDA-increase	2%	7%
EDA-responses	0%	10%
CEMG (sd)	6%	11%
ZEMG (activity)	10%	17%
Temperature-increase	0%	5%

in comparison to the nine-point valence and arousal scales. Similar to factor analyses, loss of information here can be due to the fact that the dimensional model constitutes some sort of underlying structure of a categorical approach.

5.2 Objective Film Data and Subjective Rating Data

Several parameters that differentiated between films did not differentiate between subjective emotional states. Analysis of subjective ratings showed a strong effect for the happy and sad conditions, but few for others. This bias towards happy and sad differentiation could be observed for film also and the authors propose that this is due to the fact that happy and sad are the two states (and films, respectively) that differ from each other most. In a valence-arousal-plane happy is located in quadrant 1 (top right), while sadness is located in quadrant 3 (bottom left). Other emotional states induced in the experiment only differ from one another in either valence or arousal, while anger and fear do not differ in one of the dimensions at all. This greater similarity obviously makes differentiation a lot harder.

However, there were other films where a differentiation based on physiological reactions was possible, which are worth a discussion: Zygomatic muscle activity appeared to be a very valid parameter for detecting something like happiness. It significantly differentiated the induced emotion of film 1 from all other emotional states. Temperature was especially relevant for film 5, something like contentment. In contrast, heart rate and even more so electrodermal activity appear to be useful in a more general sense. Both – combined or individually – are important parameters for the differentiation of a number of groups, e.g. happiness/sadness, happiness/anger, contentment/anger, fear/anger, fear/sadness and fear/contentment. Corrugator muscle activity was again a very specific parameter.

It is apparent that film and rating ANOVAS are very different. Film ANOVA led to a much greater amount of significant results. This indicates that – at least when a basic emotion model is utilized – objective data on induced emotions is superior over subject's self-assessment. We do not assume that really all of our subjects had so very different emotional reactions to the induction material, but instead believe that rating differences are due to different standards of evaluation. Emotion words and pictures from the basic emotion scale were apparently interpreted individually. An aggravating factor specific to our experiment was a non-representative sample. Subjects scored above-average for rationality and control, while answering slightly below average for extraversion. This indicates that self-assessment might not have been perfectly reliable.

5.3 Classification

SVM analyses led to very satisfactory results, especially for the basic emotion model. Correct estimations were made in up to 72.5% of the time for film 1 (happiness) with guessing probability of 20% in the 'one out of five' model. Film 2 (anger), 3 (fear), and 4 (sadness) were also classified fairly well with correct estimations up to 60%. Even the estimation for film 5 (contentment) with 52.5% was still 2.6 times greater than guessing probability. Naturally, estimation rates dropped when more categories were taken into account with the self-assessment, but when guessing probability (12.5% in the 'one out of eight' model) is taken into account, differences are not as large after all. However, a slight difference remains and in the end 'film' still seemed to form a better basis for classification analysis than self-assessment. Film-wise estimation rates were three times greater than guessing probability on average while they were about 2.7 times greater for subjective ratings.

Estimation rates for the dimensional model were inferior to those for the basic emotion model with a range from 65 to 82% and a guessing probability of 50%. This finding confirms the results of the statistical analyses, in which the basic emotion model accounted for larger explained variance.

5.4 Rating Experience

Results of the post-experimental questionnaire did not yield any differences between the two approaches. Preference and difficulty ratings were approximately balanced and advantages were stated for both scales.

6 Outlook

Following the results reported in this study, the authors suggest to utilize subjective ratings all along the stimulus design in order to evaluate and check the subjective validity of the material. However, since subjective measures in this field of research are strongly biased by inter-individual differences in nomenclature interpretation, additional variance to the already largely varying physiological data may lead to decreased effect detection. A more stable and comparable result can be reached by using evaluated material that is also the base for data variance analysis. In the study reported films were used to induce different emotional states. Comparisons based on films led to a larger selectivity than those based on subjective ratings.

The selection algorithm developed so far can now be applied to a standardized setting for demonstrating the overall system usage, i.e., the emotional state of a person can be measured and used to trigger a message such as 'This movie is funny, I would recommend it' in the private context. In real life such a situation is quite controllable since a person watching a movie usually sits in a chair and concentrates. For more lively scenarios, the algorithms will have to be trained with a higher noise-ratio in semi-controlled and finally in field trials. In doing so, adjustments will have to be made on a scenario-by-scenario basis.

For the development of ambient intelligent systems, two variants of system training can be proposed: Firstly, the subjective rating can be applied in various situations by the user him-/herself. Inter-individual differences and the above mentioned bias are not influential when the systems can be customized. Secondly, and less obtrusive can be a learning algorithm that is supported by additional context information besides the emotional state and therewith correlates certain situations (places, things, individuals, etc.) with the user's affective data. This, however, is a hard challenge for the development of such systems. Yet, it would depict a true integration of context information.

Following our literature review, voice parameters seem to offer additional predictive value for affective state recognition. The unobtrusive measurement via microphone could be easily utilized for ambient intelligence. In order to measure these data, however, another test setting has to be chosen in order to ensure voice samples valid enough for analysis. Besides the advantage of easy usage, this is also a disadvantage of the measure as such: the user has to talk for a sufficient time period.

The following research will be dedicated to additional data collection for the detection-algorithm learning-process including an improved, more focussed emotion induction. Besides SVM, other algorithms will be tested (e.g., neural networks and fuzzy clustering).

References

1. Dey, A.K.: Understanding and Using Context. Personal and Ubiquitous Computing Journal 5, 4–7 (2001)
2. Forest, F., Oehme, A., Yaici, K., Verchère-Morice, C.: Psycho-Social Aspects of Context Awareness in Ambient Intelligent Mobile Systems. In: 15th IST Mobile & Wireless Communication Summit, Myconos (2006),
   http://www.ist-esense.org/index.php?id=149
3. Ax, A.: The physiological differentiation between fear and anger in humans. Psychosomatic Medicine 55, 433–442 (1953)
4. Ekman, P., Levenson, R.W., Friesen, W.: Autonomic nervous system activity distinguishes among emotions. Science 221, 1208–1210 (1983)
5. Palomba, D., Stegagno, L.: Physiology, perceived emotion and memory: responding to film sequences. In: Birbaumer, N., Öhmann, A. (eds.) The Structure of Emotion, pp. 158–168. Hogrefe & Huber Publishers (1993)
6. Fredrickson, B.L., Mancuso, R.A., Branigan, C., Tugade, M.M.: The undoing effect of positive emotions. Motivation and Emotion 24, 237–257 (2000)
7. Christie, I.C.: Multivariate discrimination of emotion-specific autonomic nervous system activity. MSc Thesis, Virginia Polytechnic Institute and State University (2002)
8. Nasoz, F., Alvarez, K., Lisetti, C.L., Finkelstein, N.: Emotion recognition from physiological signals for presence technologies. International Journal of Cognition, Technology, and Work 6 (2003)
9. Ekman, P.: An argument for basic emotions. Cognition and Emotion 6(3/4) (1992)
10. Johnstone, T., Scherer, K.R.: Vocal communication of emotion. In: Lewis, M., Haviland-Jones, J. (eds.) Handbook of Emotions, 2nd edn., pp. 220–235. Guilford Press, New York (2000)

11. Levenson, R.W., Ekman, P., Friesen, W.V.: Voluntary facial action generates emotion-specific autonomic nervous system activity. Psychophysiology 27, 363–384 (1999)
12. Palomba, D., Sarlo, M., Agrilli, A., Mini, A., Stegagno, L.: Cardiac response associated with affective processing of unpleasant film stimuli. International Journal of Psychophysiology 36, 45–57 (1999)
13. Bradley, M., Greenwald, M.K., Hamm, A.O.: Affective picture processing. In: Birbaumer, N., Öhmann, A. (eds.) The Structure of Emotion, pp. 48–65. Hogrefe & Huber Publishers, Toronto (1993)
14. Detenber, B.H., Simons, R.F., Bennett, G.G.: Roll 'em!: the effects of picture motion on emotional responses. Journal of Broadcasting and Electronic Media 21, 112–126 (1998)
15. Anttonen, J., Surakka, V.: Emotions and heart rate while sitting on a chair. In: CHI 2005 Conference Proceedings, pp. 491–499. ACM Press, New York (2005)
16. Peter, C., Herbon, A.: Emotion Representation and Physiology Assignments in Digital Systems. Interacting With Computers 18, 139–170 (2006)
17. Russell, J.A.: A circumplex model of affect. Journal of Personality and Social Psychology 39, 1161–1178 (1980)
18. Russell, J.A., Feldman Barrett, L.: Core Affect, Prototypical Emotional Episodes, and Other Things Called Emotion: Dissecting the Elephant. Journal of Personality and Social Psychology 76(5), 805–819 (1999)
19. Russel, J.A.: How shall an emotion be called? In: Plutchik, R., Conte, H. (eds.) Circumplex Models of Personality and Emotion, APA, Washington, pp. 205–220 (1997)
20. Herbon, A., Peter, C., Markert, L., van der Meer, E., Voskamp, J.: Emotion studies in HCI – a new approach. In: Proceedings of the 2005 HCI International Conference, Las Vegas (2005)
21. Ritz, T., Thöns, M., Fahrenkrug, S., Dahme, B.: Airways, respiration, and respiratory sinus arrhythmia during picture viewing. Psychophysiology 42, 568–578 (2005)
22. Feldman Barrett, L.: Discrete Emotions or Dimensions? The Role of Valence Focus and Arousal Focus. Cognition and Emotion 12(4), 579–599 (1998)
23. Mahlke, S., Minge, M.: Consideration of Multiple Components of Emotions on Human-Technology Interaction. In: Peter, C., Beale, R. (eds.) Affect and Emotion in Human-Computer Interaction. LNCS, vol. 4868. Springer, Heidelberg (2008)
24. Lang, P.J.: Behavioral treatment and bio-behavioral assessment: Computer applications. In: Sidowsky, J.B., Johnson, J.H., Williams, T.A. (eds.) Technology in mental health care delivery systems, pp. 119–137. Ablex, Norwood (1980)
25. Peretz, I.: The nature of music from a biological perspective. Cognition 100, 1–32 (1998)
26. Prkachin, K.M., Williams-Avery, R.M., Zwaal, C., Mills, D.E.: Cardiovascular changes during induced emotion: an application of Lang's theory of emotional imagery. Journal of Psychosomatic Research 47, 255–267 (1999)
27. Neumann, S.A., Waldstein, S.R.: Similar patterns of cardiovascular response during emotional activation as a function of affective valence and arousal and gender. Journal of Psychosomatic Research 50, 245–253 (2001)
28. Malik, M., Bigger, J., Camm, A., Kleiger, R.: Heart rate variability - Standards of measurement, physiological interpretation, and clinical use. European Heart Journal 17, 354–381 (1996)
29. Cook, E.W., Lang, P.J.: Affective judgement and psychophysiological response. Dimensional covariation in the evaluation of pictorial stimuli. Journal of psychophysiology 3, 51–64 (1989)
30. Roedema, T.M., Simons, R.F.: Emotion-processing deficit in alexithymia. Psychophysiology 36, 379–387 (1999)
31. Vapnik, V.N.: The Nature of Statistical Learning Theory. Springer, New York (1999)

Consideration of Multiple Components of Emotions in Human-Technology Interaction

Sascha Mahlke[1] and Michael Minge[2]

[1] Centre of Human-Machine-Systems,
Technische Universität Berlin
sascha.mahlke@zmms.tu-berlin.de
[2] Centre of Human-Machine-Systems,
Technische Universität Berlin
michael.minge@zmms.tu-berlin.de

Abstract. The study of users' emotional behavior as an important aspect of the user experience has been receiving increasing attention for the past few years. In this paper we discuss the multi-component character of emotions and its consideration in the area of human-technology interaction. Based on the approach proposed by Scherer [1], various aspects of emotions were investigated in an interactive context: subjective feelings, physiological activation, motor expression, cognitive appraisals, and behavioral tendencies. In an experiment emotion-related changes were detected for a number of emotional components by using a variety of methods: rating scales for subjective feelings, electromyography of facial muscles, heart rate, electrodermal activity, performance data and questionnaires on cognitive appraisals. Results are discussed with respect to the correlation between the components and their associated methods. We suggest that a combination of methods provides a comprehensive basis for analyzing emotions as an aspect of the user experience.

1 Introduction

A necessary precondition for studying emotions and affect as part of the user experience is the assessment of product-driven emotional reactions. To measure emotional reactions, a variety of methods can be applied. They range from physiological measures, such as heart rate and electrodermal activity (EDA), electromyography (EMG) or pupil responses, and the analysis of facial expressions captured by video, to various kinds of survey methods, like questionnaires, interviews, etc. No single parameter can index emotional states unambiguously. Psychological research suggests that emotions represent a complex phenomenon consisting of reactions on various component levels [2, 3]. Therefore the assessment of emotional reactions can be improved by combining methods that are associated with different components of emotions.

2 Multiple Component Character of Emotions

Most methodological approaches to emotions in human-technology interaction still fail to account for this central feature of human emotions, namely their multi-component

C. Peter and R. Beale (Eds.): Affect and Emotion in HCI, LNCS 4868, pp. 51–62, 2008.
© Springer-Verlag Berlin Heidelberg 2008

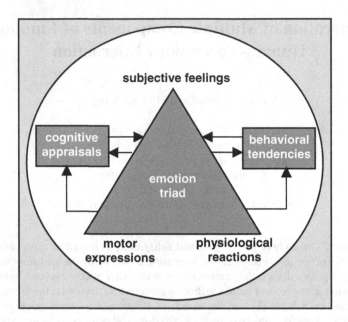

Fig. 1. Five components of human emotions according to Scherer [1]

character. The assumption is emphasized by a number of psychological theories that define emotions as complex phenomena consisting of changes in different relevant subsystems. Different models exist that describe the relevant components of emotions. Izard [4] proposed an *emotion triad* that comprises subjective feelings, physiological activation, and motor expressions. In a model by Scherer [1] this triad is connected to two other components, i.e. cognitive appraisals and behavioral tendencies (Figure 1). Other authors integrate motor expressions and behavioral tendencies in one component and name it as conative [5] or behavioral [2]. Irrespective of the exact composition of these models they presume that all components are important for understanding human emotions.

Scherer [6] goes a step further and connects each of the components to an organismic subsystem. Additionally, he proposes each of the systems to have a special emotion function. Cognitive appraisals are relevant for the evaluation of objects and events. The subjective feeling component's function is the monitoring of internal state and organism-environment interaction. Physiological reactions represent activation and regulation processes both of the neuroendocrine and the autonomic system. The role of behavior tendencies is to prepare reactions, while motor expressions serve to communicate behavior tendencies.

3 Methods Related to the Components of Emotional User Reactions

In the previous section we proposed a multi-component model to assess emotional user reactions. The question remains which approaches exist to measure emotion-related changes for the five components. Without doubt, there is a remarkable diversity of methods and assessment scales. Therefore in this section, we discuss a selected variety of quantitative measurement approaches and consider their application in previous research in human-technology interaction.

3.1 Assessments of Subjective Feelings

To assess subjective feelings, a variety of self-assessment scales is available which assume that the individual is the best source of information on the emotions they experience [7, 8]. The *SAM* scales (Self-Assessment-Manikin), introduced by Lang [9], consist of pictures of manikins for each of the dimensions *valence*, *arousal* and *dominance*. The manikins represent five states from happy to unhappy, excited to calm and controlled to control. Individuals rate their feeling either on a manikin or in the space between two manikins, which results in nine graduations per dimension. The non-verbal assessment is supposed to reduce intercultural differences, especially those that result from semantic verbalizing of emotions.

The *affect grid* [10] is a semantic questionnaire to assess a human's emotional state. In contrast to SAM, the affect grid is a single scale questionnaire. It consists of a 9 x 9-matrix which is surrounded by eight adjectives describing emotional feelings. The adjectives are arranged by the dimensions activation (high, low) and valence (positive, negative), like the ones in Russell's circumplex model of emotion (1980). Individuals are instructed to rate their feeling by setting a cross in one field of the matrix.

3.2 Measurements of Physiological Reactions

Several methods can be used to gain information on physiological reactions. The most promising way to determine emotional connotations is the measure of electrodermal activity (EDA). Common parameters are *skin conductance response* (SCR), *skin resistance response* (SRR) and *skin potential response* (SPR). The EDA is merely controlled by sympathic activation. Previous research suggests that higher decreases in EDA are correlated with more negatively valanced situations [11, 12].

A second way to gain information on physiological activation is to record heart activity by an electrocardiogram. There are a variety of parameters for analyzing and interpreting the raw signal. Common time-related parameters are *heart rate, inter-beat-interval* and *heart rate variability* [13]. However, these show inconsistent results for predicting emotional valence in human-computer interaction. While Ward & Marsden [11] describe a decrease of heart rate in negative valenced situations, other authors found a positive correlation between heart rate and valence [14]. Summarizing, heart activity seems to be a more reliable indicator for arousal and mental workload than for emotional valence [13].

Finally, *pupillometry* is the study of the dilatation of the pupil. Previous research suggests consistently that, like heart activity, pupillometry is a powerful measure for autonomic responses and mental workload. The more demanding a process is, the larger the pupil is supposed to be [15]. Additionally, Hess & Polt [16] found a significant correlation between dilatation and the valence of a stimulus. Thus, more pleasant stimuli are susceptible for generating more dilated pupils.

3.3 Measurements of Motor Expressions

Measurements of motor expressions are related to facial and body expression, gestures and speech characteristics. Especially, the relation between emotions and facial expressions has been studied extensively. The Facial Action Coding System (FACS) is one approach to assess facial expression. It is based on the analysis of 44 facial muscles that are activated single or in combination by an individual. A trained person categorizes the observed pattern of activity in respect to the six culture-independent basic emotions fear, anger, joy, disgust, grief, and surprise [17]. To gain reliable information, FACS needs an intensive training in observation. Video-computer-based analysis of facial activity does not yet lead to comparable results [18].

Electromyography (EMG) measures spontaneous muscle activity and is another way to study facial expression. Sensors are placed on the muscle regions and detect sensitively minimal voltage caused by activity. Facial EMG studies have found that activity of the corrugator supercilii muscle, which lowers the eyebrow and is involved in producing frowns, varies inversely with the emotional valence of presented stimuli and reports of emotional state. The activity of the zygomaticus major muscle, which controls smiling, is positively associated with positive emotional stimuli and positive affect [19, 20].

Another approach based on measuring motor expressions is the analyses of speech characteristics, like speed, intensity, melody, and loudness. Empirical research suggests that these qualities are highly correlated with emotional feelings, and are therefore reliable indicators for emotional reactions [21].

3.4 Assessments of Cognitive Appraisals

Different approaches examine the role of cognition in the development process of emotions [5, 22, 23, 24]. In other words, they deal with the problem that the same situation can induce different emotions depending on how a person interprets the situation. All theories of cognitive appraisals of emotions offer a set of dimensions that are proposed to be relevant for the interpretation of a situation in relation to the development of emotions. Although the proposed dimensions differ to some extent, efforts have been recently made to find an integrative model of cognitive appraisals [25].

Based on the appraisal dimensions quantitative and qualitative methods can be used [26]. A quantitative approach is the *GAF* (Geneva appraisal questionnaire) by Scherer [6]. The items of the GAF represent the five dimensions of Scherer's cognitive appraisal theory: intrinsic pleasantness, novelty, goal conduciveness, coping potential, and norm/self compatibility [1]. Novelty is connected to familiarity and predictability of the occurrence of a stimulus, while the intrinsic pleasantness dimension describes whether a stimulus event is likely to result in positive or negative emotion. A goal relevance check establishes the importance of a stimulus for the momentary hierarchy of goals/needs. The dimension of coping potential relates to the extent an event can be controlled or influenced by an agent, and norm/self compatibility is connected to internal and external standards.

Additionally, various qualitative methods can be used. The thinking aloud method that is very common in human-technology interaction can also be used to gain appraisal-related information. People are encouraged to state and describe every emotional reaction they feel during interaction with a technological system. The statements have to be recorded properly, analyzed by a qualitative procedure and related to the appraisal dimension. To prevent non-ecological interaction between usage and assessment, the thinking aloud method can be applied retrospectively, e.g. by presenting a video confrontation that took place after interaction completion.

3.5 Measurements of Behavioral Tendencies

Scherer defines the role of behavior tendencies as preparing for reactions. Indicators of these reactions can be measured in different ways. Behavioral measures as performance related variables have a long tradition in human-technology interaction research. Central indicators of performance are *speed of reaction* (e.g. the time required for single input operations or completing a defined goal), the *accuracy* of reaching a goal, the *number of errors* and the *number of creative ideas* during interaction with a system. Findings of Partala & Surakka [27] indicate that behavioral data is related to EMG values. The results demonstrated that the less the corrugator supercilii muscle was activated during interaction with a usable designed system, the higher was the rate of successful and goal conductive reactions. As indicators of behavioral tendencies, also unspecific questionnaires about the *intention of use* or the *intention of purchase* can be mentioned. However, these indicators are connected with some problems of reliability [3].

Summarizing, we discussed a number of methods that can be associated with the five components of emotion. The question remains to what extent a combination of methods based on the component approach offers a comprehensive way to understand different aspects of the emotional user experience in the context of HCI.

4   An Empirical Study of Multiple Components of Emotions

The aim of the following study was to investigate the relations that exist between the five components of an emotional experience in an interactive context. Therefore we composed a combination of various methods representing the full range of components of Scherer's model. Emotional-related changes on the components were recorded while participants interacted with two versions of a computer-based simulation of a mobile phone.

4.1   Method

Participants: Thirty individuals (15 men, 15 women) with an average age of 25.9 years took part in the study. Most of them were students at Technische Universität Berlin. They were familiar with usage of mobile phones and had moderate to high computer experience. Participants were paid for taking part in the study based on their performance.

Stimuli: As stimuli we designed two versions of a computer-based simulation of a mobile phone that we varied in the degree of quality in use. To induce differences in emotional user reactions, we varied the user interface in multiple ways according to Mentis & Gay [28]. Therefore, the less usable version had a rather complex and less self-descriptive menu hierarchy, e.g. it consisted of more irrelevant menu keys that were named in an uncommon way. Moreover, the display colors showed a disadvantageous contrast and we used a type of rather small characters. Finally, system reactions of the less usable version were delayed.

Independent variables: To measure emotion-related changes on the components, we recorded heart rate, electrodermal activity, electromyographic activity of zygomaticus major and corrugator supercilii and the time required for input operations to gain information on physiological reactions, motor expressions and behavioral tendencies during task completion. Furthermore, we used the dimensions activation and valence of SAM (Self Assessment Manikin) that participants filled in after completing each task. To collect data on cognitive appraisals, we presented a video of the user's interaction phase and used both retrospective thinking aloud method and a short questionnaire based on the Geneva appraisal questionnaire [6].

Procedure: At the beginning, sensors for measuring physiological reactions and facial expressions were attached and baseline values were recorded. The prototypes of mobile phones were presented on a computer monitor. A mouse was used as input device. Two sets of five tasks typical for mobile phone usage were chosen to be used in the experiment (see Table 1). Tasks ranged from short ones, like "reduce the volume of your mobile phone", to more complex ones, like "add a new number to your contact list".

Table 1. Tasks given to the participants

Task set 1	Task set 2
a) Reduce the volume of your ringtone.	a) Set the speaker on.
b) Set the date: "2005/09/02".	b) Set the alarm clock: "09:00 a.m.".
c) Add the following number to your contact list: "02698673250".	c) Set a divert to the phone number: "02705434860".
d) Call "Anton".	d) Delete the number of "Andrea".
e) Create and send a short message: "See us at 3" to "0254332890".	e) Create and send a short message: "Where are you" to "02543328905".

Participants started with one version and completed the first set of tasks. Then they switched to the other system to solve the remaining tasks. Maximum time for each task was two minutes. Heart rate, EDA and EMG were measured during task completion. After each task, participants filled in the SAM scales. After the electrodes were removed, we started the video confrontation. The participants watched their video-taped task completion behavior and were asked to think aloud what they felt during system use. After the presentation of each task they filled in the short appraisal questionnaire. To ensure a realistic emotional involvement, participants were paid depending on their performance. They started with a credit of 15 Euro, which was reduced by 1 Euro whenever a task could not be completed. Participants were informed about each reduction and were constantly aware of the amount of money that was left. A session lasted about 75 minutes. Time for task completion was about fifteen minutes overall.

Data reduction: Heart rate and EDA were measured as differences from the individual baseline level in order to reduce inter-individual differences and allow comparisons between subjects. For the heart rate data we converted the time series data to single points through averaging the time series for each task. Regarding EDA, we decided to interpret the amplitude of the maximum reaction value for each task in respect to the latency and recovery time of the EDA signal. The EMG data was integrated and t-transformed. All utterances received from the retrospective thinking aloud method were categorized with respect to the appraisal dimensions. Affirmative utterances were offset against negating ones and means were estimated for each dimension and all participants. For indicating the behavior intention, the time for task completion was divided by the number of inputs to get the average time per input.

4.2 Results

We first calculated a multivariate Pearson Correlation of the elements of the emotion triad (see Table 2). Correlations are rather small, but other studies on emotions showed similar correlations between physiological measures and ratings [12]. Both physiological measures as well as the measures of facial expression correlated significantly with the arousal dimension of the subjective feeling questionnaire (SAM). EDA and the activity of the corrugator supercilii and the zygomaticus major were also significantly correlated with the valence dimension. Physiological measures and facial expression measures did not correlate significantly.

Table 2. Correlations between dependent variables of the emotion triad ($*p < .05$; $**p < .01$)

	SAM - valence	SAM - arousal	Heart rate	EDA	corrugator supercilii
SAM - arousal	**-0.32****				
Heart rate	0.02	**0.25****			
EDA	**-0.14***	**0.26****	0.01		
corrugator supercilii	**-0.16****	**0.12***	0.11	0.01	
zygomaticus major	**0.19****	**0.25****	0.06	0.06	0.10

The results demonstrate a significant correlation between the valence dimension and the arousal dimension of SAM ($r = -0.32$, $p < .01$). This connection of the two theoretically independent dimensions may be caused by the stimuli we chose. The "ill-designed" version led to high arousing reactions with negative valence, while positive and low arousing emotions were experienced when the well-designed version was used. On the other hand, no significant correlations were found between the data recorded through the two methods of physiological measurements, i.e. EDA and heart rate.

Regarding the two methods we used to assess cognitive appraisals, we also found differences. Correlations between intrinsic pleasantness, goal/need conduciveness, and coping potentials lie between $r = 0.44$ and $r = 0.71$ and were highly significant ($p < .001$). On the other hand, no significant correlations were found on the dimensions of novelty and norm/self compatibility.

In another step, we analyzed the relations between the elements of the emotion triad and the other two components. The dimensions of the appraisal questionnaire were highly correlated with the valence dimension of the self-assessment manikin (see Table 3). Valence correlated positively with pleasantness ($r = 0.73$), goal/need conduciveness ($r = 0.64$), coping potential ($r = 0.64$), and norm/self compatibility ($r = 0.64$). Valence and novelty were negatively correlated ($r = -0.44$). All correlations were statistically significant ($p < .01$). Smaller correlations could be found between the arousal dimension of subjective feeling component and the appraisal dimensions. Physiological and motor expression data correlated with some of the appraisal dimensions slightly between $r = 0.13$ and $r = 0.23$. The correlation between the data gained with the retrospective think aloud method and the emotion triad differed for the two appraisal dimensions novelty and norm/self compatibility. Correlations were smaller for these dimensions with the respect to all components of the emotion triad.

The average time per input – our measure of the behavioral component – was significantly higher in situations that were experienced as less pleasant, goal conductive, capable and norm/self compatibility (see Table 4). The behavioral data also correlated with the valence and arousal dimension of the subjective feeling component ($r = -0.23$ and $r = 0.14$). No significant correlations were found between the behavioral component and the physiological or expressive ones (see Table 5).

Table 3. Correlations between dependent variables of the emotion triad and data from the cognitive appraisal questionnaire ($*p < .05$; $**p < .01$)

	SAM - valence	SAM - arousal	Heart rate	EDA	corrugator supercilii	zygomaticus major
pleasantness	0.73**	-0.36**	-0.06	0.13*	-0.19**	-0.23**
novelty	-0.44**	0.41**	0.04	0.19**	0.07	0.18**
goal relevance	0.61**	-0.31**	-0.15*	0.10	-0.15*	-0.25**
coping potential	0.64**	-0.34**	0.11	0.08	-0.15*	-0.23**
norm/self capability	0.64**	-0.28**	0.06	0.08	-0.14*	-0.23**

Table 4. Correlations between dependent variables of the cognitive appraisal questionnaire and the behavioral component data (*$p < .05$; **$p < .01$)

	pleasantness	novelty	Goal relevance	coping potential	norm/self capability
time per input	-0.31**	0.16**	-0.33**	-0.35**	-0.30**

Table 5. Correlations between dependent variables of the emotion triad and the behavioral component data (*$p < .05$; **$p < .01$)

	SAM – valence	SAM - arousal	Heart rate	EDA	corrugator supercilii	zygomaticus major
time per input	-0.23**	0.14*	0.07	< 0.01	0.03	0.08

4.3 Discussion

The results support the assumption that emotional user experience is determined by a number of different but related components. Summarizing the correlations between the components, we found high correlations between cognitive appraisal and subjective feeling data. Both are connected significantly but with smaller correlations to the other three components of emotions. No significant correlations were found between physiological and expressive reactions, and both components also did not show any connection to behavioral tendencies.

Looking at the correlations in more detail the results regarding valence are consistent with our expectations. Measures showed lower EDA values and less activity of corrugator supercilii when experienced emotions were rated as rather positive. These results are consistent with earlier findings [11, 27]. Moreover, EDA measures and heart rate correlated positively with the arousal dimension.

Although the detected pattern of correlations is rather coherent and consistent, not all methods led to expected results. Especially, our results regarding the activity of the zygomaticus major differ from most other studies, which found higher activity in relation to positive emotions [27]. Instead, our data points in the same direction as other experiments which also detected high activity of the zygomaticus major for negative emotions [29]. Hence, it seems that the activity of the zygomaticus major is not a reliable indicator for positive feelings. An alternative explanation could be that we did not induce strong positive emotions in our setting. These results point to an area for future research concerning emotional expressiveness in different situations of interactive system usage.

Another point for discussion is the extent of the correlations we found between subjective feeling, physiological and expressive measures. Although, other studies on emotions showed similar correlations between physiological measures and ratings and discussed this as a problem of emotion research [12], these results may not only be caused by measurement uncertainties, but also by the theoretical premise that the components of emotions represent different aspects of emotions that are only correlated in a specific way. The second assumption would lead to the conclusion that only a combination of measures gives a good description of the quality of an experienced emotion.

Another aspect concerns the relevance of cognitive appraisals and the behavioral component as parts of emotional user reactions. Appraisal processes of emotions in human-technology interaction have rarely been studied experimentally. Summarizing, the results of our study suggest that goal conductive, capable and norm/self compatible appraisals are associated with positive emotions. Although, we found high correlations between subjective feelings and cognitive appraisals, it can be argued that both components are qualitative different and therefore are necessary to fully understand emotional user reactions. While subjective feelings describe the quality of an experienced emotion, cognitive appraisals provide information about a person's interpretation of a specific situation.

With respect to behavioral tendencies, our study hints at an interesting point concerning the efficiency of system usage. Since the average time required per input was significantly higher for the system with usability flaws, it can be argued that just the design of the system caused these differences in performance. On the other, also negative emotions may have contributed to slowing down the user. More experiments are necessary to strengthen this assumption.

5 Conclusion and Outlook

Based on the approach of Scherer [1], we proposed to measure different components of a user's emotional experience by a combination of self assessment ratings, physiological and expression measures as well as cognitive appraisal questionnaire and analysis of behavioral data. In addition, we presented a study that demonstrated the measurement of multiple components of emotions in an interactive context. Although this combination seems to offer a sound methodological basis for future experimental studies of emotions in the context of human-technology interaction, some further questions remain unanswered.

A main question triggered by the multi-component approach is which components need to be measured to get acceptable results regarding emotions as one aspect of the user experience. Is the measurement of subjective feeling data in user experience research settings sufficient, and what advantages are offered by an incorporation of physiological and expressive data? Our suggestion is that the answer depends on the required accuracy of the data on user's emotional state. The more components are measured the more data is available to interpret the user's reactions. The information gained from the components can sometimes be contradictory, but should deliver more reliable results than if only one component is measured. On the other hand the effort is higher the more components are used. We propose the measurement of e.g. only subjective feeling data to be enough for rough estimations if an emotional user reaction is positive or negative. However, to understand emotional user reactions in more detail the study of more than one component is needed.

Theories on the role of cognitive appraisals have been developed to understand cognitive aspects of emotional experiences [6, 23]. But can their assessment also be helpful to be support for design decisions in human-technology interaction? Studying the influence of instrumental and non-instrumental quality perceptions on emotional user reactions is a first step to answering this question [30].

A final question concerns dynamic aspects of emotional user experience and the question how user reactions develop over time. Carbon, Hutzler & Minge [31] combined repeated measurements of aesthetics with eye-tracking and pupillometry data. We think that also in the context of user experience repeated measurement of perceived usability is a rather neglected aspect. Hassenzahl & Sandweg [32] showed that e.g. memory effects have a strong influence on summary assessments of perceived usability. In future research we hope that physiological and expressive data can help to improve understanding of dynamic aspects of emotional user experience.

Acknowledgements

This research was supported by the German Research Foundation (DFG) as part of the Research Training Group 'Prospective Engineering of Human-Technology Interaction' (no. 1013).

References

1. Scherer, K.R.: On the nature and function of emotion: A component process approach. In: Scherer, K.R., Ekman, P. (eds.) Approaches to emotion, pp. 293–317. Erlbaum, Hillsdale (1984)
2. Larsen, R.J., Fredrickson, B.L.: Measurement issues in emotion research. In: Kahnemann, D., Diener, E., Schwarz, N. (eds.) Well-Being - the foundations of hedonic psychology, New York, Russel Sage Foundation, pp. 40–60 (1999)
3. Brave, S., Nass, C.: Emotion in HCI. In: Jacko, J., Sears, A. (eds.) The Human-Computer-Interaction Handbook, pp. 81–96. Lawrence Erlbaum, Erlbaum (2003)
4. Izard, C.E.: Human Emotions. Plenum Press, New York (1977)
5. Lazarus, R.S.: Emotion and adaptation. Oxford University Press, New York (1991)
6. Scherer, K.R.: Appraisal considered as a process of multi-level sequential checking. In: Scherer, K.R., Schorr, A., Johnstone, T. (eds.) Appraisal processes in emotion: Theory, methods, research, pp. 92–120. Oxford University Press, New York (2001)
7. Mehrabian, A., Russell, J.A.: An approach to environmental psychology. MIT Press, Cambridge (1974)
8. Russell, J.A.: A circumplex model of affect. Journal of Personality and Social Psychology 39, 1281–1288 (1980)
9. Lang, P.J.: Behavioral treatment and bio-behavioral assessment: Computer applications. In: Sidowski, J.B., Johnson, H., Williams, T.A. (eds.) Technology in Mental Health Care Delivery Systems, Norwood NJ, pp. 119–137. Ablex Publishing, Greenwich (1980)
10. Russell, J.A., Weiss, A., Mendelsohn, G.A.: The Affect Grid: A single-item scale of pleasure and arousal. Journal of Personality and Social Psychology 57, 493–502 (1989)
11. Ward, R.D., Marsden, P.H.: Physiological responses to different WEB page designs. International Journal of Human-Computer Studies 59, 199–212 (2003)
12. Herbon, A., Peter, C., Markert, L., van der Meer, E., Voskamp, J.: Emotion studies in HCI - a new approach. In: HCII 2005 proceedings, Lawrence Erlbaum, Mahwah (2005)

13. Fahrenberg, J.: Physiologische Grundlagen und Messmethoden der Herz-Kreislaufaktivit at Physiological fundamentals and measuring methods of cardiovascular activity. In: Rösler, F. (ed.) Grundlagen und Methoden der Psychophysiologie, pp. 317–454. Gottingen, Hogrefe (2001)
14. Bradley, M.M., Greenwald, M.K., Hamm, A.O.: Affective Picture Processing and the semantic differential. Journal of Behavioural Therapy and Experimental Psychiatry 25, 204–215 (1993)
15. Beatty, J.: Task-evoked pupillary responses, processing load, and the structure of processing resources. Psychological Bulletin 91, 276–292 (1982)
16. Hess, E.H., Polt, J.M.: Pupil Size in Relation to Interest Value of Visual Stimuli. Science 132, 250–349 (1960)
17. Ekman, P.: Are there basic emotions. Psychological Review 99, 550–553 (1992)
18. Cohen, I., Garg, A., Huang, T.S.: Emotion Recognition from Facial Expressions using Multilevel HMM (2000), http://www.ifp.uiuc.edu/~iracohen/publications/mlhmmemotions.pdf
19. Cacioppo, J.T., Petty, R.E., Losch., M.E., Kim, H.S.: Electromyographic activity over facial muscle regions can differentiate the valence and intensity of affective reactions. Journal of Personality and Social Psychology 50, 260–268 (1986)
20. Dimberg, U.: Facial electromyography and emotional reactions. Psychophysiology 19, 643–647 (1990)
21. Banse, R., Scherer, K.R.: Acoustic Profiles in Vocal Emotion Expression. Journal of Personality and Social Psychology 70, 614–636 (1996)
22. Smith, C.A., Ellsworth, P.C.: Patterns of cognitive appraisal in emotion. Journal of Personality and Social Psychology 48, 813–838 (1985)
23. Ortony, A., Clore, G.L., Collins, A.: The cognitive structure of emotions. Cambridge University Press, Cambridge (1988)
24. Frijda, N.H.: The Laws of Emotion. American Psychologist 43, 349–358 (1988)
25. Ellsworth, P.C., Scherer, K.R.: Appraisal processes in emotion. In: Davidson, R.J., Goldsmith, H., Scherer, K.R. (eds.) Handbook of the Affective Sciences, pp. 572–595. Oxford University Press, New York (2004)
26. Schorr, A.: Subjective measurment in appraisal research: present state and future perspectives. In: Scherer, K.R., Schorr, A., Johnstone, T. (eds.) Appraisal Processes in Emotion: Theory, Methods, Research, pp. 331–349. Oxford University Press, New York (2001)
27. Partala, T., Surakka, V.: The effects of affective interventions in human-computer interaction. Interacting with Computers 16, 295–309 (2004)
28. Mentis, H., Gay, G.: User Recalled Occurrences of Usability errors: Implications on the User Experience. In: CHI 2003 extended abstracts, pp. 736–737. ACM Press, New York (2003)
29. Lang, P.J., Greenwald, M.K., Bradley, M.M., Hamm, A.O.: Looking at pictures: Affective, facial, visceral, and behavioral reactions. Psychophysiology 30, 261–273 (1993)
30. Mahlke, S., Thüring, M.: Studying Antecedents of Emotional Experiences in Interactive Contexts. In: CHI 2007 proceedings, pp. 915–918. ACM Press, New York (2007)
31. Carbon, C.-C., Hutzler, F., Minge, M.: Innovativeness in design investigated by eye movements and pupillometry. Psychology Science 48, 173–186 (2006)
32. Hassenzahl, M., Sandweg, N.: From Mental Effort to Perceived Usability: Transforming Experiences into Summary Assessments. In: CHI 2004 extended abstracts, pp. 1283–1286. ACM Press, New York (2004) .

Auditory-Induced Emotion:
A Neglected Channel for Communication
in Human-Computer Interaction

Ana Tajadura-Jiménez[1] and Daniel Västfjäll[1,2]

[1] Division of Applied Acoustics, Chalmers University of Technology, Göteborg, Sweden
[2] Department of Psychology, Göteborg University, Göteborg, Sweden
Ana.Tajadura@chalmers.se, psydave@psy.gu.se

Abstract. Interpreting and responding to affective states of a user is crucial for future intelligent systems. Until recently, the role of sound in affective responses has been frequently ignored. This article provides a brief overview of the research targeting affective reactions to everyday, ecological sounds. This research shows that the subjective interpretation and meaning that listeners attribute to sound, the spatial dimension, or the interactions with other sensory modalities, are as important as the physical properties of sound in evoking an affective response. Situation appraisal and individual differences are also discussed as factors influencing the emotional reactions to auditory stimuli. A study with heartbeat sounds exemplifies some of the introduced ideas and research methodologies, and shows the potential of sound in inducing emotional states.

Keywords: Auditory induced-emotion, sound quality, self-representation sounds, embodiment, emotional intelligence.

1 Introduction

Human communication is essentially emotional: most human interactions with the surrounding environment entail affective processes, a natural predisposition of our organism to feel either attraction or rejection towards the objects, people or even ideas involved in these interactions [1]. Emotions have a great impact on human behavior, since they influence processes such as perception, attention, learning, memory or decision-making [2]. The same mechanisms are activated in individual's interaction with all forms of media [3]. Thus, an efficient human-computer interaction (HCI) is highly dependant on the ability of computer-based applications to express emotions, interpret users' affective states and understand the role of external and internal influences on affective responses [4].

The link between HCI and emotional reactions is becoming an important new research area. While relatively much research has addressed the relation between visual media content and affective reactions, research on the link between auditory form/content and emotions is an under-researched area. It is also well established that sounds evoke emotions and can provide affective information, perhaps more effectively

C. Peter and R. Beale (Eds.): Affect and Emotion in HCI, LNCS 4868, pp. 63–74, 2008.

than many other forms of information channels that are available to HCI designers and researchers [5]. In our everyday life, sound often elicits emotional reactions in the listener. People can be startled by the sudden sound of a door slamming or a thunder in a storm, annoyed by the noise of cars in the street, pleased by the sound of a water stream in the forest, tired after a full day of work in a noisy environment, etc. Nowadays, sounds are used in many HCI scenarios. For instance, auditory information/feedback in the form of earcones (abstract musical sounds) and auditory icons (a sound caricature of the intended action the user is supposed to take or has taken) are used in desktop computers and many other applications. In some systems (i.e. vehicles and working environments) sounds are used to convey different forms of alerts and warnings. Today, many of these signals have to be learned through statistical association between the sound going off and an event taking place. Designing sounds that immediately convey affective information (i.e. danger) and create an affective reaction (i.e. mild fear or anxiety) also helps facilitate correct action [6].

If we consider that humans are continuously exposed to sound, both in real world and when interacting with many media applications, it seems surprising that so little is known about how users respond to affective auditory stimuli. Therefore, there is a great need for a theory, a systematic approach and a consensus for measuring human emotional responses to sound [7]. Understanding the role of sound in evoking human affective responses might improve our quality of life by helping to design spaces and media applications which are emotionally optimized.

This article provides some examples of the research targeting affective reactions to everyday sounds. Up to date, research in this area has been trying to connect physical sound properties and basic emotions [7]. However, it seems more meaningful to divide ongoing research on affective reactions to sounds into several main categories including: 1) physical determinants, 2) psychological determinants, 3) spatial determinants and 4) cross-modal determinants [8].

Psychological determinants concern other variables related to subjective interpretation and meaning that should be considered because different sources evoke different subjective evaluations [9] (e.g. dog barking vs. rock music). Spatial determinants deal with the role of the auditory space in creating an emotional response (for instance, the barking dog will have different emotional effects if the spatial cues would suggest that the space is small versus big). Finally, cross-modal effects concern the relation between different modalities in producing an affective reaction [10]. While much research still is needed to fully understand the different determinants of affective reactions to different categories of sounds, we highlight these four categories in the presented case study. We show how reproduction parameters and meaning of sound, apart from physical features, can affect emotional experience.

2 Research on Affective Reactions to Sound

Frequently, emotional experience has been defined as either discrete feeling states or states that can be placed along dimensions of experience [7, 11]. The discrete approach assumes the existence of a limited number of fundamental emotions [12] which are universal, survival-related, spontaneous, uncontrollable, not necessarily consciously perceived [13] and combinable to form other more complex emotions.

These fundamental emotions entail psychological and physiological changes which influence our attention, cognitive appraisal, behavior, facial and/or voice expressions [14], nervous system activity [15-16], self-reported experience, etc. On the contrary, other researchers prefer to characterize emotions using a dimensional model of affect [17-18] where emotional reactions can be placed in an affective space. The two dimensions most commonly used are *hedonic valence* (pleasantness) and *arousal* (activation, intensity or readiness to act) [7, 19-20]. Eventually, a third dimension, *dominance* (potency), can be added to form an affective space. For an insight on other theoretical aspects of affect and emotion please refer to [21-24] in this volume.

2.1 Physical Determinants

Regardless of the theoretical assumptions, research on affective reactions to sound has mainly explored physical determinants. Most work in this area has been carried out by sound designers for specific applications (e.g. car industry). In this framework, it is common to talk in terms of *sound quality* referring to "the adequacy of a sound in the context of a specific technical goal or task" [25]. For many years, research on sound design for systems has focused on the affective state of *annoyance*. Annoyance correlates moderately with objective metrics such as equivalent dB(A) level for community noise, and with psychoacoustics metrics such as loudness, sharpness and roughness [26-27]. *Equal pleasantness contours* for tones varying in frequency and intensity have been developed [28]. For instance, low frequencies are preferred when intensity is below 60 dB, otherwise high frequencies are more pleasant; for 50 dB of loudness, tones with frequencies between 200 and 1000 Hz are preferred [7]. It has also been argued [1, 29] that intensity of sound and arousal might be analogous, since increasing loudness results in an increase in the orienting response. This assumption holds until a level where the intensity of the sound becomes highly aversive (85–90 dB(A) in [1]; see also [9, 30-31]).

2.2 Psychological Determinants

Even though the physical properties of the sound undoubtedly play a big role on the affective reactions induced, research on ecological sounds, i.e. sounds surrounding us in everyday environments, has shown that other psychological factors, related to subjective interpretation, need to be considered. Ecological sounds can be divided on artificial and natural sounds. Studies with artificial sounds comprise, for instance, the experiments by Bisping [32-33] with sounds in the interior of a car, or the ones by Västfjäll et al. [7] with sounds in the interior of a commercial aircraft. These studies showed the validity of a two-dimensional space (with pleasantness and either powerfulness [32-33] or activation [7] as coordinates) to classify different affective reactions to artificial sound. In addition, Bisping reported that the different classifications of the engine sounds in the affective space were mainly based in the envelope of the low frequency components. Västfjäll et al. found significant correlations between affective reactions and perceptual and cognitive ratings: pleasantness correlated with loudness and naturalness of the reproduced sound, while activation was related to sharpness (high frequency components), fluctuation strength (amplitude- and frequency modulation between 15 and 300 Hz) and prominence ratio (tonal vs. noise spectra components). Their experiments also showed that pleasantness increases with loudness and audibility of tones, while activation increases with noise spectra level.

Natural sounds have been also characterized in terms of their affective quality. For instance, Björk's [34] studies placed 15 natural sounds in the valence-arousal dimensional space and Jäncke et al. [9] observed the physiological effect of environmental sounds with different valences (bird song, church bell and baby's crying). In a more ambitious project, Bradley and Lang [35] used graphical scales and psychophysiological measures to characterize the affective experience when exposed to sixty naturally acoustic stimuli. Physiological changes showed to be highly correlated with self-reported emotional reactions in terms of valence, arousal and dominance. In addition, they looked at a physical determinant, the equivalent sound level, and found almost no correlation with valence ratings (r = .07) and only a moderate one with activation ratings (r = .38). These correlations only accounted for 14% of the variance, thus supporting the suggestion made in this article that emotional reactions are due to other aspects of the stimuli apart from physical properties. The set of digitized sounds used by Bradley and Lang [17], together with their normative affective ratings, served to develop the *International Affective Digitized Sounds* (IADS) for use in emotions research [36].

Human speech and vocal cues are more complex acoustic stimuli which are frequently included in human-computer interfaces and have also been often used in emotion research (e.g. emotional speech synthesis [37]; prosody of speech [38]; see also [39-41], in this volume). Wexler et al. [42] designed an experiment with semantically emotional words. Emotional and neutral words were overlapped to form dichotic stimulus pairs and presented in such a way that in many cases emotional words were not consciously heard. Physiological measures (electroencephalography and facial electromyography) provided evidence that emotional processing occurred even in the cases where words did not reached conscious awareness. In another study, Hietanen et al. [43] explored how tendencies to approach or withdraw varied in response to vocal affective expressions. Results suggested that emotional expressions may be contained in vocal cues. In human social interaction, vocal cues are as important as visual cues, and human speech contains many features (melody, rate, pauses, intonation, etc.) which inform us about the speaker's affective state. It should however be noted that vocal cues often exhibit the same properties as sounds [5, 44].

A particular case of ecological sounds is *self-representation sounds* [45] which can be associated with a person's own body (e.g. heartbeat, breathing) and its embodied activity (e.g. footsteps, chewing or smoking). These sounds increase body awareness in listeners and they might have a stronger potential for inducing an emotional experience. In [46], adding naturally breath intake sounds to synthetic speech aided listeners to recall sentences. Eating has been described in [47] as an emotional experience which involves *"being aware of and listening to the crunch of each bite and noise of the chewing sound in your head"*. Fast heartbeat sounds have been shown to increase self-reported arousal (e.g. [48]). In particular, body sounds such as a heartbeat may force a listener to physiologically mimic the external auditory stimulation, due both to the fundamental tendency of our organism to couple internal biophysiological rhythm to external auditory drivers, and also to additional cognitive effects (self-identification with that sound or empathy, see next section, [49] and references therein). These changes at the physiological level can affect one's emotional experience (e.g. [50-51]) or induce a particular mood state.

Finally, music has the ability both to *express* and to *produce* emotions in listeners, even though it does not have obvious implications for our life goals [52]. Its role in evoking emotions is still not understood, but music is already used in many applications which try to elicit affective responses such as film music, marketing and music therapy [53]. There are a number of studies giving evidence of emotional responses to music (for an extensive overview see [54]; see also [55], in this volume). In general, results of these studies indicate that judgments of musical emotions are quick, innate, hard-wired and automatic, i.e. attention does not need to be involved.

2.3 Spatial Determinants

New media applications, such as computer games, home theatre systems or virtual reality, incorporate the most advanced digital sound reproduction systems. However, there are few studies exploring the impact of sound rendering or spatial reproduction techniques on emotional responses. In [1] the startle response when using auditory probes presented by means of different techniques was measured; binaural sound or monaural sound stimulating either the left or right ear were tested. Their results showed that binaural cues have the largest startle effect. It was also found that the monaural-left ear stimulation was more effective in producing a startle effect than the right ear. The authors suggested that this finding might be due to dominance of the right-hemisphere when processing affective stimuli. Other studies have also shown a bigger sensitivity of the left ear to emotional speech and music (see [1] and references therein).

The experienced emotions and the subjective sense of presence in auditory virtual environments were investigated in [56]. Presence can be defined as the sensation of 'being there' in mediated environments such as virtual reality, simulators, cinema, television, etc. [57]. In this study, mono, stereo and six-channel loudspeaker reproductions were used. Results showed that emotion and presence were unavoidably linked, and that they both increase when improving sound spatial resolution (see also [58-60]).

Another study on this topic compared the loudspeaker and headphone reproduction conditions when listening to news [61]. In was hypothesized that the close sound condition (headphones) would provide a more immersive experience and shorten the interpersonal distance between the user and the news anchor, thus providing a more intense, arousing and pleasant experience. Generally, results showed that the headphone listening was preferred over loudspeakers, even being judged as 'less realistic' by the participants. However, no significant differences in elicited arousal were found between both conditions.

2.4 Cross-Modal Determinants

Recent studies in multisensory research have shown that information which is only available in one sensory modality is in many cases integrated and used by other sensory modalities (for a recent review see [62]). This is also true for emotional information. An example can be found in the multisensory integration of the information expressing emotions in seen faces and heard speech, where the perceived hedonic valence of stimuli in one sensory modality is altered by the valence of stimuli in other sensory modality [10]. Another study [63] showed how emotional arousal evoked by pictures depicting threatening stimuli (snakes and spiders) is transferred to the tactile modality. Similarly, results from the Bradley and Lang experiment with natural sounds described above [35] were similar to the ones obtained with pictorial stimuli what proves that affective processing and reactivity are not sensory modality specific. Future research needs to address the issue of how emotion is transferred or interact between sensory modalities.

2.5 Other Determinants

The ongoing mood can affect the responses to subsequent emotional events (situation appraisal). For instance, pre-existing cognitive processes and emotional states may influence the judgment of an auditory event [25]. The study reported in [64] successfully showed that both current mood and individual noise sensitivity are as important as noise characteristics when judging noise annoyance. It has been also shown [1] that affective responses can vary in magnitude depending on the previously induced emotional state: a reflex with the same valence than the current emotional state will be increased and inhibited otherwise.

Individual differences, such as personality traits, may also play a role in the response to sound. In studies considering factors such as speech rate, loudness and distance to sound [61], it was shown that people preferentially process auditory stimuli emotionally congruent with their personality traits. In the same way that speech can express a variety of emotional states (e.g. arousal is revealed in increased pitch, loudness and rate), and individual characteristics (e.g. fast speech can be related to extraversion), people tend to prefer voices which matches their personality traits or their current emotional state. This can be extrapolated to other audio characteristics (e.g. background music) and to media messages (see [61] and references therein).

3   Affecting Emotions Using Heartbeat Sounds

To illustrate the concepts introduced above, in this section we report on a recent study [65] carried out in our laboratory which highlights aspects corresponding to the four categories of determinants of affective reactions. The motivation of this study was found in the theory that a specifically induced physiological state can influence one's emotional responses to stimuli (e.g. [50]). We tested how the presentation of heartbeat sounds might alter participants' own heartbeat and, in turn, affect their emotional attitude to pictures. In particular, the study explored the specific effect on emotional experience of the perceived distance to heartbeat sounds. For this purpose, distant versus close sound reproduction conditions (loudspeakers versus headphones) were included in the design. It was hypothesized that when heartbeat sounds are perceived close, it would be more likely that subjects identify them with their own heartbeat (as if they integrated them in their own body-image).

Twenty-four naïve participants, eighteen male (mean age 24.4; SD = 4.6) took part in the experiment. All subjects reported having normal hearing. They were informed that during the experiment they would be exposed to heartbeat sounds.

In each trial heart beat sounds were presented during 50 seconds, and subjects' task was to rate a photograph viewed during the last 6 seconds of the trial. Heart beat sounds could be presented at a medium or high rate (60 versus 110 beats per minute), and at close or far distance (headphones versus loudspeakers). Sound level was set at approximately 60 dB(A). Silence conditions were also included as a baseline for comparisons. 34 photographs, with positive or negative valence, were selected from the International Affective Picture System (IAPS, a set of normative pictures rated in an arousal/valence/dominance dimensional affective scale [66]), according to their medium-arousal value (5 on a 9-point scale) and valence (moderate negative and positive valence – 3 and 7 respectively on a 9-point scale) and presented on a flat projection screen placed at 1.7 meters distance from participants (768x576 pixels resolution and 33°×26° field-of-view).

Participants' peripheral heartbeat signals were collected by means of a heart rate sensor attached to an earclip. Self-reported valence and arousal ratings for the pictures were collected by using the Self-Assessment manikin (SAM), a 9-point pictorial scale developed by Lang [67]. Finally, a free-recall task for the photographs shown was implemented at the end of the experiment and memory performance scores were collected.

Results showed a small but significant ($p < 0.05$) effect of sound on physiology (heart beat changes around one beat per minute after forty seconds of heartbeat sound presentation). The influence of sound was significant as observed on the emotional responses to pictures: fast heart rate made people rate pictures as more arousing, and increased memory performance, while slow heart rate showed a relaxing effect when facing negative pictures. As hypothesized, there was a stronger effect of rate for the close sound reproduction condition (headphones); the effect was observed both at the physiological level and on the self-reported arousal ratings.

In summary, the presented results give further support to the idea of the amodal character (in terms of sensory modality) of affective reactions, since here sounds affected emotional judgments of visual stimuli. They also suggest that the emotion eliciting power of auditory modality is influenced by the perceived distance, with close stimulation being more affective than distant one. Close is intimate, arousing, engaging [3]. Moreover, this study highlights the possibility of considering the affective power of self-representation sounds or other stimuli related to one's body (here body sounds). Future research needs to clarify whether the effects found can be accounted only to the distance cues or to the fact that the sound used was from the *self-representation* category. The implications of these findings for the design of media applications are discussed in the next section.

4 Conclusions

Traditionally visual domain has captured the main interest in multimedia applications. In search of pictorial realism other sensory modalities were often neglected. However, there is evidence to affirm that people are much more sensitive to audio fidelity than to visual fidelity [3]. This means that sound may compensate for visual imperfections. Therefore, audiovisual applications can be optimized by making use of audio technologies, which tend to be technically less complex than visual rendering systems. In particular, sound might be considered in the design of affective human-computer interfaces. Sound is capable of eliciting a full range of emotions, which can vary according to factors such as the physical properties of the acoustical signal, the subjective interpretation and meaning of the sound, sound rendering techniques (the spatial dimension), situation appraisal and as a result of cross-modal interaction with other sensory modalities.

An open question in this area is the possibility for reliable predictions of the emotional response to sound. Research has shown that it is possible to separate cognitive evaluations and emotional reactions to auditory stimuli, and thus, in theory we might potentially establish a relation between sound physical properties and affective response [7]. When considering the meaning attributed to sound, this article provides some examples showing that both artificial and natural sounds have an affective power which is not only dependant on the physical properties. For instance, self-representation sounds like a heartbeat, breath or footsteps might facilitate self-identification with that sound (an embodied experience) and this might induce strong affective processes. In particular, this type of sounds might be used in the design of multimodal virtual environments, where research has already shown that visual cues representing one's body increase engagement [68]. In these virtual environments, self-representation sounds would form part of a user's multimodal virtual body [45].

Sound spatial dimension (resolution, distance to sound) has also been mentioned as a determinant of listener's emotional arousal. Arousing or intense emotional experiences accompany engagement in media applications [69], something desired, for instance, in e-learning environments, because arousal and positive experiences facilitate memory for events and encourage users to go on with the tasks [70].

In addition, the result of using different sensory modalities in combination needs to be considered, given the amodal character of emotional processes. Future research should also consider other factors which may influence emotional reactions to auditory stimuli, such as situation appraisal and individual differences, personality traits or individual goals.

Although the present review covers only a small sample of everyday sounds, the principles considered here are likely to be virtually extended to any kind of sound perception, and therefore, to the design of any system interacting with humans. Research in human affective responses might help to improve our quality of life by contributing to the design of spaces, objects and applications which are *emotionally optimized*. For instance, our personal everyday life can be enhanced by including affective human-computer interfaces in workplace systems, because they increase motivation and persistency of users [70-71] (see also [72], in this volume); in the area of health they can help in telemedicine applications (see [73], in this volume) or in tools to fight against stress (see [74], in this volume) or fear (e.g. of public speaking [75]); in e-learning environments, they may enhance memory [70]; and they can even be useful in telerobotics, where adding an affective value make people understand and empathize with the tasks and needs of robots [76] (see also [40], in this volume).

Acknowledgments. The work presented in this paper was supported by the EU grant PRESENCCIA-IST-2006-27731 (www.presenccia.org). We thank Dr. Aleksander Väljamäe, anonymous reviewers and editors for their helpful feedback in the manuscript preparation.

References

1. Lang, P.J., Bradley, M.M., Cuthbert, B.N.: Emotion, Attention, and the Startle reflex. Psychological Review 97, 377–395 (1990)
2. Phelps, E.A., LeDoux, J.E.: Contributions of the Amygdala to Emotion Processing: From Animal Models to Human Behavior. Neuron 48, 175–187 (2005)
3. Reeves, B., Nass, C.: The Media Equation: How People Treat Computers, Television, and New Media Like Real People and Places. Cambridge University Press, New York (1996)
4. Picard, R.W., Daily, S.B.: Evaluating Affective Interactions: Alternatives to Asking What Users Feel. In: CHI Workshop on Evaluating Affective interfaces: Innovative Approaches, Portland (April 2005)
5. Juslin, P., Västfjäll, D.: All Emotions are not Created Equal: Mechanism Underlying Musical Emotions. Behavioral Brain Sciences (in press)
6. Sköld, A., Bergman, P., Västfjäll, D., Tajadura-Jiménez, A., Larsson, P.: Emotional Reactions to Information and Warning Sounds. Acta Acustica (submitted)
7. Västfjäll, D., Kleiner, M.: Emotion in Product Sound Design. In: Proceedings of Journées Design Sonore, Paris, March 20-21 (2002)
8. Västfjäll, D., Tajadura-Jiménez, A., Väljamäe, A., Juslin, P.: Non-Vocal, Non-Musical Determinants of Auditory Induced Emotions (in preparation)
9. Jäncke, L., Vogt, J., Musial, F., Lutz, K., Kalveram, K.T.: Facial EMG Responses to Auditory Stimuli. International Journal of Psychophysiology 22, 85–96 (1996)
10. De Gelder, B., Bertelson, P.: Multisensory Integration, Perception and Ecological Validity. Trends in Cognitive Sciences 7, 460–467 (2003)
11. Levenson, R.W.: Human emotions: A functional view. In: Ekman, P., Davidson, R.J. (eds.) The Nature of Emotion: Fundamental Questions, pp. 123–126. Oxford University Press, New York (1994)
12. Lazarus, R.S.: Emotion and Qdaptation. Oxford University Press, New York (1991)
13. Shiv, B., Fedorikhin, A.: Heart and Mind in Conflict: Interplay of Affect and Cognition in Consumer Decision Making. Journal of Consumer Research 26, 278–282 (1999)
14. Ekman, P., Friesen, W.V., Ancoli, S.: Facial Signs of Emotional Experience. Journal of Personality and Social Psychology 39, 1125–1134 (1980)
15. LeDoux, J.E.: The Emotional Brain: The mysterious Underpinnings of Emotional Life. Simon & Schuster, New York (1996)
16. Levenson, R.W.: Emotion and the Autonomic Nervous System: A Prospectus for Research on Autonomic Specificity. In: Wagner, H. (ed.) Social Psychology: Perspectives of Theory and Clinical Applications, pp. 17–42. Wiley, London (1988)
17. Wundt, W.: Lectures on Human and Animal Psychology. Macmillan, New York (1896) (J.E. Creighton & E.B Titchener, Trans.)
18. Osgood, C., Suci, G., Tannenbaum, P.: The Measurement of Meaning. University of Illinois Press, Urbana (1957)
19. Lang, P.J.: The Emotion Probe: Studies of Motivation and Attention. American Psychologist 50, 372–385 (1995)
20. Russell, J.A.: The Circumplex Model of Affect. Journal of Personality and Social Psychology 39, 1161–1178 (1980)
21. Palen, L., Bølen, S.: Don't Get Emotional. In: Peter, C., Beale, R. (eds.) Affect and Emotion in Human-Computer Interaction. LNCS, vol. 4868. Springer, Heidelberg (2008)
22. Bainbridge, W.S.: Computational Affective Sociology. In: Peter, C., Beale, R. (eds.) Affect and Emotion in Human-Computer Interaction. LNCS, vol. 4868. Springer, Heidelberg (2008)

23. Lichtenstein, A., Oehme, A., Kupschick, S., Jürgensohn, T.: Comparing Two Emotion Models for Deriving Affective States from Physiological Data. In: Peter, C., Beale, R. (eds.) Affect and Emotion in Human-Computer Interaction. LNCS, vol. 4868. Springer, Heidelberg (2008)

24. Mahlke, S., Minge, M.: Consideration of Multiple Components of Emotions in Human-Technology Interaction. In: Peter, C., Beale, R. (eds.) Affect and Emotion in Human-Computer Interaction. LNCS, vol. 4868. Springer, Heidelberg (2008)

25. Blauert, J., Jekosch, U.: Sound-Quality Evaluation: A Multi-Layered Problem. Acta Acustica 83, 747–753 (1997)

26. Guski, R.: Psychological Methods for Evaluating Sound Quality and Assessing Acoustic Information. Acta Acustica 83, 765–774 (1997)

27. Widman, U.: Aurally Adequate Evaluation of Sounds. In: Proc. of Euro Noise, vol. 98, pp. 29–46 (1998)

28. Todd, N.: Evidence for a Behavioral Significance of Saccular Acoustic Sensitivity in Humans. Journal of the Acoustical Society of America 110, 380–390 (2001)

29. Sokolov, E.N.: Perception and the Conditioned Reflex. Pergamon Press, Oxford (1963)

30. Dimberg, U.: Facial Electromyography and Emotional Reactions. Psychophysiology 27(5), 481–494 (1990)

31. Kjellberg, A., Skoldstrom, B., Tesarz, M., Dallner, M.: Facial EMG Responses to Noise. Percept Mot Skills 79(3 Pt 1), 1203–1216 (1994)

32. Bisping, R.: Emotional Effect of Car Interior Sounds: Pleasantness and Power and their Relation to Acoustic Key Features. SAE paper 951284, 1203–1209 (1995)

33. Bisping, R.: Car Interior Sound Quality: Experimental Analysis by Synthesis. Acta Acustica 83, 813–818 (1997)

34. Björk, E.A.: The Perceived Quality of Natural Sounds. Acustica 57, 185–188 (1985)

35. Bradley, M.M., Lang, P.J.: Affective Reactions to Acoustic Stimuli. Psychophysiology 37, 204–215 (2000)

36. Bradley, M.M., Lang, P.J.: International Affective Digitized Sounds (IADS): Stimuli, Instruction Manual and Affective Ratings (Tech. Rep. No. B-2). Gainesville, FL: The Center for Research in Psychophysiology. University of Florida (1999)

37. Schröder, M.: Emotional Speech Synthesis: A Review. In: Proceedings of Eurospeech 2001, Scandinavia (2001)

38. Hermann, T., Ritter, H.: Sound and Meaning in Auditory Data Display. Proceedings of the IEEE 92(4) (2004)

39. Vogt, T., André, E., Wagner, J.: Automatic Recognition of Emotions from Speech: a Review of the Literature and Recommendations for Practical Realisation. In: Peter, C., Beale, R. (eds.) Affect and Emotion in Human-Computer Interaction. LNCS, vol. 4868. Springer, Heidelberg (2008)

40. Jones, C., Deeming, A.: Affective Human-Robotic Interaction. In: Peter, C., Beale, R. (eds.) Affect and Emotion in Human-Computer Interaction. LNCS, vol. 4868. Springer, Heidelberg (2008)

41. Jones, C., Sutherland, J.: Acoustic Emotion Recognition for Affective Computer Gaming. In: Peter, C., Beale, R. (eds.) Affect and Emotion in Human-Computer Interaction. LNCS, vol. 4868.Springer, Heidelberg (2008)

42. Wexler, B.E., Warrenburg, S., Schwartz, G.E., Janer, L.D.: EEG and EMG Responses to Emotion-Evoking Stimuli Processed Without Conscious Awareness. Neuropsychologia 30(12), 1065–1079 (1992)

43. Hietanen, J.K., Surakka, V., Linnankoski, L.: Facial Electromyographic Responses to Vocal Affect Expressions. Psychophysiology, 35, 530–536 (1998)

44. Scherer, K.R.: Acoustic Concomitants of Emotion Dimensions: Judging Affect from Synthesized Tone Sequences. In: Weitz, S. (ed.) Nonverbal Communication: Readings with Commentary, pp. 249–253. Oxford University Press, New York (1974)
45. Väljamäe, A., Larsson, P., Västfjäll, D., Kleiner, M.: Sound Representing Self-Motion in Virtual Environments Enhances Linear Vection. Presence: Teleoperators and Virtual Environments (to appear)
46. Whalen, D.H., Hoequist, C.E., Sheffert, S.M.: The Effects of Breath Sounds on the Perception of Synthetic Speech. Journal of Acoustic Society of America 97, 3147–3153 (1995)
47. Albers, S.: Eating Mindfully: How to End Mindless Eating and Enjoy a Balanced Relationship with Food. New Harbinger Publications (2003)
48. Woll, S.B., McFall, M.E.: The Effects of False Feedback on Attributed Arousal and Rated Attractiveness in Female Subjects. Journal of Personality 47, 214–229 (1979)
49. Scherer, K.R., Zentner, M.R.: Emotional Effects of Music: Production Rules. In: Juslin, P.N., Sloboda, J.A. (eds.) Music and Emotion: Theory and Research. Oxford University Press, New York (2001)
50. James, W.: The Principles of Psychology. Holt, New York (1890)
51. Schachter, S., Singer, J.E.: Cognitive, Social and Physiological Determinants of Emotional State. Psychol. Review 69, 379–399 (1962)
52. Juslin, P.N., Västfjäll, D.: Lost in a Feeling? A Model that can Guide the Study of Music and Emotion (submitted)
53. Thaut, M.H.: Neuropsychological Processes in Music Perception and their Relevance in Music Therapy. In: Unkeler, R.F. (ed.) Music Therapy in the Treatment of Adults with Mental disorders, pp. 3–31. Schirmer books, New York (1990)
54. Juslin, P.N., Sloboda, J.A.: Music and Emotion. In: Theory and Research. Oxford University Press, New York (2001)
55. Loviscach, J., Oswald, D.: In the Mood: Tagging Music with Affects. In: Peter, C., Beale, R. (eds.) Affect and Emotion in Human-Computer Interaction. LNCS, vol. 4868. Springer, Heidelberg (2008)
56. Västfjäll, D.: The Subjective Sense of Presence, Emotion Recognition, and Experienced Emotions in Auditory Virtual Environments. CyberPsychology & Behavior 6(2), 181–188 (2003)
57. Freeman, J., Avons, S.E., Pearson, D.E., Ijsselsteijn, W.A.: Effects of Sensory Information and Prior Experience on Direct Subjective Ratings of Presence. Presence: Teleoperators and Virtual Environments 8(1), 1–13 (1999)
58. Frijda, N.H.: Emotions are Functional, Most of the Time. In: Ekman, P., Davidson, R.J. (eds.) The nature of emotion, pp. 112–122. Oxford University Press, New York (1994)
59. Hendrix, C., Barfield, W.: The sense of Presence Within Auditory Virtual Environments. Presence: Teleoperators and Virtual Environments 3, 290–301 (1996)
60. Larsson, P., Väjamäe, V.D., Kleiner, M.: Auditory Induced Presence in Mediated Environments and Related Technology. In: Biocca, F., IJsselsteijn, W.A., Freeman, J.J. (eds.) Handbook of Presence. Lawrence Erlbaum, Mahwah (in press)
61. Kallinen, K., Ravaja, N.: Comparing Speakers versus Headphones in Listening to News from a Computer: Individual Differences and Psychophysiological Responses. Computers in Human Behavior 23, 303–317 (2007)
62. Spence, C., Driver, J. (eds.): Crossmodal Space and Cross-modal Attention. Oxford University Press, Oxford (2004)
63. Poliakoff, E., Miles, E., Li, X., Blanchette, I.: The effect of Visual Threat on Spatial Attention to Touch. Cognition 102(3), 405–414 (2007)

64. Västfjäll, D.: Influences of Current Mood and Noise Sensitivity on Judgments of noise annoyance. The Journal of Psychology 136, 357–370 (2002)
65. Tajadura-Jiménez, A., Väljamäe, A., Västfjäll, D.: Self-Representation in Mediated Environments: The Experience of Emotions Modulated by Auditory-Vibrotactile Heartbeat (in press)
66. Lang, P.J., Bradley, M.M., Cuthbert, B.N.: International Affective Picture System (IAPS): Affective Ratings of Pictures and Instruction Manual. Technical Report A-6. Univ. Florida, Gainesville, FL (2005)
67. Lang, P.J.: Behavioral Treatment and Bio-Behavioral Assessment: Computer Applications. In: Sidowski, J.B., Johnson, J.H., Williams, T.A. (eds.) Technology in Mental Health Care Delivery Systems, pp. 119–137. Ablex Publishing, Norwood (1980)
68. Slater, M., Usoh, M.: Body Centred Interaction in Immersive Virtual Environments. In: Magnenat Thalmann, N., Thalmann, D. (eds.) Artificial Life and Virtual Reality, pp. 125–148. John Wiley and Sons, Chichester (1994)
69. Watson, D., Tellegen, A.: Toward a Consensual Structure of Mood. Psychological Bulletin 98, 219–235 (1985)
70. Graf, C., Niebuhr, S., Kohler, K.: Enhancing Business Software through Fun-of-Use: A Pattern-based approach. In: Position Paper for Workshop on The Role of Emotion in HCI 2006, London, September 12-15 (2006)
71. Walkinshaw, O.: A Photo a Day: Is it Work, Rest or Play? In: Position Paper for Workshop on The Role of Emotion in HCI 2006, London (September 12-15, 2006)
72. Harbich, S., Hassenzahl, M.: Beyond Task Completition in the Workplace: Execute, Engage, Evolve, Expand. In: Peter, C., Beale, R. (eds.) Affect and Emotion in Human-Computer Interaction. LNCS, vol. 4868. Springer, Heidelberg (2008)
73. Creed, C., Beale, R.: Simulated Emotion in Affective Embodied Agents. In: Peter, C., Beale, R. (eds.) Affect and Emotion in Human-Computer Interaction. LNCS, vol. 4868. Springer, Heidelberg (2008)
74. Millard, N., Hole, L.: In the Moodie: Using Affective Widgets to Help Contact Centre Advisors Fight Stress. In: Peter, C., Beale, R. (eds.) Affect and Emotion in Human-Computer Interaction. LNCS, vol. 4868. Springer, Heidelberg (2008)
75. Pertaub, D.P., Slater, M., Barker, C.: An Experiment on Public Speaking Anxiety in Response to Three Different Types of Virtual Audience. Presence: Teleoperators and Virtual Environments 11, 68–78 (2002)
76. Shick, A.: Duckie and Dudle: a preliminary demonstration using affective display to communicate task status. In: Position Paper for Workshop on the Role of Emotion in HCI 2006: Engage, London, September 12-15 (2006)

Automatic Recognition of Emotions from Speech: A Review of the Literature and Recommendations for Practical Realisation

Thurid Vogt, Elisabeth André, and Johannes Wagner

Multimedia Concepts and Applications, University of Augsburg, Augsburg, Germany
{vogt,andre,wagner}@informatik.uni-augsburg.de

Abstract. In this article we give guidelines on how to address the major technical challenges of automatic emotion recognition from speech in human-computer interfaces, which include audio segmentation to find appropriate units for emotions, extraction of emotion relevant features, classification of emotions, and training databases with emotional speech. Research so far has mostly dealt with offline evaluation of vocal emotions, and online processing has hardly been addressed. Online processing is, however, a necessary prerequisite for the realization of human-computer interfaces that analyze and respond to the user's emotions while he or she is interacting with an application. By means of a sample application, we demonstrate how the challenges arising from online processing may be solved. The overall objective of the paper is to help readers to assess the feasibility of human-computer interfaces that are sensitive to the user's emotional voice and to provide them with guidelines of how to technically realize such interfaces.

1   Introduction

Automatic emotion recognition from speech has in the last decade shifted from a side issue to a major topic in human computer interaction and speech processing. The aim is to enable a very natural interaction with the computer by speaking instead of using traditional input devices and not only have the machine understand the verbal content, but also more subtle cues such as affect that any human listener would easily react to. This can be used in spoken dialogue systems, e.g. in call center applications. However, so far real-time emotion recognition has scarcely been attempted and if so, only in prototypical applications, as there are still many problems that are not yet solved appropriately.

In this article, we focus on technical challenges that arise when equipping human-computer interfaces with the ability to recognize the user's vocal emotions. Therefore, we will start with a short introduction into the acoustic properties of voice that are relevant for emotions as identified by psychological studies and move on to a discussion of databases with emotional speech. To give the reader an idea of how to employ information on the user's emotional state in human-computer interfaces, we then present a number of promising application

C. Peter and R. Beale (Eds.): Affect and Emotion in HCI, LNCS 4868, pp. 75–91, 2008.

fields. After that, we address the three main parts of automatic emotion recognition, namely finding appropriate audio units, feature extraction, and classification, that pose the hardest problems. Last, we exemplify the major difficulties of real-time emotion recognition by means of a sample application. The overall objective of the paper is to help readers to assess the feasibility of human-computer interfaces that are sensitive to the user's emotional voice and to provide them with guidelines of how to technically realize such interfaces.

2 Acoustic Measures of Emotion in Speech

Information on emotion is encoded in all aspects of language, in what we say and in how we say it, and the 'how' is even more important than the 'what'. This article focuses on the phonetic and acoustic properties of affective spoken language. The vocal parameters that have been best researched by psychological studies in relation to emotion and which are also intuitively the most important ones are prosody (pitch, intensity, speaking rate) and voice quality. Murray and Arnott [1] wrote an often cited review of literature on emotions in speech and refer to a number of studies which seemingly have identified unambiguous acoustic correlates of emotions as displayed in Table 1. These show prosody and voice quality to be most important to distinguish between emotions according to human perception. In particular pitch and intensity seem to be correlated to activation, so that high pitch and intensity values imply high, low pitch and intensity values low activation.

Table 1. Some variations of acoustic variables observed in relation to emotions, summarised from [1]

Emotion	Pitch	Intensity	Speaking rate	Voice quality
Anger	high mean, wide range	increased	increased	breathy; blaring timbre
Joy	increased mean and range	increased	increased	sometimes breathy; moderately blaring timbre
Sadness	normal or lower than normal mean, narrow range	decreased	slow	resonant timbre

The automatic recognition of emotion seems straight-forward when looking at Table 1. However, this is unfortunately not the case. First of all, psychological studies often get their insights from data of test persons *acting* to be in an emotional state. There, this clear mapping from acoustic variables might even be possible in a number of cases, though even when acting, intra- and inter-speaker variations are higher, as the expressivity of emotions is also dependent on the personality or the mood. In everyday human computer interaction, however, the occurring emotions are very spontaneous. There, these variations are considerably higher as these are not any more prototypical emotions but may be shaded, mixed, or weak and hardly distinguishable. This makes the task much harder, so that further acoustic features need to be investigated. Of course, personalised emotion recognition, that is from only one speaker, is more reliable. Further evidence of the differences of acted and spontaneous emotions has been supplied by Wilting *et al.* who showed in human listening tests that the perception of acted emotions is different than that from natural emotions [2]. In an experiment based on the Velten mood induction method [3] they had one group of test persons utter a set of positive or negative emotional sentences, and another group that was told to utter the same sentences, but act positively for the negative sentences, and negatively for the positive sentences. After the experiment, the first group stated that they actually felt positive or negative, while the other group felt neutral. Furthermore, in a perception experiment, listeners judged acted emotions to be stronger than natural emotions which suggests that actors tend to exaggerate. So, assumptions that hold for acted emotions do not necessarily transfer to natural emotions which are obviously of greater interest to human-computer interaction.

3   Databases

Databases with emotional speech are not only essential for psychological studies, but also for automatic emotion recognition, as standard methods are statistical and need to learn by examples. Generally, research deals with databases of acted, induced or completely spontaneous emotions. Of course, the complexity of the task increases with the naturalness. So at the beginning of the research on automatic vocal emotion recognition, which started seriously in the mid-90s, work began with acted speech [4] and shifts now towards more realistic data [5,6]. Prominent examples for acted databases are the Berlin database of emotional speech [7] and the Danish Emotional Speech corpus (DES) [8] which hold recordings of 10 resp. 4 test persons that were asked to speak sentences of emotionally neutral content in 7 resp. 5 basic emotions. Induced data is for instance the SmartKom corpus [9] and the German Aibo emotion corpus [10] where people where recorded in a lab setting fulfilling a certain task that was intended to elicit e.g. anger or irritation in the subjects without them knowing that their emotional state was of interest. The call center communication dealt with by Devillers and colleagues [5] is fully realistic as it is obtained from live recordings.

   The labeled emotions in the databases — and consequently also the emotions that are going to be recognised — can be a classic set of basic emotions like joy, anger, sadness, disgust. Alternatively, emotion states can be placed within a dimensional model of two or three affective dimensions (see Fig. 1). The dimensions are usually valence (from positive to negative) and arousal (from high to low), sometimes a third dimension like stance (from open to close) is added. A dimensional model allows for a continuous description which is very suitable

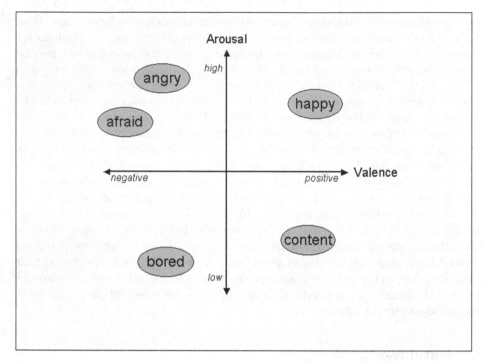

Fig. 1. A two-dimensional emotion space with a valence and an arousal axis. Basic Emotions are marked as areas within the space.

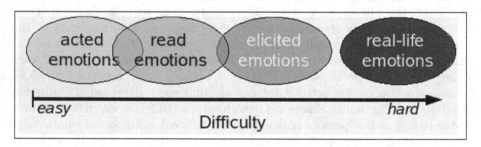

Fig. 2. Types of databases used for emotion recognition and their difficulty

for spontaneous emotions. However, for automatic recognition, this is usually mapped onto the four quadrants positive/high, positive/low, negative/high and negative/low [11,12], since it increases the complexity of the recognition task. Recently, Grimm et al. [13] used a regression technique to classify into a continuous three-dimensional emotion space. There are also only few databases available that are labeled using a dimensional model (e. g. the SAL – Sensitive Artificial Listener database [14]).

Often, the set of emotions is application driven, and can then contain for instance boredom, frustration, or even motherese (baby-talk) [15]. Other less obvious settings are the distinction between problem and no problem in a dialogue [16], or the detection of engagement [12]. The term "emotion" is thus interpreted widely and would rather comprise all affect related user states that occur in human-computer interaction. However, the more realistic the data is, the smaller is the number of classes that can feasibly be processed. Figure 2 illustrates how the difficulty of emotion recognition increases with the type of data used.

4 Applications

Call centre conversations belong to the most popular applications for approaches to the automated recognition of emotions from speech. On the one hand, a system may provide human operators with information regarding the emotions their voice might portray. That is, the system serves as a kind of "Affective Mirror" [17] that helps users to improve their interaction skills. An example includes the Jerk-O-Meter that monitors attention (activity and stress) in a phone conversation, based on speech feature analysis, and gives the user feedback allowing her to change her manners if deemed appropriate [18]. On the other hand, mechanisms for detecting emotions may be employed to sort voice messages according to the emotions portrayed by the caller. Among other things, a dialogue system may deploy knowledge on emotional user states to select appropriate conciliation strategies and to decide whether or not to transfer the caller to a human agent. An example includes the emotion-ware voice portal currently under development at T-Systems [19]. Furthermore, information on the caller's emotional state may be used to predict system error rates. Riccardi and Hakkani-Tür [20] investigate how the user's emotional state affects the accuracy of the AT&T "How May I Help You?" spoken dialogue system and conclude that the detection of the caller's emotional state may be beneficial for the adaptation of the system's dialogue strategies. In the case of anger, the performance of the dialogue system tends to go down, for example. This knowledge may again be used to select appropriate repair strategies.

Recently, methods for the recognition of emotions from speech have also been explored within the context of computer-enhanced learning. The motivation behind these approaches is the expectation that the learning process may be improved if a tutoring system adapts its pedagogical strategies to a student's emotional state. For instance, Ai and colleagues [21] consider features extracted from the dialogue between the tutor and the student, such as the prosody of speech, as well as features relating to user and system performance for the emotion recognition process in the ITSpoke tutoring system.

Starting in the last years, research has been conducted to explore the feasibility and potential of emotionally aware in-car systems. This work is motivated by empirical studies that provide evidence of the dependencies between a driver's performance and his or her emotional state. Emotion recognition from speech in cars has so far been investigated e.g. in the Emotive Driver project [22], and in the FERMUS project, a cooperation with the automobile industry (DaimlerChrysler and BMW) [23] where, however, experiments have been restricted to data collection and evaluation of driving simulators scenarios.

Finally, emotion detection has a high potential in games [24] and for giving feedback in human-robot interaction [25,26].

Summing up, it may be said that there is a large application potential for emotion-aware speech recognition systems. Nevertheless, the wide-spread exploitation of such systems is still impeded by great technical issues that need to be solved. As we will see later, especially online emotion recognition from speech which is in most cases necessary in real-time human-computer interaction poses great challenges. One possibility to mitigate such problems is the reduction to few emotional states. For instance, Burkhardt and colleagues distinguish between low and high anger as well as neutrality while Riccardi and Hakkani-Tür consider positive and negative user states only. The ITSpoke tutoring system uses the additional user and system performance features to enhance robustness.

5   Automatic Speech Emotion Recognition

A speech emotion recognition system consists of three principal parts, as shown in figure 3: signal processing, feature calculation and classification. Signal processing involves digitalisation and potentially acoustic preprocessing like filtering, as well as segmenting the input signal into meaningful units. Feature calculation is concerned with identifying relevant features of the acoustic signal with respect to emotions. Classification, lastly, maps feature vectors onto emotion classes through learning by examples. In the following we will discuss audio segmentation, feature extraction and classification in more detail pointing out differences between acted and spontaneous speech which is obviously of higher relevance for human-computer interfaces.

5.1   Audio Segmentation

The goal of the audio segmentation is to segment a speech signal into units that are representative for emotions. These are usually linguistically motivated middle-length time intervals such as words or utterances. Though the decision on

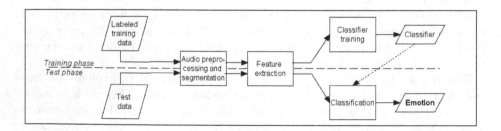

Fig. 3. Overview of a speech emotion recognition system

which kind of unit to take is evidently important, it has not received much attention in past research on emotion recognition. Most approaches so far have dealt with utterances of acted emotions where the choice of unit is obviously just one utterance, a well-defined linguistic unit with no change of emotion within in this case. However, in spontaneous speech this kind of obvious unit does not exist. Neither is the segmentation into utterances straight-forward nor can a constant emotion be expected over an utterance. Generally speaking, a good emotion unit has to fulfill certain requirements. In particular, it should be (1) long enough to reliably calculate features by means of statistical functions and (2) short enough to guarantee stable acoustic properties with respect to emotions within the segment: For features calculated from global statistics over an extraction unit, these units need to have a minimum length. The more values statistical measures are based on, the more expressive they are. On the other hand all alterations of the emotional state should possibly be captured, so the unit should be short enough that no change of emotion is likely to happen within. In addition, it should be so short that the acoustic properties of the segment with respect to emotions are stable, so that expressive features can be derived. This is particularly important for features based on statistical measures, since e. g. the mean value of a very inhomogeneous segment yields an inadequate description. So a compromise has to be found for these two contradicting requirements.

So far, only few attempts have been undertaken to compare different types of units. In [27], we compared utterances, words, words in context and fixed time intervals and found larger, linguistically motivated units tending to be better. Batliner et al. [16] grounded their features on words with a varying number of context words. In addition to simple word-level recognition, they also mapped word results onto turns and on chunks within the turns using two different strategies. In a qualitative analysis of this they found both advantages and disadvantages of smaller units than turns, but they have not further quantitatively explored it.

Generally, it strongly depends on the data which unit fits best. Most commonly dialogue turns, utterances or phrases as e. g. in [5,28,6,29,30] have been used, but also words [16,31].

5.2   Feature Extraction

The second step for an emotion classification system is the extraction of relevant features. Its aim is to find those properties of the digitised and preprocessed acoustic signal that are characteristic for emotions and to represent them in a n-dimensional feature vector. So far, there is not yet a general agreement on which features are the most important ones and good features seem to be highly data dependent [5,27]. However, a high number of features is often not beneficial because most classifiers are negatively influenced by redundant, correlated or irrelevant features. As a consequence, most approaches compute a high number of features and apply then, in order to reduce the dimensionality of the input data, a feature selection algorithm that chooses the most significant features of the training data for the given task. Alternatively, a feature reduction algorithm like principal components analysis (PCA) can be used to encode the main information of the feature space more compactly. The start set of features consisted originally mainly of pitch and energy related features, and these continue to be the prominent features. Formants and Mel Frequency Cepstral Coefficients (MFCC) are also frequently found. Durational and pause related features are noted in several papers, as well as different types of voice quality features. Spectral measures and parametric representations other than MFCCs are less common, but include wavelets, Teager energy operator (TEO) based features, log frequency power coefficients (LFPC) and linear prediction cepstral coefficients (LPCC).

The raw pitch, energy, etc. contours can be used as is, and are then called short-term features, or more often, the actual features are derived from these acoustic variables by applying (statistic) functions over the sequence of values within an emotion segment, thus called global statistics features. This could be e.g. mean pitch of a word or an utterance; further statistical measures are typically maximum, or minimum, etc. of the segment, but also regression, derivations or other more complex functions. The choice of feature type also determines the type of classifier. For global statistics features, a static classifier like Support Vector Machines (SVM), processing one instance at a time has to be used. Short-term features require a dynamic classifier such as Hidden Markov Models (HMM). One can say, that in the first case, dynamic properties of emotions should be captured by the features, while in the latter case, they are dealt with by the classifier.

Some suprasegmental acoustic phenomena may also be considered as global emotion features. Batliner et al. [32] and Devillers et al. [5] used those, among them hyper-clear speech, pauses inside words, syllable lengthening, off-talk, resp. disfluency cues, inspiration, expiration, mouth noise, laughter, crying, unintelligible voice. Though these have been mainly annotated by hand, automatic extraction would also be possible in some cases.

Furthermore, meta-data can be used to enhance recognition accuracy as e.g. applied by Litman and colleagues [6]: They collected a corpus from a spoken dialogue tutoring system in the physics domain and hence incorporated into their feature set further application dependent knowledge like the respective speaker, the gender and which of five available physics problems was treated.

Unfortunately, it is rarely possible to compare features across published work, since conditions vary a lot and even slight changes in the general set-up can make results incomparable. E.g. most researchers use their own recordings, and different data or particularly data types have a huge impact on the comparability between two approaches. As for now, there don't exist standard databases that could be used for benchmarking. For one database, 50% accuracy may be excellent for a 4-class problem, while for another database, recognition rates of 70% to 80% can be reached. This does not mean that the database in the former case was not well designed, but rather that it is a harder task and that can be due to many factors. A rule of thumb for natural emotions is that recognition rate is not much more than twice chance level, so for a 4-class problem, 50% is good.

Classifiers, target classes, speaker types also differ in the various publications on automatic emotion recognition, so that from a comparison of the literature no general statement can be made on which features are most successful. Of course, comparisons of features within publications are made, e. g. through relevance ranking by the information gain of single features [29,30] or by rank in a sequential selection method [28,33]. Relevance ranking usually has the goal to see the salience of single features, usually per feature type. However, a single feature's relevance does not necessarily imply usefulness in a set of features. Another strategy is to have groups of features (e. g. prosodic, lexical, etc.) and to look at the different performance of the groups or combinations of groups e. g. [6,32,34]. No general conclusion can be drawn from the work on feature evaluation, but pitch features have on various occasions shown not to be that important as previously assumed [27,28,29,30]. As for now, this has however not been confirmed for other emotion classification tasks. The CEICES (Combining Efforts for Improving automatic Classification of Emotional user States) initiative [15] is therefore aimed at finding a more general evaluation of features by providing a database under fixed conditions and having different sites use their own features and classifiers.

5.3   Classification

After the feature calculation, each input unit is represented by a feature vector, and the problem of emotion recognition can now be considered a general data mining problem. So, in principle, any statistical classifier that can deal with high-dimensional data can be used, but static classifiers like support vector machines, neural networks, and decision trees for global statistics features, and HMM for short-term features as a dynamic modeling technique are most commonly found in the literature on emotional speech recognition. All these classifiers need training data to learn parameters.

Static classification has been more prevalent than dynamic classification in the work on emotion recognition. It has proved to be successful for acted data, but for more natural data, recognition accuracy is only useful in a problem with very few emotion classes. Recent approaches try to enhance the recognition accuracy by a multi-layered classification approach, like having several steps of classifying two groups of the target emotion classes and always further splitting the "winning" group in two as in the cascade-bisection process [35] or automatically separating male and female voice before the actual emotion classification [36].

Dynamic classification with HMMs is used less often than static classification, but is thought to be advantageous for better capturing the temporal activity incorporated in speech. So far, HMMs have almost exclusively been applied to acted data, though they might even better be suited for natural emotions. An HMM is a stochastic finite automaton, where each state models some characteristics of the input signal and where the probability to pass to the next state only depends from the previous state (cf. Fig. 4). In order to use HMMs for speech emotion recognition, usually a single HMM is trained for each emotion and an unknown sample is classified according to the model which describes the derived feature sequence best. Beside the use of appropriate speech features, the architecture of the HMM has main influence on its ability to capture those emotional cues that help to distinguish among different emotions. In [37] we examined the three parameters that are important for the model topology, number of states, connectivity and output probabilities (discrete or continuous and number of mixtures). Although it turned out that finding general tendencies was rather difficult, since on the one hand quite different parameters sometimes gained the same results, whereas on the other hand a slight parameter sometimes caused a very different performance, we could conclude that for the model topology, a medium number of 5 to 10 states per model is most often successful, and for the output probabilities, this was the case for continuous probability densities with a low number of mixtures. With respect to the connectivity of the states, we found high connectivity not necessarily to be more suitable. Results showed also that the network design seems to be relatively independent of the source of speech (acted vs. spontaneous) and the segmentation level (word vs. utterance).

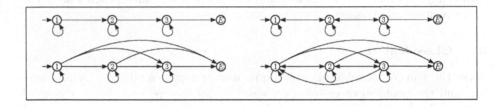

Fig. 4. Some HMM topologies that are suitable for emotion recognition

A direct comparison of static and dynamic classification is difficult since not the same features can be used, so it is difficult to say if just the features have been chosen more favorable or if really the classifier has been superior. Dynamic classification is very promising, but currently, for static classification more feature types can be exploited (e. g. suprasegmental acoustic features like jitter or shimmer to measure voice quality), so that overall, the latter performs better. However, when the feature set is restricted to the same feature types, for instance only MFCCs and energy, HMMs often outperform static modeling techniques [37].

The quality of a classifier can be determined in comparison to human raters in listening tests or to other classification algorithms. The former is more meaningful for practical purposes and shows also the complexity of the particular tasks but it usually involves much effort to conduct such a study. Human rating performance has been reported in different studies to be around 65% [38,39] which is also supported by the findings of [40] in a psychological study, about 70% [41,42], or 80% [43,44]. Interestingly, the automatic classification results presented in these papers reach about the same level or even exceed it. These figures, however, concern acted speech. For spontaneous emotions the gap would supposedly be larger, though figures like this are more difficult to obtain for these databases. When labeling spontaneous emotions, the "true" emotion is not known but established by agreement between the labelers. A perception test can only tell the relation between this ground truth and further listeners. But, as said before, a good recognition rate for natural emotions is about twice chance level.

As a general tendency it can be observed that sophisticated classifiers do achieve higher recognition rates than simple classifiers but not much. SVM is the most popular and the most often successfully applied algorithm, so it can be considered a kind of standard.

6 Emotion Recognition in Real-Time Human-Computer Interaction: A Practical Example

The previous section focused on a systematic evaluation of static and dynamic classification for robust emotion recognition from speech. Characteristic of these approaches was that emotion recognition was done offline. That is both the training as well as the testing was performed using pre-recorded corpora whereby time was not considered as a critical factor.

In this section, we discuss challenges that arise when analyzing and responding to emotional signals in real-time while the user interacts with an application. We illustrate our ideas by means of a simple demo application where a user converses with an embodied conversational agent. The agent does not analyse the meaning of the user's verbal utterances, but instead just interprets the user's emotive cues from speech and responds to them emotionally, for example, by showing empathy when the user's voice conveys sadness. It is not supposed to take the initiative in a conversation, rather its role is that of a sensitive listening agent that gives facial and verbal feedback according to the emotions the human dialogue partner conveys with her voice. An important consideration is how often and how fast this feedback should be given. The facial feedback directly adapts to each processed emotion unit. If an emotion is directly repeated, the intensity of the facial expression increases. After a random number of repetitions, verbal feedback is given. However, outliers, that is e. g. a single occurrence of boredom in a long sequence of recognised joy, are ignored.

The approach is quite similar to the work described in [26] where we equipped an anthropomorphic robot torso with our emotional speech recognition component. The robot mirrors the emotions happiness, fear and neutral as recognised from user speech by facial expressions. A user study revealed that users perceived the emotional mimicry as a sign for the robot reacting more adequately to emotional aspects of a situation and recognising emotion better as compared to a robot reacting without emotion recognition. However, our overall objective is now the creation of rapport between the virtual agent and the human user by providing the agent with emotional sensitivity [45] as opposed to direct mimicry [26]. Furthermore, we analyse continuous dialogue instead of single utterances. Finally, the agent's feedback is not restricted to facial expressions, but may also include verbal comments, such as "That sounds wonderful!".

In Fig. 5, a user is engaged in a dialogue with the Greta agent from Pelachaud and colleagues [46]. The user is reporting on a positive event that happened to her to which Greta responds with a cheerful facial expression.

Fig. 5. Affective conversation with the Greta agent

Real-time emotion recognition is a great challenge for current methodology as apparently demands concerning robustness and accuracy are very high. Additionally, adequate response times are essential for human-computer interaction, as it becomes confusing for the user if he has to wait and there is no direct reaction. Thus, the recognition process needs to be very fast to enhance usability. Note that we are concerned here only with the test phase of the classifier (cf. Fig. 3), as training can be done offline and is not required to be especially fast.

The first issue we faced is the fast segmentation of the continuously incoming audio signal into meaningful, consistent segments. We found a voice activity detection with no in-between pauses longer than 1000 ms to be a good compromise between speed and accuracy. Pauses in the voice activity approximate phrase breaks, though the resulting segments may not be linguistically sound. However, this segmentation requires no further knowledge and is thus very fast. Furthermore, automatic linguistic segmentation by speech recognition, besides being time-consuming, is still very error-prone on spontaneous dialogue, which can easily have negative influence on the emotion recognition, too.

Concerning the features, we decided for global statistics features as more varied feature types can be exploited with this approach. In most related work of offline emotion recognition, some features used to classify emotions rely on manual labeling such as phrase accent annotation or word transcription which is obviously not possible in a fully automatic system. We limited our feature set to only fully automatically computable features without any linguistic knowledge. We computed features based on pitch, energy, MFCCs, the frequency spectrum, duration and pauses which resulted in a vector of 1316 features. Then, in order to reduce dimensionality and to improve and speed up classification, a sequential feature selection was applied ending up with 20 features related to pitch, MFCCs and energy that are most relevant for the given training data. The procedure is equivalent to the one described in [27]. There we showed that good feature sets differ significantly depending on the data type, whether it's acted or spontaneous, so a feature selection is a very beneficial step. Furthermore, we did not find the high degree of automation in the feature extraction to be a disadvantage and we assume the large number of features provided to the selection process to be responsible for this.

For classification, a Naive Bayes classifier was used. Though this is a very simple classifier, it has the advantage of being very fast without performing much worse than more sophisticated classifiers such as support vector machines.

To train the classifier, we used the Berlin emotional speech database [7] which was already introduced in section 3. As mentioned before, it holds very proto-typical, acted emotions. The available emotions are fear, anger, joy, boredom, sadness, disgust as well as neutral. However, for our application better results are achieved if the set is restricted, e. g. to joy, boredom, neutral. In general, the more training and test data resemble, the better the results on the test data are. In this case, the training database is quite different from the expected test data, as it is acted and recorded in a very different setting. In our sample application we can expect people to exaggerate their emotions rather than being completely natural. On the other hand, having test speakers in the training data, thus per-sonalising the emotion recognition in some way, would of course improve results. However, data acquisition is laborious and users would often not be willing to do so.

Even though we had to restrict ourselves to few emotion classes and recog-nition rates were lower than for offline processing, we have evidence that users prefer a listening agent with emotional sensitivity over a listening agent without such a behavior. Due to the more subtle emotional response by the Greta agent, we expect a stronger effect than in the experiment reported in [26] where we compared a robot with and without emotion recognition. A formal experiment testing this hypothesis is currently under preparation.

7 Conclusion

The integration of approaches to the automated evaluation of vocal emotions into human-computer interfaces presents great challenges since emotions have to be recognized in real-time while the user is interacting with an application. These challenges affect audio segmentation to find appropriate units for emotions, extraction of emotion relevant features, classification of emotions, and training databases with emotional speech. By means of a sample application with a virtual agent giving affective feedback in a dialogue with a human user, we outlined solutions to each of the problems.

Audio segmentation can be performed by voice activity detection which is a fast segmentation method not requiring high-level linguistic knowledge. Feature extraction may only rely on automatically computable properties of the acoustic signal, but this is not a major limitation, if the approach of calculating a multitude of possible features and then selecting the most relevant ones for the given training data is taken. For classification, in principle any statistical classifier can be used with sophisticated classifiers being superior in accuracy, but simple and thus fast classifiers are often sufficient. The speech database used to train the classifier should be adjusted to the particular application as much as possible. Best is a specifically designed database with the same scenario as occurring during testing and possibly even including test speakers. Since this is often not feasible, it is also practical to switch to general databases. Furthermore, the restriction to few (maximally 3) classes is strongly suggested.

Designers of human-computer interfaces should consider carefully how to use information on the user's emotional state in the envisioned application context and what impact erroneous recognition results may have. In this paper, we have sketched some application fields, such as self monitoring systems, where the automated evaluation of vocal emotions seems promising and beneficial.

Acknowledgements

This work was partially supported by the European Community (EC) within the network of excellence Humaine IST-507422, the eCIRCUS project IST-4-027656-STP and the Callas project IST-034800. The authors are solely responsible for the content of this publication. It does not represent the opinion of the EC, and the EC is not responsible for any use that might be made of data appearing therein.

References

1. Murray, I., Arnott, J.: Toward the simulation of emotion in synthetic speech: A review of the literature on human vocal emotion. Journal of the Acoustical Society of America 93(2), 1097–1108 (1993)
2. Wilting, J., Krahmer, E., Swerts, M.: Real vs. acted emotional speech. In: Proceedings of Interspeech 2006 — ICSLP, Pittsburgh, PA, USA (2006)
3. Velten, E.: A laboratory task for induction of mood states. Behavior Research & Therapy 6, 473–482 (1968)
4. Dellaert, F., Polzin, T., Waibel, A.: Recognizing emotion in speech. In: Proceedings of ICSLP, Philadelphia, USA (1996)

5. Devillers, L., Vidrascu, L., Lamel, L.: Challenges in real-life emotion annotation and machine learning based detection. Neural Networks 18(4), 407–422 (2005)
6. Litman, D.J., Forbes-Riley, K.: Predicting student emotions in computer-human tutoring dialogues. In: Proceedings of the 42nd Annual Meeting of the Association for Computational Linguistics (ACL), Barcelona, Spain (2004)
7. Burkhardt, F., Paeschke, A., Rolfes, M., Sendlmeier, W.F., Weiss, B.: A database of German emotional speech. In: Proceedings of Interspeech 2005, Lisbon, Portugal (2005)
8. Engberg, I.S., Hansen, A.V.: Documentation of the Danish Emotional Speech Database (DES). Technical report. Aalborg University, Aalborg, Denmark (1996)
9. Schiel, F., Steininger, S., Türk, U.: The SmartKom multimodal corpus at BAS. In: Proceedings of the 3rd Language Resources & Evaluation Conference (LREC) 2002, Las Palmas, Gran Canaria, Spain, pp. 200–206 (2002)
10. Batliner, A., Hacker, C., Steidl, S., Nöth, E., D'Arcy, S., Russell, M., Wong, M.: "You stupid tin box" - children interacting with the AIBO robot: A cross-linguistic emotional speech corpus. In: Proceedings of the 4th International Conference of Language Resources and Evaluation LREC 2004, Lisbon, pp. 171–174 (2004)
11. Tato, R., Santos, R., Kompe, R., Pardo, J.M.: Emotional space improves emotion recognition. In: Proceedings International Conference on Spoken Language Processing, Denver, pp. 2029–2032 (2002)
12. Yu, C., Aoki, P.M., Woodruff, A.: Detecting user engagement in everyday conversations. In: Proceedings of Interspeech 2004 — ICSLP, Jeju, Korea, pp. 1329–1332 (2004)
13. Grimm, M., Kroschel, K., Harris, H., Nass, C., Schuller, B., Rigoll, G., Moosmayr, T.: On the necessity and feasibility of detecting a driver's emotional state while driving. In: International Conference on Affective Computing and Intelligent Interaction, Lisbon, Portugal, pp. 126–138 (2007)
14. Kollias, S.: ERMIS — Emotionally Rich Man-machine Intelligent System. (2002) retrieved: 09.02.2007, http://www.image.ntua.gr/ermis/
15. Batliner, A., Steidl, S., Schuller, B., Seppi, D., Laskowski, K., Vogt, T., Devillers, L., Vidrascu, L., Amir, N., Kessous, L., Aharonson, V.: Combining efforts for improving automatic classification of emotional user states. In: IS-LTC 2006, Ljubljana, Slovenia (2006)
16. Batliner, A., Fischer, K., Huber, R., Spilker, J., Nöth, E.: How to find trouble in communication. Speech Communication 40, 117–143 (2003)
17. Picard, R.W.: Affective Computing. MIT Press, Cambridge (1998)
18. Madan, A.: Jerk-O-Meter: Speech-Feature Analysis Provides Feedback on Your Phone Interactions (2005), retrieved: 28.06.2007, http://www.media.mit.edu/press/jerk-o-meter/
19. Burkhardt, F., van Ballegooy, M., Englert, R., Huber, R.: An emotion-aware voice portal. In: Electronic Speech Signal Processing Conference, Prague, Czech Republic (2005)
20. Riccardi, G., Hakkani-Tür, D.: Grounding emotions in human-machine conversational systems. In: Proceedings of Intelligent Technologies for Interactive Entertainment, INTETAIN, Madonna di Campiglio, Italy (2005)
21. Ai, H., Litman, D.J., Forbes-Riley, K., Rotaru, M., Tetreault, J., Purandare, A.: Using system and user performance features to improve emotion detection in spoken tutoring dialogs. In: Proceedings of Interspeech 2006 — ICSLP, Pittsburgh, PA, USA (2006)

22. Jones, C., Jonsson, I.: Using Paralinguistic Cues in Speech to Recognise Emotions in Older Car Drivers. In: Peter, C., Beale, R. (eds.) Affect and Emotion in Human-Computer Interaction. LNCS, vol. 4868. Springer, Heidelberg (2008)
23. Schuller, B., Rigoll, G., Grimm, M., Kroschel, K., Moosmayr, T., Ruske, G.: Effects of in-car noise-conditions on the recognition of emotion within speech. In: Proc. of the DAGA 2007, Stuttgart, Germany (2007)
24. Jones, C., Sutherland, J.: Acoustic Emotion Recognition for Affective Computer Gaming. In: Peter, C., Beale, R. (eds.) Affect and Emotion in Human-Computer Interaction. LNCS, vol. 4868. Springer, Heidelberg (2008)
25. Jones, C., Deeming, A.: Affective Human-Robotic Interaction. In: Peter, C., Beale, R. (eds.) Affect and Emotion in Human-Computer Interaction. LNCS, vol. 4868. Springer, Heidelberg (2008)
26. Hegel, F., Spexard, T., Vogt, T., Horstmann, G., Wrede, B.: Playing a different imitation game: Interaction with an empathic android robot. In: Proc. 2006 IEEE-RAS International Conference on Humanoid Robots (Humanoids 2006) (2006)
27. Vogt, T., André, E.: Comparing feature sets for acted and spontaneous speech in view of automatic emotion recognition. In: Proceedings of International Conference on Multimedia & Expo., Amsterdam, The Netherlands (2005)
28. Fernandez, R., Picard, R.W.: Classical and novel discriminant features for affect recognition from speech. In: Proceedings of Interspeech 2005, Lisbon, Portugal (2005)
29. Oudeyer, P.Y.: The production and recognition of emotions in speech: features and algorithms. International Journal of Human-Computer Studies 59(1–2), 157–183 (2003)
30. Schuller, B., Müller, R., Lang, M., Rigoll, G.: Speaker independent emotion recognition by early fusion of acoustic and linguistic features within ensembles. In: Proceedings of Interspeech 2005, Lisbon, Portugal (2005)
31. Nicholas, G., Rotaru, M., Litman, D.J.: Exploiting word-level features for emotion recognition. In: Proceedings of the IEEE/ACL Workshop on Spoken Language Technology, Aruba (2006)
32. Batliner, A., Zeißler, V., Frank, C., Adelhardt, J., Shi, R.P., Nöth, E.: We are not amused - but how do you know? User states in a multi-modal dialogue system. In: Proceedings of Eurospeech 2003, Geneva, Switzerland, pp. 733–736 (2003)
33. Kwon, O.W., Chan, K., Hao, J., Lee, T.W.: Emotion recognition by speech signals. In: Proceedings of Eurospeech 2003, Geneva, Switzerland, pp. 125–128 (2003)
34. Lee, C.M., Narayanan, S.S.: Toward detecting emotions in spoken dialogs. IEEE Transaction on speech and audio processing 13(2), 293–303 (2005)
35. Zhang, S.,, P.: C.C., Kong, F.: Automatic emotion recognition of speech signal in mandarin. In: Proceedings of Interspeech 2006 — ICSLP, Pittsburgh, PA, USA (2006)
36. Vogt, T., André, E.: Improving automatic emotion recognition from speech via gender differentiation. In: Proc. Language Resources and Evaluation Conference (LREC 2006), Genoa (2006)
37. Wagner, J., Vogt, T., André, E.: A systematic comparison of different hmm designs for emotion recognition from acted and spontaneous speech. In: International Conference on Affective Computing and Intelligent Interaction (ACII), Lisbon, Portugal, pp. 114–125 (2007)
38. Nwe, T.L., Foo, S.W., De Silva, L.C.: Speech emotion recognition using hidden markov models. Speech Communication 41, 603–623 (2003)

39. Petrushin, V.A.: Creating emotion recognition agents for speech signal. In: Dautenhahn, K., Bond, A.H., Canamero, L., Edmonds, B. (eds.) Socially Intelligent Agents. Creating Relationships with Computers and Robots, pp. 77–84. Kluwer Academic Publishers, Dordrecht (2002)
40. Scherer, K.R., Banse, R., Walbott, H.G., Goldbeck, T.: Vocal clues in emotion encoding and decoding. Motivation and Emotion 15, 123–148 (1991)
41. Polzin, T.S., Waibel, A.H.: Detecting emotions in speech. In: Proceedings of Cooperative Multimodal Communications, Tilburg, The Netherlands (1998)
42. Polzin, T.S., Waibel, A.H.: Emotion-sensitive human-computer interfaces. In: Workshop on Speech and Emotion, Newcastle, Northern Ireland, UK, pp. 201–206 (2000)
43. Lee, C.M., Yildirim, S., Bulut, M., Kazemzadeh, A.: Emotion recognition based on phoneme classes. In: Proceedings of Interspeech 2004 — ICSLP, Jeju, Korea (2004)
44. Nogueiras, A., Moreno, A., Bonafonte, A., No, J.M.: Speech emotion recognition using hidden markov models. In: Proceedings of Eurospeech, Aalborg, Denmark (2001)
45. Gratch, J., Okhmatovskaia, A., Lamothe, F., Marsella, S., Morales, M., van der Werf, R.J., Morency, L.P.: Virtual rapport. In: 6th International Conference on Intelligent Virtual Agents, Marina del Rey, USA (2006)
46. de Rosis, F., Pelachaud, C., Poggi, I., Carofiglio, V., de Carolis, B.: From Greta's mind to her face: modelling the dynamics of affective states in a conversational embodied agent. International Journal of Human-Computer Studies 59, 81–118 (2003)

Emotion Recognition through Multiple Modalities: Face, Body Gesture, Speech

Ginevra Castellano[1,*], Loic Kessous[2], and George Caridakis[3]

[1] InfoMus Lab, DIST - University of Genova, Viale Causa 13, I-16145, Genova, Italy
Ginevra.Castellano@unige.it
[2] Department of Speech, Language and Hearing, University of Tel Aviv,
Sheba Center, 52621, Tel Aviv, Israel
kessous@post.tau.ac.il
[3] Image, Video and Multimedia Systems Laboratory,
National Technical University of Athens,
9, Heroon Politechniou str., 15780, Athens, Greece
gcari@image.ece.ntua.gr

Abstract. In this paper we present a multimodal approach for the recognition of eight emotions. Our approach integrates information from facial expressions, body movement and gestures and speech. We trained and tested a model with a Bayesian classifier, using a multimodal corpus with eight emotions and ten subjects. Firstly, individual classifiers were trained for each modality. Next, data were fused at the feature level and the decision level. Fusing the multimodal data resulted in a large increase in the recognition rates in comparison with the unimodal systems: the multimodal approach gave an improvement of more than 10% when compared to the most successful unimodal system. Further, the fusion performed at the feature level provided better results than the one performed at the decision level.

Keywords: Affective body language, Affective speech, Emotion recognition, Multimodal fusion.

1 Introduction

A challenging research issue and one that has been of growing importance to those working in human-computer interaction is to endow a machine with an emotional intelligence. Such a system must be able to create an affective interaction with users: it must have the ability to perceive, interpret, express and regulate emotions [1]. In this case, recognising users' emotional state is one of the main requirements for computers to successfully interact with humans [2]. Many works in affective computing do not combine different modalities into a single system for the analysis of human emotional behaviour: different channels of information (mainly facial expressions and speech) are considered independently to each other. Further, there have been only a few attempts to also consider the integration of information from body movement and

---

* Ginevra Castellano is now at the Department of Computer Science, Queen Mary, University of London, UK (ginevra@dcs.qmul.ac.uk).

C. Peter and R. Beale (Eds.): Affect and Emotion in HCI, LNCS 4868, pp. 92–103, 2008.
© Springer-Verlag Berlin Heidelberg 2008

gestures. Nevertheless, Sebe et al. [3] and Pantic et al. [4] highlight that an ideal system for automatic analysis and recognition of human affective information should be multimodal, as the human sensory system is. Moreover, studies from psychology highlight the need to consider the integration of different behaviour modalities in human-human communication [5] [6].

In this paper we present a multimodal approach for the recognition of eight acted emotional states (anger, despair, interest, pleasure, sadness, irritation, joy and pride). Our approach integrates information from facial expressions, body movement and gestures and speech: we trained and tested a model with a Bayesian classifier, using a multimodal corpus with ten subjects collected during the Third Summer School of the HUMAINE EU-IST project, held in Genova in September 2006. In the following sections we describe the approach by focusing on the analysis performed for each of the three modalities considered in this work. We then compare different strategies to perform the data fusion for the multimodal emotion recognition.

2 Related Work

Emotion recognition has been investigated with three main types of databases: acted emotions, natural spontaneous emotions and elicited emotions. The best results are generally obtained with acted emotion databases because they contain strong emotional expressions. Literature on speech (see for example Banse and Scherer [7]) shows that the majority of studies have been conducted with emotional acted speech. Feature sets for acted and spontaneous speech have recently been compared by [8]. Generally, few acted-emotion speech databases have included speakers with several different native languages. More recently, some attempts to collect multimodal data were made: some examples of multimodal databases can be found in [9] [10] [11].

In the area of unimodal emotion recognition, there have been many studies using different, but single, modalities. Facial expressions [12] [13], vocal features [14] [15], body movements and postures [16] [17] [18], physiological signals [19] have been used as inputs during these attempts, while multimodal emotion recognition is currently gaining ground [20] [21] [22]. Nevertheless, most of the work has considered the integration of information from facial expressions and speech and there have been relatively a few attempts to combine information from body movement and gestures in a multimodal framework. Gunes and Piccardi [23] for example fused at different levels facial expressions and body gestures information for bimodal emotion recognition. Further, el Kaliouby and Robinson [24] proposed a vision-based computational model to infer acted mental states from head movements and facial expressions.

A wide variety of machine learning techniques have been used in emotion recognition approaches [2] [12]. Especially in the multimodal case [4], they all employ a large number of audio, visual or physiological features, a fact which usually impedes the training process; therefore, it is necessary to find a way to reduce the number of utilised features by picking out only those related to emotion. One possibility in this direction is to use neural networks, since they enable us to pinpoint the most relevant features with respect to the output, usually by observing their weights. An interesting work in this area is the sensitivity analysis approach by Engelbrecht et al. [25]. Sebe et al. [3] highlight that probabilistic graphical models, such as Hidden Markov Models, Bayesian networks and Dynamic Bayesian networks are very well suited for fusing different sources of information in multimodal emotion recognition and can also handle noisy features and missing values of features all by probabilistic inference.

In this work we combine a wrapper feature selection approach and a Bayesian classifier. The former reduces the number of features and the latter was used both for unimodal and multimodal emotion recognition.

3 Collection of Multimodal Data

The corpus used in this study was collected during Third Summer School of the HUMAINE EU-IST project, held in Genova in September 2006. The overall recording procedure was based on the GEMEP corpus [10], a multimodal collection of portrayed emotional expressions: we simultaneously recorded data on facial expressions, body movement and gestures and speech.

3.1 Subjects and Set-Up

Ten participants of the summer school distributed as evenly as possible concerning their gender participated to the recordings. Subjects represented five different nationalities: French, German, Greek, Hebrew, Italian.

In terms of the technical set-up, two DV cameras (25 fps) recorded the actors from a frontal view. One camera recorded the actor's body and the other one was focused on the actor's face (Figure 1).

(a)   (b)

Fig. 1. Camera views of (a) face and (b) body

We chose such a setup because the resolution required for the extraction of facial features is much larger than the one for body movement detection or hand gesture tracking. This could only be achieved if one camera zoomed in on the actor's face. We adopted some restrictions concerning the actor's behaviour and clothing. Long sleeves and a covered neck were preferred since the majority of the hand and head detection algorithms are based on colour tracking. Further, a uniform background was used to make the background subtraction process easier. As for the facial features extraction process we considered some prerequisites such as the lack of eyeglasses, beards, and moustaches.

For the voice recordings we used a direct-to-disk computer-based system. The speech samples were directly recorded on the hard disk of the computer using sound editing software. We used an external sound card connected to the computer by IEEE 1394 High Speed Serial Bus (also known as FireWire or i.Link). A microphone mounted on the actors' shirt was connected to an HF emitter (wireless system emitter) and the receiver was connected to the sound card using a XLR connector (balanced audio connector for high quality microphones and connections between equipments). The external sound card included a preamplifier (for two XLR inputs) that was used in order to adjust the input gain and to minimise the impact of signal-to-noise ratio of the recording system. The sampling rate of the recording was 44.1 kHz and the quantization was 16 bit, mono.

3.2 Procedure

Participants were asked to act eight emotional states: anger, despair, interest, pleasure, sadness, irritation, joy and pride, equally distributed in the space valence-arousal (see Table 1).

During the recording process one of the authors had the role of director guiding the actors through the process. Participants were asked to perform specific gestures that exemplify each emotion. The director's role was to instruct the subject on the procedure (number of gestures' repetitions, emotion sequence, etc.) and details of each emotion and emotion-specific gesture. For example, for the despair emotion the subject was given a brief description of the emotion (e.g. "facing an existential problem without solution, coupled with a refusal to accept the situation") and if the subject had required more details he would be given an example of a situation in which the specific emotion was present. All instructions were provided based on the procedure used during the collection of the GEMEP corpus [10]. For selecting the emotion-specific gestures we have borrowed ideas from a figure animation research area dealing with posturing of a figure [26] and came up with the gestures shown in Table 1.

Table 1. The acted emotions and the *emotion-specific gestures*

Emotion	Valence	Arousal	Gesture
Anger	Negative	High	Violent descend of hands
Despair	Negative	High	Leave me alone
Interest	Positive	Low	Raise hands
Pleasure	Positive	Low	Open hands
Sadness	Negative	Low	Smooth falling hands
Irritation	Negative	Low	Smooth go away
Joy	Positive	High	Circular italianate movement
Pride	Positive	High	Close hands towards chest

As in the GEMEP corpus [10], a pseudo-linguistic sentence was pronounced by the actors during acting the emotional states. The sentence "Toko, damato ma gali sa" was designed in order to fulfil different needs. First, as the different speakers have different native languages, using a specific language was not so adequate to this study. Then we wanted the sentence to include phonemes that exist in all the languages of all the speakers. Also, the words in the sentence are composed of simple diphones ('ma' and 'sa'), two ('gali' 'toko') or three diphones ('damato'). Then, the vowels included ('o' , 'a' , 'i') are vowels that are relatively distant in a vowel space, for example the vowel triangle, and have a pronunciation mostly similar in all the languages of the group of speakers. We suggested the speakers a meaning for the sentence. 'Toko' is supposed to be the name of a person, who the speakers/users are interacting with. We chose for this word two stop consonants (also known as plosives or stop-plosives) /t/ and /k/ and two identical vowels /o/. This was done in order to allow the study of certain acoustic correlates. Then 'damato ma gali sa' is supposed to mean something like 'can you open it'. The word 'it' could correspond to a folder, a file, a box, a door or whatever.

Each emotion was acted three times by each actor, so that we collected 240 posed gestures, facial expressions and speech samples.

4   Feature Extraction

4.1   Face Feature Extraction

As first step the face was located, so that approximate facial feature locations could be estimated from the head position and rotation. The face was segmented focusing on the following facial areas: left eye/eyebrow, right eye/eyebrow, nose and mouth. Each of those areas, called feature-candidate areas, contains the features whose boundaries need to be extracted for our purposes. Inside the corresponding feature-candidate areas precise feature extraction was performed for each facial feature, i.e. eyes, eyebrows, mouth and nose, using a multi-cue approach, generating a small number of intermediate feature masks. Feature masks generated for each facial feature were fused together to produce the final mask for that feature. The mask fusion process uses anthropometric criteria [27] to perform validation and weight assignment on each intermediate mask; all the feature's weighted masks are then fused to produce a final mask along with confidence level estimation.

Since this procedure essentially locates and tracks points in the facial area, we chose to work with MPEG-4 FAPs (Facial Animation Parameters) and not Action Units (AUs), since the former are explicitly defined to measure the deformation of these feature points. Measurement of FAPs requires the availability of a frame where the subject's expression is found to be neutral. This frame is called the *neutral frame* and is manually selected from video sequences to be analysed or interactively provided to the system when initially brought into a specific user's ownership. The final feature masks were used to extract 19 Feature Points (FPs) [28]; Feature Points obtained from each frame were compared to FPs obtained from the neutral frame to estimate facial deformations and produce the FAPs. Confidence levels on FAP estimation were derived from the equivalent feature point confidence levels. The FAPs were used along with their confidence levels to provide the facial expression estimation.

In accordance with the other modalities, facial features needed to be processed so as to have one vector of values per sentence. FAPs originally correspond to every frame in the sentence. A way to imprint the temporal evolution of the FAP values was to calculate a set of statistical features over these values and their derivatives. The whole process was inspired by the equivalent process performed in the acoustic features.

4.2   Body Feature Extraction

Tracking of body and hands of the subjects was done using the EyesWeb platform [29]. Starting from the silhouette and the hands blobs of the actors, we extracted five main expressive motion cues, using the EyesWeb Expressive Gesture Processing Library [30]: quantity of motion and contraction index of the body, velocity, acceleration and fluidity of the hand's barycenter. Data were normalised according to the behaviour shown by each actor, considering the maximum and the minimum values of each motion cue in each actor, in order to compare data from all the subjects.

Automatic extraction allows to obtain temporal series of the selected motion cues over time, depending on the video frame rate. For each profile of the motion cues we selected then a subset of features describing the dynamics of the cues over time. Based on the model proposed in [31] we extracted the following dynamic indicators of the motion cues temporal profile: initial and final slope, initial and final slope of the main peak, maximum value, ratio between the maximum value and the duration of the main peak, mean value, ratio between the mean and the maximum value, ratio between the absolute maximum and the biggest following relative maximum, centroid of energy, distance between maximum value and centroid of energy, symmetry index, shift index of the main peak, number of peaks, number of peaks preceding the main one, ratio between the main peak duration and the whole profile duration. This process was made for each motion cue of all the videos of the corpus, so that each gesture is characterised by a subset of 80 motion features.

4.3 Speech Feature Extraction

The set of features that we used contains features based on intensity, pitch, MFCC (Mel Frequency Cepstral Coefficient), Bark spectral bands, voiced segment characteristics and pause length. The full set contains 377 features. The features from the intensity contour and the pitch contour were extracted using a set of 32 statistical features. This set of features was applied both to the pitch and intensity contour and to their derivatives. Not any normalisation was applied before feature extraction. In particular, we didn't perform user or gender normalisation for pitch contour as it is often done in order to remove difference between registers. We considered the following 32 features: maximum, mean and minimum values, sample mode (most frequently occurring value), interquartile range (difference between the 75th and 25th percentiles), kurtosis, the third central sample moment, first (slope) and second coefficients of linear regression, first, second and third coefficients of quadratic regression, percentiles at 2.5%, 25%, 50%, 75%, and 97.5%, skewness, standard deviation, variance. Thus, we have 64 features based on the pitch contour and 64 features based on the intensity contour. This feature set was used originally for inspecting a contour such as a pitch contour or a loudness contour, but these features are also meaningful for inspecting evolution over time or spectral axis. Indeed, we also extracted similar features on the Bark spectral bands as done in [32]. Further, we extracted 13 MFCCs using time averaging on time windows, as well as features derived from pitch values and lengths of voiced segments, using a set of 35 features applied to both of them. Finally, we extracted features based on pause (or silence) length and non-pauses lengths (35 each).

5 Unimodal and Multimodal Emotion Recognition

In order to compare the results of the unimodal and the multimodal systems, we used a common approach based on a Bayesian classifier (BayesNet) provided by the software Weka, a free toolbox containing a collection of machine learning algorithms for data mining tasks [33]. In Figure 2 we show an overview of the framework we propose:

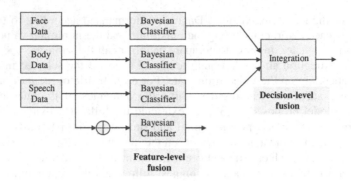

Fig. 2. Overview of the framework

As shown in the left part of the diagram, a separate Bayesian classifier was used for each modality (face, gestures, speech). All sets of data were normalised. Features discretisation based on Kononenko's MDL (minimum description length) criterion [34] was done to reduce the learning complexity. A wrapper approach to feature subset selection (which allows to evaluate the attribute sets by using a learning scheme) was used in order to reduce the number of inputs to the classifiers and find the features that maximise the performance of the classifier. A best-first search method in forward direction was used. Further, in all the systems, the corpus was trained and tested using the cross-validation method.

To fuse facial expressions, gestures and speech information, two different approaches were implemented (right of Figure 2): feature-level fusion, where a single classifier with features of the three modalities is used; and decision-level fusion, where a separate classifier is used for each modality and the outputs are combined a posteriori. In the second approach the output was computed combining the posterior probabilities of the unimodal systems. We made experiments using two different approaches for the decision-level fusion. The first approach consisted of selecting the emotion that received the highest probability in the three modalities (*best probability* approach). The second approach (*majority voting plus best probability*) consisted of selecting the emotion that corresponds to the majority of 'voting' from the three modalities; if a majority was not possible to define (for example when each unimodal system gives in output a different emotion), the emotion that received the highest probability in the three modalities was selected.

6 Results

6.1 Emotion Recognition from Facial Expressions

Table 2 shows the confusion matrix of the emotion recognition system based on facial expressions. The overall performance of this classifier was 48.3%. The most recognised emotions were anger (56.67%), irritation, joy and pleasure (53.33%). Pride is misclassified with pleasure (20%), while sadness is misclassified with irritation (20%), an emotion in the same valence-arousal quadrant.

Table 2. Confusion matrix of the emotion recognition system based on facial expressions

a	b	c	d	E	f	g	h		
56.67	3.33	3.33	10	6.67	10	6.67	3.33	a	Anger
10	**40**	13.33	10	0	13.33	3.33	10	b	Despair
6.67	3.33	**50**	6.67	6.67	10	16.67	0	c	Interest
10	6.67	10	**53.33**	3.33	6.67	3.33	6.67	d	Irritation
3.33	0	13.33	16.67	**53.33**	10	0	3.33	e	Joy
6.67	13.33	6.67	0	6.67	**53.33**	13.33	0	f	Pleasure
6.67	3.33	16.67	6.67	13.33	20	**33.33**	0	g	Pride
3.33	6.67	3.33	20	0	13.33	6.67	**46.67**	h	Sadness

6.2 Emotion Recognition from Gestures

Table 3 shows the performance of the emotion recognition system. The overall performance of this classifier was 67.1%. Anger and pride are recognised with very high accuracy (80 and 96.67% respectively). Sadness was partly misclassified with pride (36.67%).

Table 3. Confusion matrix of the emotion recognition system based on gestures

a	b	c	d	e	f	g	h		
80	10	0	3.33	0	0	6.67	0	a	Anger
3.33	**56.67**	6.67	0	0	0	26.67	6.67	b	Despair
3.33	0	**56.67**	0	6.67	6.67	26.67	0	c	Interest
0	10	0	**63.33**	0	0	26.67	0	d	Irritation
0	10	0	6.67	**60**	0	23.33	0	e	Joy
0	6.67	3.33	0	0	**66.67**	23.33	0	f	Pleasure
0	0	0	3.33	0	0	**96.67**	0	g	Pride
0	3.33	0	3.33	0	0	36.67	**56.67**	h	Sadness

6.3 Emotion Recognition from Speech

Table 4 displays the confusion matrix of the emotion recognition system based on speech. The overall performance of this classifier was 57.1%. Anger and sadness are classified with high accuracy (93.33 and 76.67% respectively). Despair obtained a very low recognition rate and was mainly confused with pleasure (23.33%).

Table 4. Confusion matrix of the emotion recognition system based on speech

a	b	c	d	e	f	g	h		
93.33	0	3.33	3.33	0	0	0	0	a	Anger
10	**23.33**	16.67	6.67	3.33	23.33	3.33	13.33	b	Despair
6.67	0	**60**	10	0	16.67	3.33	3.33	c	Interest
13.33	3.33	10	**50**	3.33	3.33	13.33	3.33	d	Irritation
20	0	10	13.33	**43.33**	10	3.33	0	e	Joy
3.33	6.67	6.67	6.67	0	**53.33**	6.67	16.67	f	Pleasure
3.33	10	3.33	13.33	0	13.33	**56.67**	0	g	Pride
0	6.67	3.33	10	0	3.33	0	**76.67**	h	Sadness

6.4 Feature-Level Fusion

Table 5 displays the confusion matrix of the multimodal emotion recognition system. The overall performance of this classifier was 78.3%, which is much higher than the performance obtained by the most successful unimodal system, the one based on gestures. The diagonal components reveal that all the emotions, apart from despair, can be recognised with over 70% accuracy. Anger was the emotion recognised with highest accuracy, as in all the unimodal systems.

Table 5. Confusion matrix of the multimodal emotion recognition system

a	b	c	d	e	f	g	h		
90	0	0	0	10	0	0	0	a	Anger
0	**53.33**	3.33	16.67	6.67	0	10	10	b	Despair
6.67	0	**73.33**	13.33	0	3.33	3.33	0	c	Interest
0	6.67	0	**76.67**	6.67	3.33	0	6.67	d	Irritation
0	0	0	0	**93.33**	0	6.67	0	e	Joy
0	3.33	3.33	13.33	3.33	**70**	6.67	0	f	Pleasure
3.33	3.33	0	3.33	0	0	**86.67**	3.33	g	Pride
0	0	0	16.67	0	0	0	**83.33**	h	Sadness

6.5 Decision Level Fusion

The approach based on decision-level fusion obtained lower recognition rates than that based on feature-level fusion. The performance of the classifier was 74.6%, both for the *best probability* and for the *majority voting plus best probability* approaches.

Table 6 shows the performance of the system with decision level integration using the *best probability* approach. Anger was again the emotion recognised with highest accuracy, but the recognition rate of the majority of emotions decreases with respect to the feature-level integration.

Table 6. Decision level integration with *best probability* approach

a	b	c	d	e	f	g	h		
96,67	0	0	0	0	0	3,33	0	a	Anger
13,33	**53,33**	6,67	0	0	3,33	13,33	10	b	Despair
3,33	0	**60**	3,33	10	13,33	6,67	3,33	c	Interest
13,33	6,67	6,67	**60**	0	3,33	0	10	d	Irritation
0	0	10	3,33	**86,67**	0	0	0	e	Joy
6,67	3,33	0	0	0	**80**	6,67	3,33	f	Pleasure
3,33	0	6,67	0	0	10	**80**	0	g	Pride
3,33	3,33	0	10	0	3,33	0	**80**	h	Sadness

7 Discussion and Conclusions

We presented a multimodal framework for analysis and recognition of emotion starting from expressive faces, gestures and speech. We trained and tested a model with a Bayesian classifier, using a multimodal corpus with eight acted emotions and ten subjects of five different nationalities.

We tested our approach on a dataset of 240 samples for each modality (face, body, speech). Considering the performances of the unimodal emotion recognition systems, the one based on gestures appears to be the most successful, followed by the one based on speech and then the one based on facial expressions. We note that in this study we used *emotion-specific gestures*: these are gestures that are selected so as to express each specific emotion. An alterative approach which may also be of interest would be to recognise emotions from different expressivities of the same gesture (one not necessarily associated with any specific emotion) performed under different emotional conditions. This would allow good comparison with contemporary systems based on facial expressions and speech and will be considered in our future work. Fusing multimodal data greatly improved the recognition rates in comparison with the unimodal systems: the multimodal approach gave an improvement of more than 10% compared to the performance of the system based on gestures. Further, the fusion performed at the feature level showed better performances than the one performed at the decision-level, highlighting the processing of input data in a joint feature space as the most successful approach in this case.

We can conclude that using three different modalities greatly increases the recognition performance of an automatic emotion recognition system. That is helpful also when some values for features of some modalities are missing. On the other hand, humans use more than one modality to recognise emotions and process signals in a complementary manner, so it is expected that an automatic system shows a similar behaviour. This study considered a restricted set of data, collected from a relatively small group of subjects. Nevertheless, it represents a first attempt to fuse together three different synchronised modalities, which is still uncommon in current research. Future work will consider new multimodal recordings with a larger and more representative set of subjects, as well as the investigation of the mutual relationship between audio-visual information.

Acknowledgments. The research work has been realised in the framework of the EU-IST Project HUMAINE (Human-Machine Interaction Network on Emotion), a Network of Excellence (NoE) in the EU 6th Framework Programme (2004–2007).

References

1. Picard, R.: Affective computing. MIT Press, Boston (1997)
2. Cowie, R., Douglas-Cowie, E., Tsapatsoulis, N., Votsis, G., Kollias, S., Fellenz, W., Taylor, J.G.: Emotion recognition in human-computer interaction. IEEE Signal Processing Magazine (January 2001)
3. Sebe, N., Cohen, I., Huang, T.S.: Multimodal Emotion Recognition. Handbook of Pattern Recognition and Computer Vision. World Scientific, Singapore (2005)
4. Pantic, M., Sebe, N., Cohn, J., Huang, T.S.: Affective Multimodal Human-Computer Interaction. In: ACM Multimedia, Singapore, pp. 669–676 (November 2005)
5. Scherer, K.R., Wallbott, H.G.: Analysis of Nonverbal Behavior. In: Handbook Of Discourse: Analysis, ch.11, vol. 2. Academic Press, London (1985)
6. Scherer, K.R., Ellgring, H.: Multimodal Expression of Emotion: Affect Programs or Componential Appraisal Patterns? Emotion 7(1) (2007)

7. Banse, R., Scherer, K.R.: Acoustic Profiles in Vocal Emotion Expression. Journal of Personality and Social Psychology, 614–636 (1996)
8. Vogt, T., André, E.: Comparing feature sets for acted and spontaneous speech in view of automatic emotion recognition. In: IEEE International Conference on Multimedia & Expo (ICME 2005) (2005)
9. Gunes, H., Piccardi, M.: A Bimodal Face and Body Gesture Database for Automatic Analysis of Human Nonverbal Affective Behavior. In: Proc. of ICPR 2006 the 18th International Conference on Pattern Recognition, Hong Kong, China, August 20–24 (2006)
10. Bänziger, T., Pirker, H., Scherer, K.: Gemep - geneva multimodal emotion portrayals: a corpus for the study of multimodal emotional expressions. In: Deviller, L., et al. (eds.) Proceedings of LREC 2006 Workshop on Corpora for Research on Emotion and Affect, Genoa. Italy, pp. 15–19 (2006)
11. Douglas-Cowie, E., Campbell, N., Cowie, R., Roach, P.: Emotional speech: towards a new generation of databases. Speech Communication 40, 33–60 (2003)
12. Pantic, M., Rothkrantz, L.J.M.: Automatic analysis of facial expressions: The state of the art. IEEE Trans. on Pattern Analysis and Machine Intelligence 22(12), 1424–1445 (2000)
13. Ioannou, S., Raouzaiou, A., Tzouvaras, V., Mailis, T., Karpouzis, K., Kollias, S.: Emotion recognition through facial expression analysis based on a neurofuzzy network. Neural Networks 18(4), 423–435 (2005)
14. Cowie, R., Douglas-Cowie, E.: Automatic statistical analysis of the signal and prosodic signs of emotion in speech. In: Proc. International Conf. on Spoken Language Processing, pp. 1989–1992 (1996)
15. Scherer, K.R.: Adding the affective dimension: A new look in speech analysis and synthesis. In: Proc. International Conf. on Spoken Language Processing, pp. 1808–1811 (1996)
16. Camurri, A., Lagerlöf, I., Volpe, G.: Recognizing Emotion from Dance Movement: Comparison of Spectator Recognition and Automated Techniques. International Journal of Human-Computer Studies 59(1-2), 213–225 (2003)
17. Bianchi-Berthouze, N., Kleinsmith, A.: A categorical approach to affective gesture recognition. Connection Science 15(4), 259–269 (2003)
18. Castellano, G., Villalba, S.D., Camurri, A.: Recognising Human Emotions from Body Movement and Gesture Dynamics. In: Proc. of 2nd International Conference on Affective Computing and Intelligent Interaction, Lisbon (2007)
19. Picard, R.W., Vyzas, E., Healey, J.: Toward machine emotional intelligence: Analysis of affective physiological state. IEEE Trans. on Pattern Analysis and Machine Intelligence 23(10), 1175–1191 (2001)
20. Pantic, M., Rothkrantz, L.J.M.: Towards an Affect-sensitive Multimodal Human-Computer Interaction. Proceedings of the IEEE 91(9), 1370–1390 (2003)
21. Busso, C., Deng, Z., Yildirim, S., Bulut, M., Lee, C.M., Kazemzaeh, A., Lee, S., Neumann, U., Narayanan, S.: Analysis of Emotion Recognition using Facial Expressions, Speech and Multimodal information. In: Proc. of ACM 6th int'l Conf. on Multimodal Interfaces (ICMI 2004), State College, PA, October 2004, pp. 205–211 (2004)
22. Kim, J., André, E., Rehm, M., Vogt, T., Wagner, J.: Integrating information from speech and physiological signals to achieve emotional sensitivity. In: Proc. of the 9th European Conference on Speech Communication and Technology (2005)
23. Gunes, H., Piccardi, M.: Bi-modal emotion recognition from expressive face and body gestures. Journal of Network and Computer Applications (2006), doi:10.1016/j.jnca.2006.09.007
24. el Kaliouby, R., Robinson, P.: Generalization of a Vision-Based Computational Model of Mind-Reading. In: Proceedings of First International Conference on Affective Computing and Intelligent Interfaces, pp. 582–589 (2005)

25. Engelbrecht, A.P., Fletcher, L., Cloete, I.: Variance analysis of sensitivity information for pruning multilayer feedforward neural networks. In: IJCNN 1999. International Joint Conference on Neural Networks, vol. 3, pp. 1829–1833 (1999)
26. Densley, D.J., Willis, P.J.: Emotional posturing: a method towards achieving emotional figure animation. Computer Animation, 8 (1997)
27. Young, J.W.: Head and Face Anthropometry of Adult U.S. Civilians, FAA Civil Aeromedical Institute, 1963–1993 (final report, 1993)
28. Raouzaiou, A., Tsapatsoulis, N., Karpouzis, K., Kollias, S.: Parameterized facial expression synthesis based on MPEG-4. EURASIP Journal on Applied Signal Processing 2002(10), 1021–1038 (2002)
29. Camurri, A., Coletta, P., Massari, A., Mazzarino, B., Peri, M., Ricchetti, M., Ricci, A., Volpe, G.: Toward real-time multimodal processing: EyesWeb 4.0. In: Proc. AISB 2004 Convention: Motion, Emotion and Cognition, Leeds, UK (March 2004)
30. Camurri, A., Mazzarino, B., Volpe, G.: Analysis of Expressive Gesture: The Eyesweb Expressive Gesture Processing Library. In: Camurri, A., Volpe, G. (eds.) GW 2003. LNCS (LNAI), vol. 2915. Springer, Heidelberg (2004)
31. Castellano, G., Camurri, A., Mazzarino, B., Volpe, G.: A mathematical model to analyse the dynamics of gesture expressivity. In: Proc. of AISB 2007 Convention: Artificial and Ambient Intelligence, Newcastle upon Tyne, UK (April 2007)
32. Kessous, L., Amir, N.: Comparison of feature extraction approaches based on the Bark time/frequency representation for classification of expressive speechpaper submitted to Interspeech (2007)
33. Witten, I.H., Frank, E.: Data Mining: Practical machine learning tools and techniques, 2nd edn. Morgan Kaufmann, San Francisco (2005)
34. Kononenko, I.: On Biases in Estimating Multi-Valued Attributes. In: 14th International Joint Conference on Articial Intelligence, pp. 1034–1040 (1995).

The Composite Sensing of Affect

Gordon McIntyre[1] and Roland Göcke[1,2]

[1] Research School of Information Sciences and Engineering,
Australian National University, Canberra, Australia
[2] Seeing Machines, Canberra, Australia

Abstract. This paper describes some of the issues faced by typical emotion recognition systems and the need to be able to deal with emotions in a natural setting. Studies tend to ignore the dynamic, versatile and personalised nature of affective expression and the influence that social setting, context and culture have on its rules of display. Affective cues can be present in multiple modalities and they can manifest themselves in different temporal order. Thus, fusing the feature sets is challenging. We present a composite approach to affective sensing. The term composite is used to reflect the blending of information from multiple modalities with the available semantic evidence to enhance the emotion recognition process.

1 Introduction

Recognising emotions from the modulations in another person's voice and facial expressions is perhaps one of our most important human abilities. Such interaction is inherently multimodal and for computers to adapt and respond in a natural, yet robust, manner in real-world situations demands a similar capability. This is a great challenge. *Affective sensing* is the neologism used to describe recognition of emotional cues by machines. It is the process of mapping measurable physical responses to affective states. Several studies have successfully mapped strong responses to episodic emotions such as happiness, anger and surprise. However, few studies deal with the more subtle emotions such as anxiety and depression and most research takes place in a controlled environment, ignoring the importance that social settings, culture and context play in dictating the display rules of affect.

At present, reported examples of affective sensing systems tend to be very application specific [1,2,3,4,5,6,7,8,9,10,11]. However, in a natural setting, emotions can present themselves in many ways, and in different combinations of modalities. Thus it seems that some level of semantic incorporation is essential. For instance, during a diplomatic exchange, anger is more likely to be signaled through verbal content than, say, in an incident during a football game where a player remonstrates wildly with the referee. In this paper, a novel approach is presented which integrates semantic descriptions with standard speech recognition and computer vision feature sets.

C. Peter and R. Beale (Eds.): Affect and Emotion in HCI, LNCS 4868, pp. 104–115, 2008.

The remainder of the paper is structured as follows. Section 2 discusses the physiology of emotional display. Section 3 gives a brief overview of the recognition of emotions by machines. It also motivates the discussion of the limitations in current emotion recognition due to inheriting much of its techniques from automatic speech recognition (ASR) technology. Section 4 describes how we might add semantics to the emotion recognition process. Finally, Section 5 presents conclusions and future work.

2   The Physiology of Emotions in Speech

Age, gender, culture, social setting, personality and well-being all play their part in suffusing our communication apparatus even before we begin to speak. Darwin raised the issue of whether it was possible to inhibit emotional expression [12]. This is a pertinent question in human emotion recognition and in emotion recognition by computer systems. Intentional or not, the voice and face are used in everyday life to judge verisimilitude in speakers.

2.1   Vocal Speech

Speech carries a great deal more information than just the verbal message. It can tell us about the speaker, their background and their emotional state. Changes in brain patterns result in modulations in our major anatomical systems.

Stress tenses the laryngeal muscles, in turn, tightening the vocal folds. The result is that more pressure is required to produce sound. Consequently, the fundamental frequency and amplitude, particularly with regard to the ratio of the open to the closed phase of the cycle, varies the larynx wave. The harmonics of the larynx wave vary according to the specific balance of mass, length and tension that is set up to produce a given frequency [13].

	fear	anger	sorrow	joy	disgust	surprise
speech rate	much faster	slightly faster	slightly slower	faster or slower	very much slower	much faster
pitch average	very much higher	very much higher	slightly lower	much higher	very much lower	much higher
pitch range	much wider	much wider	slightly narrower	much wider	slightly wider	
intensity	normal	higher	lower	higher	lower	higher
voice quality	irregular voicing	breathy chest tone	resonant	Breathy, blaring	grumble chest tone	
pitch changes	normal	abrupt on stressed syllable	downward inflections	smooth upward inflections	wide downward terminal inflections	rising contour
articulation	precise	tense	slurring	normal	normal	

Fig. 1. The effect of emotion on the human voice [14]

Some affective states like anxiety can influence breathing resulting in variations in sub-glottal pressure. Drying of the mucus membrane causes shrinking of the voice. Rapid breath alters the tempo of the voice. Relaxation tends to deepen the breath and lowers the voice. Changes in facial expression can also alter the sound of the voice. Figure 1 represents the typical cues to the six most common emotion categories [14].

2.2   Visual Speech

The most widely used system for explaining the facial expression of emotion is that of Ekman's Facial Action Coding System (FACS) [12] [15,16,17,18]. Facial muscles are mapped to "Action Units" that produce movement. The combinations of "Action Units" are mapped to emotional states. The changes associated with emotional expression are usually brief, i.e. a few seconds.

McNeill [19] has shown how tightly integrated and important a role gesture plays in speech. It often precedes vocal expression, exposes our inner thoughts and can disambiguate utterances. Gestures can be expressed through various body parts (e.g. hands, arms, head) as well as the entire body.

3   Recognition of Emotions by Machines

Affective sensing is an attempt to map manifestations or measurable physical responses to affective states. Non-obtrusive sensing of affect from the voice and facial expressions is commonly based on ASR technology and computer vision. ASR is concerned with the analysis of sound patterns, phonemes, words, sentences, and dialogues. However, when extended to the detection of emotions in vocal speech, the focus tends to be on prosody and energy levels.

Computer vision techniques to detect emotions from facial expressions are often used in conjunction with some codebook of muscle movements such as Ekman's FACS. FACS is typically used in conjunction with probabilistic models, e.g. Hidden Markov Models [20]. Several studies have used computer vision to detect features and build evidence of FACS Action Units [21] [22].

Several researchers have reported improved recognition of emotions when sensory cues from multiple modalities are fused [23]. In [24] facial features, prosody and lexical content in speech are fused. In his dissertation, Polzin used a similar technique, using separate, composite hidden Markov models to model each emotion [25].

However, ASR and computer vision approaches are grounded in pattern matching and statistical machines learning techniques. Hence, the premise is that samples of real world data can be matched against samples of test data. One inherent weakness in this premise, for emotion recognition, is in the elicitation method of the sample data. The topic of the elicitation of emotional speech samples has been well covered by other reviews [26,27,28], so it is only briefly covered in the next section.

3.1 Eliciting Emotional Speech Samples

Naturally Occurring Speech. To date, call centre recordings [10,29], recordings of pilot conversations, and television reports [30] have provided sensible sources of data to research emotions in speech. These types of samples have the highest ecological validity. However, aside from the copyright and privacy issues, it is very difficult to construct a database of emotional speech from this sort of naturally occurring emotional data sources. In audio samples, there are the complications of background noise and overlapping utterances. In video, there are difficulties in detecting moving faces and facial expressions. A further complication is the suppression of emotional behaviour by the speaker who is aware of being recorded.

Induced Emotional Speech. One technique introduced by Velten [31], is to have subjects read emotive texts and passages which, in turn, induce emotional states in the speaker. Other techniques include the use of Wizard of Oz setups where, for example, a dialogue between a human and a computer is controlled without the knowledge of the human [32]. This method has the benefit of providing a degree of control over the dialogue and can simulate a natural setting. The principal shortcoming of these methods is that the response to stimuli may induce different emotional states in different people.

Acted Emotional Speech. By far the most popular approach is to engage actors to portray emotions [11,33,34]. This technique provides for a lot of experimental control over a range of emotions and like the previous method provides for a degree of control over the ambient conditions.

One problem with this approach is that acted speech elicits how emotions should be portrayed, not necessarily how they are portrayed. The other serious drawback is that acted emotions are unlikely to derive from emotions in the way that Scherer *et al.* [35] describe them, i.e. episodes of massive, synchronised recruitment of mental and somatic resources to adapt or cope with a stimulus event subjectively appraised as being highly pertinent to the needs, goals and values of the individual.

3.2 Discussion on the Elicitation Methods

We display emotions in an extemporaneous symphony of modalities and with insouciant ease. Some of us are Rembrandts in concealing and revealing our feelings. Cultural, social, physiological, and contextual factors dictate the display rules of emotions. Yet, as implied in the last section, few studies ever take these factors into account. In computer science, we like to hold certain variables constant in order to find ways of explaining the change in the others. In this case, the variables that are held constant are the most important ones that contribute to the selection and production of affect.

Relatively little research into affect has been based on natural speech. In many cases, the approach to affect recognition has simply been an extension of ASR, i.e. acquiring a corpus of acted speech, then annotating sequences containing affect within the corpus. In the case of automatic recognition of episodic emotions, this approach is plausible, based on the assumption that clear-cut bursts of episodic emotion will look and sound somewhat similar in most contexts [28]. However, recognition of pervasive emotions present a much greater challenge and, intuitively, one would think that awareness of personal and contextual information needs to be integrated into the recognition process.

Fernandez and Picard [36] used eighty-seven features and concluded that the recognition rate was still below human performance. One would have to question how much extrapolation it would take to extend the ASR approach to affective sensing in a natural setting. Studies by Koike *et al.* [37] and Shigeno [38] have shown that it is difficult to identify the emotion of a speaker from a different culture and that people will predominantly use visual information to identify emotion. The implications are that the number of feature sets and the amount of training samples required to take into account natural, social, physiological, and contextual factors would be infeasible.

Richard Stibbard [39] who undertook the, somewhat difficult, Leeds Emotion in Speech Project reported,

"The use of genuine spoken data has revealed that the type of data commonly used gives an oversimplified picture of emotional expression. It is recommended that future work cease looking for stable phonetic correlates of emotions and look instead at dynamic speech features, that the classification of the emotions be reconsidered, and that more account be taken of the complex relationship between eliciting event, emotion, and expression."

In keeping with speech recognition, much of the effort to date in emotion recognition has been concerned with finding the low-level, symbolic representation and interpretation of the speech signal features. Only a handful of reports involve real-time facial feature extraction in the emotion recognition process [40] [30]. Similar points about the need to recognise emotions in natural settings, and the difficulties of doing so, were made by [41]. To address this deficiency, some level of semantic reasoning seems essential.

4   Adding Semantics to the Emotion Recognition Process

There have been some attempts at representing real-life emotions in audio-video data with non-basic emotional patterns and context features [42] [43]. [44] have shown that recognition of speech can be improved by combining a dictionary of affect with the standard ASR dictionary. [45] have developed a rule-based system for interpreting facial expressions. This recent activity in the field suggests that the incorporation of some level of semantic reasoning in the recognition process is now seen by many as a necessary evolution.

Some systems have incorporated elaborate syntax checking rules but there are fewer examples where semantics within a domain of interest has been used. Speech processing and computer vision techniques were discussed previously. An important distinction between the two is that visual information is inherently

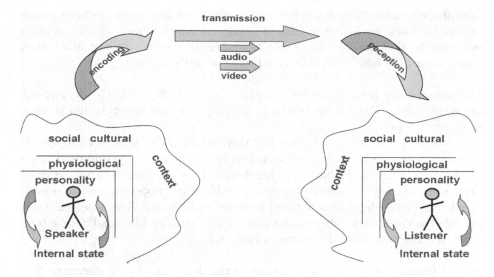

Fig. 2. A generic model of affective communication

more ambiguous and semantically impoverished [46]. The currently available computer vision techniques are still no match with human interpretation of images. However, by combining modalities with other available semantic evidence it could be possible to enhance not only the emotion recognition process but the recognition of speech.

The proposed approach consists of a generic model of affective communication and a domain *ontology* of affective communication. The model and ontology are intended to be used in conjunction as a standardised way to describe the content.

4.1   A Model for Affective Communication

Figure 2 presents a model of emotions in spoken language. Firstly, note that it includes speaker and listener, in keeping with the Brunswikian lens model as proposed by Scherer [26]. The reason for modelling attributes of both speaker and listener is that the listener's cultural and social presentation vis-à-vis the speaker may also influence judgement of emotional content. Secondly, note that it includes a number of factors that influence the expression of affect in spoken language. A brief description of the components of the model follows.

Context is linked to modality and emotion is strongly multimodal in the way that certain emotions manifest themselves favouring one modality over the other [28]. **Physiological** measurements change depending on whether a subject is sedentary or mobile. A stressful context such as an emergency hot-line, air-traffic control, or a war zone is likely to yield more examples of affect than everyday conversation.

Agent characteristics such as facial hair, whether a person wears spectacles, and their head and eye movements all affect the ability to visually detect and interpret emotions. As Scherer [26] points out, most studies are either speaker oriented or listener oriented, with most being the former. This is significant when you consider that the emotion of someone labelling affective content in a corpus could impact the label that is ascribed to a speaker's message.

Culture-specific display rules influence the display of affect [28]. Gender and age are established as important factors in shaping conversation style and content in many societies.

It might be stating the obvious but there are marked differences in speech signals and facial expressions between people of different **physiological** make up, e.g. age, gender and health. The habitual settings of facial features and vocal organs determine the speaker's range of possible visual appearances and sounds produced. The configuration of facial features, such as chin, lips, nose, and eyes, provide the visual cues, whereas the vocal tract length and internal muscle tone guide the interpretation of acoustic output [47].

Social factors temper spoken language to the demands of civil discourse [28]. For example, affective bursts are likely to be constrained in the case of a minor relating to an adult, yet totally unconstrained in a scenario of sibling rivalry. Similarly, a social setting in a library is less likely to yield loud and extroverted displays of affect than a family setting.

Internal state has been included in the model for completeness. At the core of affective states is the person and their experiences. Recent events such as winning the lottery or losing a job are likely to influence emotions.

4.2 An Application Ontology for Affective Communication

An ontology is a statement of concepts which facilitates the specification of an agreed vocabulary within a domain of interest. Creating an ontology introduces a common way of laying down the knowledge and facilitates intelligent searching and reuse of knowledge within the domain. Ontologies have been used for some time in the annotation of web pages and in the medical fields. In its simplest form it is a hierarchical database of definitions. In a more complex setup, it is a sophisticated knowledge base with embedded logic and semantic constraints.

Figure 3 shows an example application ontology for affective communication in a context of investigating dialogues. During the dialogue, various events can occur, triggered by one of the dialogue participants and recorded by the sensor system. These are recorded as time stamped instances of events, so that they can be easily identified and distinguished. In this ontology, we distinguish between two roles for each interlocutor: sender and receiver, respectively. At various points in time, each interlocutor can take on different roles. On the sensory side, we distinguish between facial, gestural, textual, speech, physiological and verbal[1] cues. This list, and the ontology, could be easily extended for other cues

---

[1] The difference between speech and verbal cues here being spoken language versus other verbal utterings.

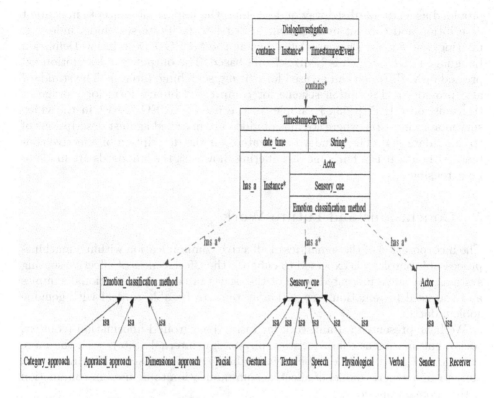

Fig. 3. An application ontology for affective sensing

and is meant to serve as an example here, rather than a complete list of affective cues. Finally, the emotion classification method used in the investigation of a particular dialogue is also recorded.

We use this ontology to describe our affective sensing research in a formal, yet flexible and extendible way. In the following section, a brief description of the facial expression recognition system developed in our group is given as an example of using the ontologies in practice.

4.3 Describing Semantics

One of the issues in emotion recognition, is that of reuse and verification of results. However, there is no universally accepted system of describing emotional content. The HUMAINE project is trying to remedy this through the definition of the Emotion Annotation and Representation Language (EARL) which is currently under design [48,49].

Another direction is that of the Moving Picture Experts Group (MPEG) who have developed the MPEG-7 standard for audio, audio-video and multimedia description [50]. MPEG-7 uses metadata structures or Multimedia Description Schemes (MDS) for describing and annotating audio-video content. These are provided as a standardised way of describing the important concepts in content description and content management in order to facilitate searching, indexing, filtering, and access. They are defined using the MPEG-7 Description Definition Language (DDL), which is XML Schema-based. The output is a description expressed in XML which can be used for editing, searching, filtering. The standard also provides a description scheme for compressed binary form for storage or transmission [51] [52] [53]. Examples in the use of MPEG-7 exist in the video surveillance industry where streams of video are matched against descriptions of training data [54]. The standard also caters for the description of affective content. Although it is a fairly modest offering, however, the standards are made to be extensible.

5   Conclusions and Future Work

The incorporation of the semantics of affective communication within a machine-processable ontology is expected to enhance the effectiveness of affective sensing systems. We have presented some of the issues in collecting emotional samples and the need for emotion recognition systems to be able to deal with genuine spoken data.

We have presented a framework for fusing background information (context, social, culture, agent characteristics, physiology, internal state), with the more traditional feature that describe an individual's emotional state. The framework consists of a generic model of affective communication to be used in conjunction with a domain ontology.

In future work, we intend to demonstrate the composite sensing of affect from multimodal cues and plan to include physiological sensors as another cue for determining the affective state of a user.

References

1. McCann, J., Peppe, S.: PEPS-C: A new speech science software programme for assessing prosody. In: The Fifth Annual Parliamentary Reception for Younger Researchers in Science, Engineering, Medicine and Technology (SET for Britain. Taking science to parliament: The 2003 great British research and R&D show), the House of Commons, London (2003)
2. Devillers, L., Vasilescu, I., Vidrascu, L.: F0 and pause features analysis for anger and fear detection in real-life spoken dialogs. Speech Prosody (2004)
3. Jones, C.M., Jonsson, I.: Automatic recognition of affective cues in the speech of car drivers to allow appropriate responses. Technical report, School of Mathematical and Computer Sciences, Heriot-Watt University, Edinburgh, UK and Department of Communication. Stanford University, California, USA (2005)
4. Jones, C.M., Jonsson, I.: Using paralinguistic cues in speech to recognise emotions in older car drivers. In: Peter, C., Beale, R. (eds.) Affect and Emotion in Human-Computer Interaction. LNCS, vol. 4868. Springer, Heidelberg (2008)
5. Breazeal, C.: Emotion and sociable humanoid robots. Int. J. Human-Computer Studies 59, 119–155 (2003)

6. Reilly, R., Moran, R., Lacy, P.: Voice pathology assessment based on a dialogue system and speech analysis. Technical report, Department of Electronic and Electrical Engineering, University College Dublin, Ireland and St James's Hospital, Dublin 8, Ireland (2000)
7. Picard, R.: Helping addicts: A scenario from 2021. Technical report (2005)
8. Kaliouby, R., Robinson, P.: Therapeutic versus prosthetic assistive technologies: The case of autism. Technical report, Computer Laboratory, University of Cambridge (2005)
9. Kaliouby, R., Robinson, P.: The emotional hearing aid: An assistive tool for children with asperger's syndrome. Technical report, Computer Laboratory, University of Cambridge (2003)
10. Petrushin, V.A.: Emotion in speech: Recognition and application to call centres. In: Artificial Neural Networks in Engineering (1999)
11. Yacoub, S., Simske, S.: X.Lin, Burns, J.: Recognition of emotions in interactive voice response systems. Technical report, HP Laboratories Palo Alto (2003)
12. Ekman, P.: Darwin, deception, and facial expression. Annals New York Academy of Sciences, 205–221 (2003)
13. Fry, D.B.: The Physics of Speech. Cambridge Textbooks in Linguistics. Cambridge University Press, Cambridge (1979)
14. Murray, I., Arnott, L.: Toward the simulation of emotion in synthetic speech. Journal Acoustical Society of America 93(2), 1097–1108 (1993)
15. Ekman, P., Friesen, W.: Unmasking the Face. Prentice Hall, Englewood Cliffs (1975)
16. Ekman, P., Oster, H.: Emotion in the human face, 2nd edn. Cambridge University Press, New York (1982)
17. Ekman, P., Rosenberg, E.L.: What the Face Reveals. Series in Affective Science. Oxford University Press, Oxford (1997)
18. Ekman, P.: Facial Expressions. In: The Handbook of Cognition and Emotion, pp. 301–320. John Wiley and Sons, Ltd., Sussex (1999)
19. McNeill, D.: Gesture and language dialectic. Technical report, Department of Psychology. University of Chicago (2002)
20. Lien, J., Kanade, T., Cohn, J., Li, C.: Automated Facial Expression Recognition Based on FACS Action Units. In: International Conference on Automatic Face and Gesture Recognition, pp. 390–395 (1998)
21. Cootes, T., Taylor, C., Cooper, D., Graham, J.: Active shape models - their training and applications. Computer Vision and Image Understanding 61(1), 38–59 (1995)
22. Nixon, M., Aguado, A.: Feature Extraction and Image Processing. MPG Books Ltd., Brodmin, Cornwall (2001)
23. Castellano, G., Kessous, L., Caridakis, G.: Emotion recognition through multiple modalities: face, body gesture, speech. In: Peter, C., Beale, R. (eds.) Affect and Emotion in Human-Computer Interaction, vol. 4868. Springer, Heidelberg (2007)
24. Fragopanagos, N., Taylor, J.: Emotion recognition in human-computer interaction. Neural Networks 18, 389–405 (2005)
25. Polzin, T.: Detecting verbal and non-verbal cues in the communication of emotions. PhD thesis, School of Computer Science. Carnegie Mellon University (2000)
26. Scherer, K.R.: Vocal communication of emotion: A review of research paradigms. Speech Communication 40, 227–256 (2003)
27. Cowie, R., Cornelius, R.: Describing the emotional states that are expressed in speech. Speech Communication 40, 5–32 (2003)
28. Cowie, R., Douglas-Cowie, E., Cox, C.: Beyond emotion archetypes: Databases for emotion modelling using neural networks. Neural Networks 18, 371–388 (2005)

29. Lee, C.M., Narayanan, S., Pieraccini, R.: Recognition of negative emotions from the speech signal. Automatic Speech Recognition and Understanding (2001)
30. Devillers, L., Abrilian, S., Martin, J.: Representing real-life emotions in audiovisual data with non basic emotional patterns and context features. Technical report, LIMSI, Centre national de la recherche scientifique, France (2005)
31. Velten, E.: A laboratory task for induction of mood states. Behaviour Research and Therapy 6, 473–482 (1968)
32. Schiel, F., Steininger, S., Türk, U.: The SmartKom Multimodal Corpus at BAS. Technical report, Ludwig Maximilans Universität München (2003)
33. Dellaert, F., Polzin, T., Waibel, A.: Recognizing emotion in speech. Technical report, School of Computer Science. Carnegie Mellon University (1995)
34. Lin, Y.L., Wei, G.: Speech emotion recognition based on hmm and svm. In: Proceedings (2005)
35. Scherer, K.R.: Humaine Deliverable D3c: Preliminary plans for exemplars: theory (2004). Retrieved October 26, 2006,
    http://emotion-research.net/publicnews/d3c/
36. Fernandez, R., Picard, R.: Classical and novel discriminant features for affect recognition from speech. In: Interspeech, Lisbon, Portugal, pp. 473–476 (2005)
37. Koike, K., Suzuki, H., Saito, H.: Prosodic parameters in emotional speech. In: International Conference on Spoken Language Processing, pp. 679–682 (1998)
38. Shigeno, S.: Cultural similarities and differences in the recognition of audiovisual speech stimuli. In: International Conference on Spoken Language Processing, 1057th edn., pp. 281–284 (1998)
39. Stibbard, R.: Vocal expression of emotions in non-laboratory speech: An investigation of the Reading/Leeds Emotion in Speech Project annotation data. PhD thesis, University of Reading, UK (2001)
40. Silva, L.D., Hui, S.: Real-time facial feature extraction and emotion recognition. In: ICICS-PCM. IEEE, Singapore (2003)
41. Ward, R., Marsden, P.: Affective computing: Problems, reactions and intentions. Interacting with Computers 16(4), 707–713 (2004)
42. Liscombe, J., Riccardi, G., Hakkani-Tür, D.: Using context to improve emotion detection in spoken dialog systems. In: EUROSPEECH 2005, 9th European Conference on Speech Communication and Technology, pp. 1845–1848 (2005)
43. Devillers, L., Vidrascu, L., Lamel, L.: Challenges in real-life emotion annotation and machine learning based detection. Neural Networks 18, 407–422 (2005)
44. Athanaselisa, T., Bakamidisa, S., Dologloua, I., Cowieb, R., Douglas-Cowie, E., Cox, C.: Asr for emotional speech: Clarifying the issues and enhancing performance. Neural Networks 18, 437–444 (2005)
45. Cowie, R., Douglas-Cowie, E., Taylor, J., Ioannou, S., Wallace, M., Kollias, S.: An intelligent system for facial emotion recognition. IEEE, Los Alamitos (2005)
46. Town, C., Sinclair, D.: A self-referential perceptual inference framework for video interpretation. In: Crowley, J.L., Piater, J.H., Vincze, M., Paletta, L. (eds.) ICVS 2003. LNCS, vol. 2626, pp. 54–67. Springer, Heidelberg (2003)
47. Millar, J.B., Wagner, M., Göcke, R.: Aspects of speaking-face data corpus design methodology. In: International Conference on Spoken Language Processing 2004, Jeju, Korea, vol. II, pp. 1157–1160 (2004)
48. Schröder, M., Devillers, L., Karpouzis, K., Martin, J.C., Pelachaud, C., Peter, C., Pirker, H., Schuller, B., Tao, J., Wilson, I.: What should a generic emotion markup language be able to represent? In: Proc. 2nd International Conference on Affective Computing and Intelligent Interaction (ACII 2007), Lisbon, Portugal (2007)

49. Schröder, M., Zovato, E., Pirker, H., Peter, C., Burkhardt, F.: W3c emotion incubator group final report. Technical report, W3C (2007)
50. MPEG-7 Committee: Retrieved June 2, 2007, http://www.m4if.org/m4if/
51. Chiariglione, L.: Introduction to MPEG-7: Multimedia Content Description Interface. Technical report, Telecom Italia Lab, Italy (2001)
52. Salembier, P., Smith, J.: MPEG-7 Multimedia Description Schemes. IEEE Transactions on Circuits and Systems for Video Technology 11, 748–759 (2001)
53. Rege, M., Dong, M., Fotouhi, F., Siadat, M., Zamorano, L.: Using MPEG-7 to build a Human Brain Image Database for Image-guided Neurosurgery. Medical Imaging 2005: Visualization, Image-Guided Procedures, and Display, 512–519 (2005)
54. Annesley, J., Orwell, J.: On the Use of MPEG-7 for Visual Surveillance. Technical report, Digital Imaging Research Center, Kingston University, Kingston-upon-Thames, Surrey, UK (2005)

Emotional Experience and Interaction Design

Youn-kyung Lim[1,*], Justin Donaldson[1], Heekyoung Jung[1], Breanne Kunz[2],
David Royer[1], Shruti Ramalingam[1], Sindhia Thirumaran[1], and Erik Stolterman[1]

[1] School of Informatics, Indiana University,
Bloomington, IN 47408
{younlim,jjdonald,jung5,dproyer,sramalin,sinthiru,
estolter}@indiana.edu
[2] Imaging & Printing Group,Hewlett-Packard Company,
Boise, Idaho 83714
breanne.kunz@hp.com

Abstract. The emotional experience of an interactive system has been the subject of a great deal of recent interest and study in the HCI community. However, many of researchers have pointed out the extreme difficulty in predicting or controlling these emotional experiences through intentional design choices. However, the user study we conducted proposes a different point-of-view than these claims. Although these emotional responses were not always tied directly to the device itself and influenced by contextual factors, we discovered that certain controllable aspects of interactive products showed clear patterns of emotion in the responses of our participants. We discuss our findings and provide implications for the design of emotional experiences in interactive devices.

Keywords: Emotion, affect, user experience, interaction design.

1 Introduction

The importance of "affect and emotion in HCI" has become increasingly significant when we face so-called "the third wave" or "the third paradigm" of HCI [6, 12]. One of the clearest comments on the notion of the third wave in HCI is introduced in Bødker's keynote article in NordiCHI 2006 [6] where she builds on Bannon's view that there is a shift "from human factors to human actors" [3]. Grudin [11] also mentioned the movement from the non-discretionary use of technologies to the discretionary use where users use technologies for personal purposes, which indicates the opening-up of this new paradigm.

As we move in this direction, researchers and professionals in HCI have started to redefine the meaning of "user-centered design" from an emphasis on efficiency and usability to a broader holistic context of human behavior. In this behavioral context, we start to adapt the terms like "human-centered" or "experience–centered" design. This

* Current address: Department of Industrial Design, KAIST, 373-1 Guseong-dong, Yuseong-gu, Daejeon 305-701, Republic of Korea, Tel.: +82-42-869-4522, Fax: +82-42-869-4510, younlim@kaist.ac.kr.

C. Peter and R. Beale (Eds.): Affect and Emotion in HCI, LNCS 4868, pp. 116–129, 2008.
© Springer-Verlag Berlin Heidelberg 2008

direction promotes the understanding of human-computer interaction as embodied in the meanings, experiences, and values relevant to personal or cultural contexts [21].

This movement has led researchers to explore the nature of human experience that emerges in interactions with technologies. This research direction has opened up deeper investigations of the meaning of affect, emotion, and experience. It is natural that this has become the trend within HCI. After all, we cannot truly design something *human-centered* without a deep understanding of the emotional experiences prevalent in our own human nature. However, it is also clear that focusing on such human aspects alone does not necessarily lead to successful design outcomes [23].

Several noted researchers have made discouraging comments in relation to emotional design practice. A few representative sentiments include: "emotion cannot be designed" [13], "… not the design quality … but what the person did with it and what the interaction meant to the person …" (p.120 in [7]), etc. Although to a certain degree these claims are true, we also must accept that *emotions are significantly influenced by the design of interactive products*. This view is demonstrated and validated by various researchers [15, 8]. Norman and Ortony [22] also clearly mentioned that emotion *can* be designed in their explanation of "emotion by design" contrasting with the notion of "emotion by accident" which obviously also exists.

We make the simple claim that *a given emotional response to an interactive design feature is not entirely predictable*, but at the same time, we show that *the various emotional responses to a given product quality are not completely random*, either. Going further, we can identify which emotions are prevalent for a given product quality, and can seek to characterize the true source and nature of these emotions, looking for commonalities among the representative population.

Before we discuss the method and results, we will define some of our terminology. The phrase "product quality" relates to product attributes such as color, size, function, interface, etc. The phrase "experience quality" relates to abstract experiential attributes such as usability, usefulness, pleasantness, etc.

Interestingly, we show the three levels of emotional experience originally proposed by Norman [20] including visceral, behavioral, and reflective levels of emotion are affected by different proportionate distributions of the product qualities. This result clearly shows that each level of emotional experience has its own characteristics and relationships with product qualities. Our promising initial results leads us to believe that we should not be discouraged to continue the search for a better understanding of how these relationships are correlated, and that such research should lead to results that would inform designers.

In this paper, we start with a discussion of the definitions of affect, emotion, and experience that help researchers and designers establish appropriate strategies for design research and design practice in HCI. The objective of our research is not to establish or discuss theory, but to understand *in which ways design influences people's emotional experiences*. However, our discussion about theories and definitions provides the background for the design of our study.

In our study, we explore the relationships between the qualities people experience and the interactive product qualities inherent in the device. From these qualities we discuss what needs to be considered in design practice when concerning the emotional aspects of HCI. Finally, we conclude with important design implications of the study results in relation to emotion in HCI.

2 Background

We have encountered and used various terms related to each other such as affect, emotion, and experience in HCI. Numerous researchers have proposed definitions of these terms as well as the relationships among them [4, 5, 8, 9, 16, 18, 19, 20]. In our research, it is critical to revisit the definitions proposed by other researchers and to re-establish an integrated perspective of those meanings, since it will explain the position we take in our research and why we selected it.

2.1 Affect and Emotion

In HCI, many researchers do not clearly identify the differences between the meanings of *affect* and *emotion*, and frequently use them as synonyms [4]. Bentley et al. [4] particularly addressed this issue and explained the key differences between the two, which we accepted for our research. In [4], they introduced the definitions suggested by other researchers and clearly identified the difference. For example, emotion is viewed as "overall feeling" that is influenced by various external and internal stimuli which include "context, past experience, recent experiences, personality, affect, and the net cognitive interpretation of these influences" (p.2 in [4]). Affect is defined more as "a short term, discrete, conscious subjective feeling" (p.3 in [4]), which shows the contrast from the meaning of emotion.

In our research, our focus is on *emotion*, as we accept this distinction. We are particularly interested in feelings that are relatively stable and shaped over longer periods of time through the experience with interactive products. Bentley et al. [4] also suggest an approach to understand emotions: "In practice, many system evaluations can account for emotion by asking the user their overall feelings regarding the system after use. This could be done through a post-use interview or questionnaire." (p.3 in [4]). We conducted a type of a post-use interview that is called "disposable camera study", which is a type of a probing technique such as the "cultural probing" technique [10]. The detailed procedure of conducting this study is introduced in Section 3.

2.2 Emotion and Experience

We did not wish to let a single theory of emotional experience constrain the probes or responses of our participants. However, we needed to have some basic framework to categorize and organize the various emotional responses that we encountered.

For this purpose, we accept Norman's three levels of emotional response [20] as a starting point for the analysis since it is one of the most comprehensive, general, and explicable definitions of emotion in HCI. The three levels include the *visceral*-level which represents "perceptually-induced reactions," the *behavioral*-level which represents "expectation-induced reactions," and the *reflective*-level which represents "intellectually-induced reactions" [22]. The visceral level of response is directly related to our physical senses. Textures, sizes, temperatures, or colors evoke different emotional responses through the physical senses. These reactions usually shape immediate feelings about the product. The behavioral level of responses mostly involves cognitive processing of the mind. The emotions at this level are formed through the process of planning, expectation, and learning. It also involves automatic responses and immediate feelings like the visceral level, but these responses are formed by the process of behavioral control over time (for a *short* period of time), not by physical sensing at a particular moment. The reflective level of responses is the most complex and challenging to fully understand. It is "the highest level of intellectual functioning in a person" (p.4 in [22]). If the other two levels are sub-conscious, this level is "conscious and self-aware" [22]. For example, the same blue color can be interpreted in different ways and result in different emotions according to different contexts—e.g. situations, cultures, and past experiences. For example, some people may not accept a blue Apple Mac Mini [2], because it would go against the recognizable color scheme that Apple Inc. has established through its brand image.

Then how is *emotion* related to *experience*? Emotion can be viewed as "a resource for understanding and communicating about what we experience" (p. 264 in [9]). That is, emotion is a significant channel for expressing experience. We can also say that emotion is what makes experience possible. It is why many of the frameworks that explain *experience* proposed by various researchers, are tightly related to Norman's three levels of emotion. McCarthy and Wright [19] defines experience with four types of "threads," including the *sensual thread of experience* which corresponds to the visceral level of emotion, the *compositional thread of experience* which corresponds to the behavioral level of emotion, the *emotional thread of experience* which corresponds to the reflective level of emotion, and the *spatio-temporal thread of experience* which is indirectly related to both the visceral level and the behavioral level. The spatial part of the spatio-temporal thread of experience is tightly related to the visceral level of emotion since the space is mostly sensed by a visual sense—i.e. the eyes. The temporal part of the spatio-temporal thread of experience is tightly related to the behavioral level since this level is induced by expectation that requires the notion of time. Another framework of pleasurable experience proposed by Jordan [16] includes *physical pleasures* that correspond to the visceral level, *physiological pleasures* that correspond to the behavioral level, and *ideological and social pleasures* that correspond to the reflective level.

In our study, we particularly focused on *emotion* as the foundation for experiences that can be verbalized directly by users and compared. The primary objective of our study is to examine how different types of interactive product qualities are related to people's emotions. The purpose of this study was to gather insights valuable to designers when designing interactive products in relation to the issues of emotions.

3 User Study: Exploring the Relationship between Interactive Product Qualities and User Experience Qualities

In this study, we were interested in analyzing interactive products that individuals have owned or used for some time—especially the ones that engender strong emotional responses. Eliciting their emotions about the products was the key aspect of this study, and we used several strategies to enable this. This approach included (1) asking interviewees to select interactive products which they liked, disliked or valued, and had used for a significant period, and (2) conducting in-depth interviews with strategically designed semantic differential questions which provided the participants a guide to express their emotional experiences in detail in relation to the three levels of emotion we explored.

3.1 Study Design and Data Analysis

We conducted a disposable camera study for twelve participants. Six participants had some background in design, as they were the students of the HCI/d master's program in the School of Informatics at Indiana University. The other six participants did not have any design background, and they were either undergraduate or graduate students in various universities. The ages ranged from early twenties to early thirties.

The disposable camera study is a type of an interview-based study that combines a picture-journaling (or probing) activity by participants. We first asked the participants to take several pictures of five to ten interactive products that they own or have frequently used. We asked them to select the products they particularly liked, disliked, or valued. This naturally led them to select the ones for which they have some strong emotional response. While we conducted the studies, we did not directly ask them to describe their "emotional experiences" since that term can be interpreted in different ways by different people. Instead, we simply asked them to freely explain any kinds of experiences and memories they have with the products they selected, while also probing for semantic differentials in a questionnaire we used during the interview (Table 1). We did not show the terms like visceral, behavioral, and reflective to the participants. We also mixed the order of these semantic differentials to minimize any bias.

Table 1. Semantic values selected for representing the three levels of emotion

The level of emotion	Contrasting semantic values	
Visceral	spicy	bland
	warm	cold
	soft	hard
	heavy	light
Behavioral	simple	complicate
	clear	ambiguous
	controllable	uncontrollable
	expectable	unpredictable
Reflective	natural	artificial
	beautiful	ugly
	sympathetic	unsympathetic
	deep	shallow
	exotic	mundane
	authentic	imitated
	precious	worthless
	novel	retro

We provided a digital camera for each participant, which they used to photograph their device. Then we met with them to talk about their pictures and to conduct in-depth interviews about the products they showed. Each interview took about an hour to an hour and half. The interview was structured in two parts: (1) general questions about their demographic information and overall impressions of the selected products in terms of why they like, dislike, and/or value the product; and (2) semantic differential questions (Table 1) that cover the three levels of emotion and extract their emotional experiences with the respective products. For this second part of the interview, we also asked why they selected a certain value for each semantic differential in terms of the corresponding *product qualities* of that specific value they assigned. We presented these semantic differentials to the participants in a random order.

The semantic values for the semantic differentials (Table 1) are very carefully selected in order to investigate how people experience emotion through the respective product qualities in terms of the three levels of emotion proposed by Norman [20]. The semantic differentials are also referred to simply as "semantic values" or "semantics" occasionally in this paper. The four semantic values for the visceral level are all related to physical senses, and the four semantic values for the behavioral level are all related to cognitive processes. We also use eight semantic values for the reflective level that all require personal reflections in order to decide the corresponding values. Therefore, a total of 16 semantic values are used for examining the participants' emotional responses toward the interactive products they selected. We intentionally selected the larger number of reflective-level semantic values so that we could have more data to characterize this complex portion of Norman's emotion framework.

We treated the beautiful-ugly dimension as an example of the reflective level since we originally accepted Hassenzahl's [14] doubtful perspective on visceral beauty. However, our data analysis from this study showed a contrasting result of this view which we will explain in detail at the next section.

We recorded all the interviews using digital audio recorders, and transcribed all the comments from the participants using the template shown in Table 2. This template is designed to extract two major types of information from the participants' comments in relation to their emotional experiences. These include (1) the qualities of the interactive products corresponding to each semantic differential question, and (2) the qualities of user experience involved in the use of the selected interactive products corresponding to each semantic differential question. We organized this information according to each semantic, numbered all 16 semantic differentials from 1 to 16, and used that number as the code to indicate each semantic (Table 2).

For the interactive product qualities, we used six types of qualities. These qualities include:

1. *Interaction* (coded as 'PI') – qualities that enable people's interactions with the product, such as interfaces.
2. *Visual* (coded as 'PV') – qualities that people can see such as colors, sizes, shapes, visual material qualities,
3. *Tactile* (coded as 'PT') – qualities that people can feel by touching or grabbing such as weight, texture, etc.
4. *Content* (coded as 'PC') – contents that are carried, accessed, or delivered by the product such as music, news, video, games, etc.
5. *Function* (coded as 'PF') – capabilities and functionality such as playing music, calling to someone, taking pictures, etc.
6. *Performance* (coded as 'PP') – qualities of how well the product performs the expected functions such as resolution, sound quality, speed, etc.

Table 2. The template used for transcribing the interview data. (The italicized texts indicate the example records we transcribed into this template).

Product name	Interactive product quality		User experience quality		Semantic differential
	Quality category	Quality description	Quality category	Quality description	
CD player	*PV* (Visual quality of the CD player)	*Shiny material*	*UXV* (Visceral experience with this visual quality)	*Not boring*	*1 [2]* (1 is the number of a semantics which is "spicy-bland" and [2] is the value between 1 (spicy) to 7 (bland) the participant selected about this particular emotional experience)

These six qualities may not cover all the possible qualities of any type of interactive product that exists in this world. However, these six qualities cover all the qualities that were mentioned by our participants from their respective product experiences. All the transcribed data from our study could be categorized with one of these types of product qualities. This framework is more comprehensive than the work by Norman and Ortony [22] who discussed the three levels of emotion only in relation to function and appearance. For the user experience qualities, we used four types including:

1. *Visceral Quality* (coded as UXV) – the visceral level of emotion that is emotional responses formed by physical senses such as "looks nice," "feel cold," etc.
2. *Cognitive Quality* (coded as UXC) – the behavioral level of emotion that is formed from cognitive processes such as "easy to use," "simple to use," "hard to figure out," etc.
3. *Usefulness Quality* (coded as UXU) – an indirect quality related to their overall needs rather than a certain specific type of emotional response, such as "fulfills what I need," "practical", "does what I want it to do," etc.
4. *Reflective and Social Quality* (coded as UXRS) – the reflective level of emotion such as "it is a trend," "creates an artificial world," "everyone has these products," etc.

The reason for extracting these user experience qualities in addition to the semantic differential values is to validate if our assumptions on the relationships between the semantic values and the three levels of emotion are appropriate. The result of this analysis is described in the next section.

The usefulness quality (UXU) is not directly related to any of the three levels of emotion, but is included to examine how this aspect of user experience is related to emotional experiences. We wanted to make sure which level of emotion is the relevant one for this quality. The analysis result for this question is also described in the next section.

For the data analysis, each analyst (total 6 analysts) transcribed two participants' data into the template, and one supervising analyst went through all the data transcribed by every analyst to make sure the data is consistent with the definitions of the product qualities and the experience qualities. Before starting the data analysis, the definitions given here were established by consensus. A total of 1,020 comments were collected from all the 12 participants, and a total of 64 interactive products were discussed.

3.2 Results

We discuss the results to understand (1) how our selections of the semantics are related to the three levels of emotion as a first examiner before we closely analyze the relationship between interactive product qualities and the three levels of emotion outcomes, (2) how usefulness-related user experience can be understood in relation to the three levels of emotion, (3) what qualities are more significant than others when people are discussing about their emotional experience with the product, and (4) whether the different levels of emotion have distinctive relationships with the different types of the interactive product qualities. This part establishes if the product qualities have a random or non-deterministic effect on emotion.

The second aspect of analysis among these four, regarding the *usefulness* experience, was specifically addressed since there has not been much examination done by researchers in HCI. One prominent previous research outcome about the relationship between perceived-usefulness and perceived-affect qualities includes Zhang and Li's work [25], but our research outcome adds further valuable insight to this relationship by examining which level of emotion the usefulness experience is most tightly related to. To the best of our knowledge this aspect has not been addressed in the literature. We find this information meaningful in terms of opening up a future research agenda, i.e. how we can define usefulness in terms of its affect on emotional experiences.

The results from each of these four aspects of analysis are explained in the following sections.

The Semantics and the Three-level Emotions. We conducted k-means cluster analysis among the semantic differentials used in the survey. The analysis was based on the numbers of comments mentioned by the participants about the different types of user experience qualities for each semantic differential pair. Each distribution of the comments in relation to the user experience qualities (i.e. UXV, UXC, UXU, and UXRS) for each semantic differential pair was compared with one another to cluster the semantic values. This method was used to examine if the original semantic-emotional groupings shown in Table 1 are clustered accordingly in our participant results.

Table 3 shows the result of this cluster analysis. As we see here, only two semantics (i.e. beautiful-ugly and deep-shallow) are clustered into other groups than what we first assumed. All the semantics related to the visceral and the behavioral levels are clustered as we originally assumed.

As we briefly mentioned in the previous section, our original assumption based on Hassenzahl's claim of "no visceral beauty" [14] needs to be re-examined according to this result. From our data, we could clearly see that the participants were discussing their experiences in the visceral level when reasoning about their selection of the value related to the beauty (the beautiful-ugly semantic). This occurred in their descriptions of colors, material feelings, shapes, sound qualities, etc. There were also several comments that were related to the reflective level such as "trendy," "cool," etc. Another interesting comment was "chemistry is ugly," mentioned by a chemical informatics major who commented about the application he/she must use for his/her work-related activities. There were also comments related to the cognitive experience such as "it is easy to use," when discussing beauty. However, the major type of experience was the visceral experience.

Table 3. K-means cluster analysis results for clustering semantics in relation to the data about user experience qualities. (*clusters that are clustered to a different group from the originally assumed one).

Clusters	Semantics	Distance
Visceral cluster	spicy-bland	.278
	warm-cold	.148
	soft-hard	.124
	heavy-light	.110
	*beautiful-ugly	.250
Behavioral cluster	simple-complicate	.101
	clear-ambiguous	.189
	controllable-uncontrollable	.158
	expectable-unpredictable	.076
	*deep-shallow	.329
Reflective cluster	natural-artificial	.327
	sympathetic-unsympathetic	.240
	exotic-mundane	.156
	authentic-imitated	.241
	precious-worthless	.239
	novel-retro	.126

For the semantic differential "deep-shallow", we originally assumed that this would lead the participants to discuss their reflective experience with the products. However, the participants mainly discussed their cognitive-level experience, indicating "if the task does not require so much thinking then it is considered shallow."

Through this analysis, we re-clustered the semantic differentials, and the following results are discussed based on this new clustering.

Usefulness and Emotional Experience. As shown in Fig. 1, we can readily see that the usefulness aspect of user experience is primarily related to the reflective-level emotion. The visceral-level emotion does not seem very influential in determining the quality of experience compared to other two levels.

Interactive Product Qualities that Matter for Emotional Experience. There were total 64 individual products selected by the participants, and the types of the products primarily include laptop computers (mentioned by 7 people), mp3 players (mentioned by 7 people), cell phones (mentioned by 7 people), TVs (mentioned by 5 people), digital cameras (mentioned by 5 people), and desktop computers (mentioned by 3 people). We first analyzed how many comments about all types of their emotional experience are mentioned for each different interactive product quality.

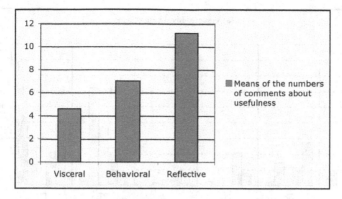

Fig. 1. The means of the numbers of comments the participants mentioned in terms of the usefulness-related experience (UXU) according to the three levels of emotion. (Each mean for each level of emotion is calculated by adding the numbers of UXU comments related to each level of emotion (following our result shown in Table 3) and dividing it with the number of the semantics relevant to each level of emotion).

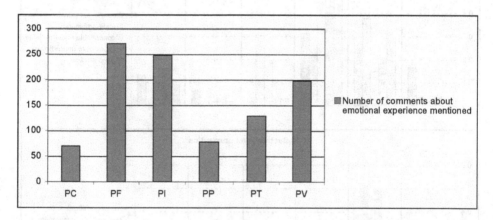

Fig. 2. The numbers of comments the participants mentioned regarding all types of their emotional experience per each type of the interactive product qualities

As shown in Fig. 2, the *functional* and *interaction* qualities are the most influential qualities when shaping people's emotional experience with interactive products, and the visceral and tactile qualities are also relatively important although they are not as significant as the functional and interaction qualities.

Interactive Product Qualities and the Three-level Emotions. We examined how each different semantic is related to the different types of the interactive product qualities (Fig. 3). The charts shown in Fig. 3(a), (b), and (c) clearly show that the three different levels of emotion are involved with a different set of the interactive product qualities as major influencers. We can clearly see that the tactile and visual qualities are tightly related to the visceral-level emotion (Fig. 3(a)) and the functional

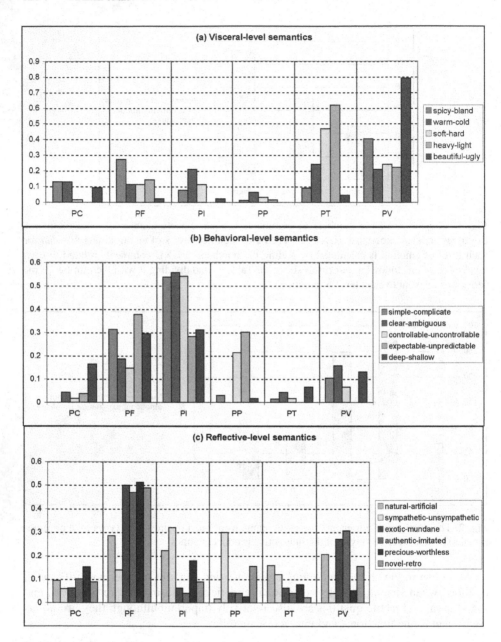

Fig. 3. The rates of the numbers of comments the participants mentioned related to each semantic differential associated to each type of the interactive product qualities

and interaction qualities are tightly related to the behavioral-level emotion (Fig. 3(b)). For the reflective-level chart (Fig. 3(c)), the distribution looks like a combination of both visceral and behavioral levels as we see the functional, interaction, tactile, and visual qualities are significant. However, the functional quality was shown as the most significant influencer in the reflective level which was not the case in other levels.

Most of the distributions are resulted as we expected except for the distribution of "sympathetic-unsympathetic", as we can see in Fig. 3(c). It is interesting since it is the only semantic that stands out for the performance quality comparing to the other semantic differentials. From people's comments, we could understand that they feel things are sympathetic when they perform as they expected—e.g. "the device is unsympathetic because it is unreliable," or when they make errors—e.g. "feels sympathetic when the machine makes mistakes."

4 Discussion and Conclusion

Our user study confirmed that interactive product qualities are important sources for emotional experiences and that they do not randomly affect the emotional experience. In conclusion, the key findings from this study can be summarized as follows:

- Norman's three levels of emotion are clearly distinguishable and influenced by different types of interactive product qualities (Fig. 3).
- Beauty can be controlled by product qualities (Fig. 3(a)).
- Usefulness is tightly related to the reflective level of emotion although it is related to other levels as well (Fig. 1).
- The functional and interaction qualities for interactive products are critical when designing emotional experiences (Fig. 2).

We would like to discuss further the results in terms of their implications in interaction design and understanding emotional experience.

Design Implications Based on the Results. From the results (especially shown in Fig. 1), we have found out that the reflective level of emotions such as *exotic-mundane, authentic-imitated, precious-worthless, novel-retro*, and *natural-artificial*, were tightly related to the experience of usefulness. When people discussed these types of semantics, they talked a lot about its usefulness—e.g. "the device is important for my music practice," "I use it a lot, I value it," etc. Although the reflective level was the primary one in relation to usefulness, people also talked about it when discussing other levels of emotional experience—e.g. when the visceral level of emotion directly affects its usefulness such as lightness of a portable device.

We also found that people mentioned functional and interactive qualities of products often when they discuss their emotional experiences with the products. In fact, it was the dominant point of discussion when compared to other qualities such as content, performance, tactile, and visual. This is an unexpected result since many of previous discussions regarding people's emotional experiences have mentioned more about people's frustration due to performance-related issues such as speed and errors [24], or about visceral emotional experiences that are tightly related to visual and tactile qualities of products [17]. From this result, we can see that, particularly for interactive products, the design of functionality and interactivity matters strongly. An example like Apple iPod [1] creates a very different emotional response compared to other types of mp3 players not just because of its look, but also because of its unique interaction quality that allows people to browse music with the wheel interface. This supports the notion that interaction quality and useful functionality are significant components to affect people's emotional experience with a given interactive products.

Implications of Understanding Emotional Experience for Interaction Design. Our study supports the fact that the three levels of emotion are clearly distinguishable in our data. Furthermore, in spite of some researchers' doubtful perspectives regarding designing for emotional experience [7, 13], our results showed that different qualities of interactive products do in fact have different roles in affecting various levels of emotion.

This tells us that there are at least three research directions potentially valuable in terms of helping designers to effectively consider and project outcomes of emotional experiences toward what they design:

1. Continuous research on developing improved models of emotion and experience (building on the previous work in HCI such as Norman's [20], Jordan's [16], and McCarthy & Wright's [19]),
2. Continuous research on the relationship between the models of emotion and a deeper understanding of interactive product qualities (similar to what is presented in this article), and
3. Research on developing useful design principles for enhancing positive emotional experiences.

As we briefly mentioned earlier in this paper, designers must not give up on accommodating or directing emotional experiences since it is apparent that how we design does in fact influence users' emotions. Although it may not be possible to fully control emotional experiences by design, our results show that it is possible to utilize our results about what types of product qualities are more tightly related to which types of emotional experiences. The results shown in Fig. 3 especially provide valuable knowledge about product qualities that can be manipulated through design in order to shape emotional experiences according to the semantic differential space. For future research, we need to continue to examine these relationships in even more depth and detail to increase the resolution of our findings.

Acknowledgments. We would like to thank all the participants to our studies.

References

1. Apple - iPod, Apple, Inc. (August 31, 2007),
   http://www.apple.com/ipod/ ipod.html
2. Apple - Mac mini, Apple, Inc. (June 21, 2007), http://www.apple.com/macmini/
3. Bannon, L.: From Human Factors to Human Actors: the Role of Psychology and Human-computer Interaction Studies in System Design. In: Greenbaum, J., Kyng, M. (eds.) Design at Work: Cooperative Design of Computer Systems, Erlbaum, pp. 25–44 (1986)
4. Bentley, T., Johnston, L., von Baggo, K.: Evaluation Using Cued-recall Debrief to Elicit Information about a User's Affective Experiences. In: Proc. of CHISIG 2005. ACM International Conference Proceeding Series, vol. 122, pp. 1–10 (2005)

5. Boehner, K., De Paula, R., Dourish, P., Sengers, P.: Affect: from information to interaction. In: Proc. of CC 2005, pp. 59–68. ACM Press, New York (2005)
6. Bødker, S.: When second wave HCI meets third wave challenges. In: Proc. of NordiCHI 2006, vol. 189, pp. 1–8. ACM Press, New York (2006)
7. Csikszentmihalyi, M.: Design and Order in Everyday Life. In: Margolin, V., Buchanan, R. (eds.) The Idea of Design, pp. 118–126. MIT Press, Cambridge (1995)
8. Desmet, P., Hekkert, P.: Framework of Product Experience. International Journal of Design 1(1), 57–66 (2007)
9. Forlizzi, J., Battarbee, K.: Understanding experience in interactive systems. In: Proc. of DIS 2004, pp. 261–268. ACM, New York (2004)
10. Gaver, B., Dunne, T., Pacenti, E.: Design: Cultural probes. Interactions 6(1), 21–29 (1999)
11. Grudin, J.: Is HCI homeless?: in search of inter-disciplinary status. Interactions 13(1), 54–59 (2006)
12. Harrison, S., Tatar, D., Sengers, P.: The Three Paradigms of HCI. In: Proc. of alt.chi CHI 2007. ACM, New York (2007)
13. Hassenzahl, M.: Emotions can be quite ephemeral; we cannot design them. Interactions 11(5), 46–48 (2004)
14. Hassenzahl, M.: Beautiful Objects as an Extension of the Self: A Reply. Human-Computer Interaction 19(4), 377–386 (2004)
15. Isbister, K., Höök, K., Sharp, M., Laaksolahti, J.: The sensual evaluation instrument: developing an affective evaluation tool. In: Proc. of CHI 2006. ACM Press, New York (2006)
16. Jordan, P.W.: Designing Pleasurable Products: An Introduction to the New Human Factors. Taylor and Francis, London (2000)
17. Krippendroff, K.: The Semantic Turn: A New Foundation for Design. CRC Taylor & Francis, Boca Raton (2005)
18. Mahlke, S.: Understanding users' experience of interaction. In: Proc. of the 2005 Annual Conference on European Association of Cognitive Ergonomics. ACM International Conference Proceeding Series, vol. 132, pp. 251–254. University of Athens (2005)
19. McCarthy, J., Wright, P.: Technology as Experience. MIT Press, Cambridge (2004)
20. Norman, D.A.: Emotional Design: Why We Love (or Hate) Everyday Things. Basic Books, New York (2005)
21. Norman, D.A.: Words matter. talk about people: not customers, not consumers, not users. Interactions 13(5), 49–63 (2006)
22. Norman, D.A., Ortony, A.: Designers and Users: Two Perspectives on Emotion and Design. In: Proc. of the Symposium on "Foundations of Interaction Design" at the Interaction Design Institute, Ivrea, Italy (2003)
23. Palen, L., Bødker, S.: Don't Get Emotional! In: Peter, C., Beale, R. (eds.) Affect and Emotion in Human-Computer Interaction. LNCS, vol. 4868. Springer, Heidelberg (2008)
24. Preece, J., Rogers, Y., Sharp, H.: Interaction Design: Beyond Human-Computer Interaction. John Wiley & Sons, Inc., Hoboken (2002)
25. Zhang, P., Li, N.: The importance of affective quality. Commun. ACM 48(9), 105–108 (2005)

How Is It for You? (A Case for Recognising User Motivation in the Design Process)

Shane Walker and David Prytherch

Birmingham City University,
Faculty of Art & Design, Corporation Street,
Gosta Green, Birmingham B4 7DX
{shane.walker,david.prytherch}@bcu.ac.uk

Abstract. This research suggests that a novel approach for extending the designers understanding of the user can be found in combining psychological and HCI perspectives. The study examines the users' emotional response to the design of software in Human-Computer Interaction (HCI), the influence it has on their attitudes and expectations of the software, and their motivation to use it. Reference to contemporary theories of human motivation and emotion in psychology, adapted for application to the user at the interface, provide a new 'lens' through which to examine the user, and to elicit new data to inform the design process. The exploration of underrepresented variables in human-computer interaction establishes the basis for additional tools and measures that can be employed by the designer to assess the success, or otherwise, of the user interface. Findings indicate that the opportunity to manage and capitalise on user interaction in the design process is under-recognised.

Keywords: Motivation, emotion, user-centred design, usability.

1 Introduction

It is likely that it will never be possible to 'know enough' about humans and the way that we behave in different environments and under different conditions, and this is particularly true of Human Computer Interaction (HCI). The immense complexity of human interaction challenges all those that work in this area.

Software design over the last 20 years has led to the predominance of engineering principles for usability and interface design, where the overall objective lies in optimising user performance and satisfaction by developing usable interfaces. Applied knowledge of human information processing has enabled designers of interfaces to exploit the strengths and support the weaknesses of human cognition, and thereby tailor the design. As new knowledge emerges on the human response, designers need to recognise and evaluate the implications for software interface design.

This paper seeks to focus on the user response (as a manifestation of the mental processes of perception, cognition and emotion) which has implications for software usability through the interactive process between humans and computers. From a design perspective there appears to be a lack of empirical research investigating the determinants of important aspects of behaviour such as emotion and motivation, and

C. Peter and R. Beale (Eds.): Affect and Emotion in HCI, LNCS 4868, pp. 130–141, 2008.

how an understanding of them may influence designers' decisions in the software design process. Picard and Klein [1] recognise the work accomplished in the educational domain, but point to a lack of focus in HCI on the needs of the user.

"...the educational domain is only one in which the role of computers has been creatively explored for attaining human goals and thereby meeting many kinds of human needs. For us, however, the challenge has been to 'pop up a level,' to begin to see the user as a complete being, and at the same time, as someone with many more needs that require satisfaction than simply the accomplishment of productivity and efficiency goals."

A 'design led' approach that acknowledges user requirements and needs at the interface can be significantly enhanced by reference to the field of psychology. The ubiquitous nature of computer technology today means it is no longer just a tool for those that are compelled to use it, or have to learn to use it, (as was the case in the 1980s) but interfaces, in particular on the Internet must appeal to a broad base of users (with varying levels of skill and ability), and should work first time to ensure the user is not 'put off' the experience. Modern psychological theories on motivation agree on a basic structure of component processes: goal directed activity, an individual's belief in their skills and the context within which they will work, and finally their emotions. Unified theories that attempt to satisfactorily explain human motivation have only been developed relatively recently; previously theories on motivation were too parochial to give generally agreed explanations for the phenomenon. Human motivation has often found itself the subject of concepts not fully understood or explained in psychology. Research within HCI on motivation (Technology Acceptance Model, (TAM) [2] supports the argument that visual communication and functionality (perceived ease of use) influence users' motivation, and change user behaviour in a way that impacts on usability. Research has shown that highly motivated users experience less anxiety, have higher perceptions of self-efficacy and more positive attitudes towards the software [3] [4].

2 Hypothesis

The authors believe that human behaviour is under-represented in the software design process and this important variable in the interaction process has consequences for interface design and usability. As with all visual communication designed to influence the viewer, the interface can embody similar techniques for persuading the user, and go much further as an interactive event with the potential to exploit behaviour patterns stimulated through perception. The authors hypothesise that the design of the interface and user experience can influence the users' behaviour and that the use of an iterative design process presents an opportunity that should be recognised and exploited. With an expanding user base, in terms of the level of experience and knowledge of many applications, together with the increasing popularity of web-based applications and requirements for accessibility, a focus on user's needs presents new opportunities for the designer. Following an extensive series of user-centred tests using recent definitions from psychology and applying these principles to HCI it is suggested that motivation, and its energising component emotion, plays a critical role in the user's perceptive, cognitive and evaluative processes, and influences choice behaviour. A predictive explanatory framework is envisaged within which motivation can be analysed, measured and evaluated for design implications. It will be possible to examine why users are motivated and de-motivated at the interface, and measure relative changes in these states. Such a framework could be used for troubleshooting and prediction in terms of the ability of the software interface to support the user.

In an attempt to bring the user and computer system closer together Picard [5] describes research that capitalises on the computer's strengths to create more meaningful interaction by enabling computers to recognise human emotion, and respond appropriately, through the use of emotional intelligence. Picard warns that too little emotion in the interaction process may be detrimental to decision-making, and she makes a comparison with patients who suffer from a lack of emotions.

This approach is supported by research at MIT [6] [7], that revealed that despite knowing the computer has particular limitations, people often respond to computers as they would to other people,

"An analogy with human-computer interaction also holds, where people think of computers as annoying and stupid, or as intimidating, and of themselves as dummies...we all know better than to treat computers like humans, and yet many of our default behaviors and responses tend in this direction." [5]

From the user's point of view, assumptions (which are a typically human characteristic) can lead to problems in the interaction process, for example, novice users are particularly susceptible to the notion that the computer must possess human-like qualities, which can open 'gaps' in the conceptual model the user has of the system. The affordances of the system [8], how the user perceives they can perform the task, can differ from how they actually need to proceed to complete the task successfully, influencing perception and behavioural response. This 'gap' can actually polarise different user groups; more experienced users can apply 'typical' computer constraints to their conceptual model, and are possibly unprepared for a more flexible, intuitive interface.

An important ingredient for a successful interface design is a well-researched design model; the design model should embody the user's task requirements, background, experience and capabilities in terms of handling information and complexity. The 'success' of the interaction process dictates the usability of the system. A simple, effective design enables the user to have a comprehensible task domain model of what the system does, and free's up the user's cognitive capacity, enabling the user to concentrate on the task in hand. This is associated with "Cognitive Load Theory" (CLT) [9] which suggests that human cognitive architecture operates by a combination of working and long term memory and that

"Working memory, in which all conscious cognitive processing occurs, can handle only a very limited number—possibly no more than two or three—of novel interacting elements." [10]

As designers, our approach to understanding human behaviour and the interaction process must recognise the evolutionary development of the user's knowledge and experience when describing the requirements of the interface for software design. The interface provides more than just sequence control, it should clearly represent the user's model of the task, and should be able reflect and facilitate complex behaviour patterns of the user. As Hooper [11], illustrates:

"The interface is the stage on which our interactions with computer systems are shown, but it is the nature of play that is of relevance, not just the physical actions of the players."

3 The Challenge for Designers

The goal of an interface to enable the user to carry out the task more effectively may benefit from observation and measurement of this process and a detailed analysis of the human response. In order to assess how far design techniques, applied to the user interface, can harmonise with human psychological needs for optimal performance (on specific tasks and attainment of goals,) we must base questions on a fundamental understanding of all the influencing variables of the interaction process, together with a clear knowledge of their relative importance. In perceptual terms, interactive computer systems are not just representations of knowledge, but interactive experiences that should seek to fully exploit the user's senses and emotions, developing new ways to deliver effective communication. This has become an important area of research and evaluation, as recent findings [12] on human behaviour, particularly emotion, have revealed its powerful effect. An investigation of the role of aesthetics on users' perception was compared with architectural design.

"The facade of the information system is what the users experience first and it is what cues the users about what is inside. Moreover the facade taints how the user perceives further interactions with the system." [12]

The interface is changed through well-researched and tested design as well as by viewing the interaction process through new 'lenses' [13]. Mental models evolve naturally through interaction with the surrounding environment. These are highly influenced by the nature of interaction in the context of a person's prior experience, knowledge and understanding. Designing for the user's needs is the new challenge for designers. The notion of technology that adapts to the needs of the individual user has been explored more recently [5] through research which examines possibilities for computers to recognise and support the user's emotional responses, helping to stimulate new contributions to the 'New HCI', a phrase coined by Hassenzahl [14]. The increasing interest in this area has led to a warning to the HCI community; Norman [15] cautions against too much emphasis on user's individual needs by suggesting that some of the best tools (not computer-based) require adaptation on the part of the user; this appears to be the antithesis of user-centred design and a warning against over-specifying the interface.

Variables during interaction that can influence user motivation lie in the gulfs between executing the task and evaluation [16]. The user evaluates their goals, their own ability to attain them, and the potential of the context (computer system) to support them in this activity. Evaluation is on-going as perception is matched against expectations. The gulf between execution and evaluation is a good indicator of how successful the interface is. These gulfs are bridged by addressing issues from either direction, the computer or the user [16]. The system designer can bridge such elements by creating interaction mechanisms that better match the psychological needs of the user, evident from the task model. In an ideal case no effort is required to bridge these elements, an invisible interface and a foolproof design model is required to achieve this, emphasising the importance of the relationship between the user's model and the design model for successful interaction. Users will have different user models and it is likely that the design model specified is based on what is considered a typical user for the application. A careful balance is required when the design is specified, highlighted by Norman [15]. Automation must concentrate on the tasks that the user need not get involved in (bridging the gulf). The system design should empower the user as too much reliance on the user to execute tasks that can be automated dilutes the user's cognitive focus on the task. As a result the user may feel the system is unworkable and can feel de-motivated and alienated from it.

A utopian 'invisible' interface would be simply a means by which someone entered the pursuit of an activity and if such an ideal existed, there may be no justification for research into HCI. The complexity of the human response makes an 'invisible' interface a difficult goal, but it is possible to come close to this ultimate tool through improved recognition of the user's requirements and needs [17]. A simple illustration might be the design of a pen. If a manufacturer came up with a design that for some people was too narrow to grip, they would have misinterpreted the user model for a pen and how the user likes to write. However, by producing a wide variety of different pens, shapes, sizes, colours, the designers are providing for a range of user models, as well as catering for emotional appeal. The user's model of the system can be described in part, by their response during use which can be observed and recorded. Information revealed about the user in this way can be limited, as not all knowledge is externalised in a form that is traditionally collected by commonly used techniques; other methodologies derived from an interdisciplinary approach are necessary to fill these 'gaps' in the user model. User motivation is a manifestation of the complexity of the human response and is fundamental for the success of the interaction process. Recognition of the role of identified stimuli of motivation can contribute to an assessment of the interface and be one of the indicators of how effectively design has addressed user centred needs and requirements.

Motivation is a response to the interaction process, illustrated in Figure 1 that leads to a positive cycle that is self-propagating, i.e. increased motivation leads to improved interaction that can lead to increased motivation. There is a notable relationship to the model proposed by Porat and Tractinsky [18].

Nielsen and Pullin [19] describe the potential impact of technology on human behaviour,

"The right technology integration can instil magic, the opposite causes disappointment, frustration and confusion."

The ability to recognise and use techniques that work to enhance user motivation at the software interface is important to all types of user. For example developing interfaces that stimulate users' motivation may be instrumental in attracting and sustaining

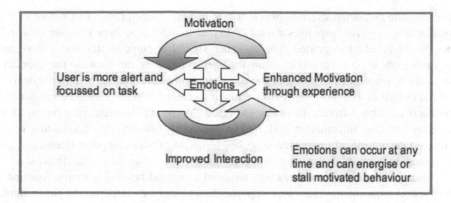

Fig. 1. Motivation and user interaction - a positive cycle

the interest of a younger audience, as they may be more prone to motivational stimuli in making assessments of whether to continue or cease activity [17]. Highly motivated users may be more likely to respond interactively with the software and thus gain a higher level of involvement and therefore understanding; the system is thus more effective at facilitating the user's task. A motivated user is more likely to overcome obstacles and any initial lack of understanding, and take a computer-based task through to completion. The enhanced energy and focus it provides the user could be viewed as motivational insurance.

Though individual users will naturally differ in their requirements and needs, extending the data collected with reference to specific psychological models of motivation will progress insights in the relationship between design and the user's experience. This new information for designers will help to re-prioritise design considerations and, most importantly, may reveal previously undetected problems relating to usability that are inaccessible to traditional user satisfaction techniques. Recent research has explored the application of certain psychological theories to software design [20], even creating systems that recognise human emotion. This work is nascent, and there is only scant research on improving our understanding of the user in the design process. Designers require a dual approach, both capitalising on what modern computers can offer in terms of processing power, speed, detailed high definition graphics, new operating systems and connectivity, and most importantly developing user-led design research to determine what qualities of the human user can (and need to) be exploited (through stimulation to create a specific response) and supported to deliver a more effective and consequently "affective" experience.

The designer's task is to define through design the interaction process between user and computer. Norman [16] developed a simple model describing user interaction as a linear sequence of events. This type of simplification delivers a sense of order to the unpredictability of human interaction. Experiencing real life practice enables innovative, useful design; the gathering of field data by testing the system with the user is an essential part of checking and re-modelling the mechanisms to cater for different user task models. It can highlight any 'gaps' between the user's model of the system and the design model. The designer will want to note whether the user response is characteristic or uncharacteristic when considering the user group. The nature of the positive and negative responses must be elicited to determine how the user's experience is enhanced or degraded. The designer should attempt to develop a designed response to these observations enabling the user to feel they can relate to the interface. There are opportunities to consider the users' individual techniques within the design, and the design model must be flexible enough to cater for those whose behaviour and approach may be different from the expected "norm". This highlights the need to correctly interpret information collected in user tests, assisting the production of an informed design model that ensures the key issues in human computer interaction are addressed, moving us closer towards the designer's goal of an 'invisible' interface.

A useable system is, in many cases required to extend beyond a simple functional interface; it must incorporate other opportunities to support users' needs, for example the human need to be creative or other personal goals. Usability will suffer if the user is searching for opportunities that don't exist. Moran [21] proposes the notion that computers are over-formal, and formalise our behaviour and constrain our thinking in ways that are not necessarily productive, partly due to the fact that in many cases, the way users interact has in part, already been predetermined by the designer. Moran believes that computers need to be as informal as pencil and paper.

"There seem to be natural structures for certain kinds of activities. But a lot of activities aren't easy to structure, particularly creative activities, where I think computers haven't helped us nearly as much as I would like to see. I would like computers to aid and liberate thinking, not constrain it."

The overall style and approach of the design concept can have a dramatic impact on users' behaviour and interaction. An example of this might be the difference in attitude of many Apple Macintosh users in comparison with IBM PC compatible and early Microsoft Windows users. Turkle [22] describes the evolving two cultures of personal computing that had developed by the late 1980s,

"IBM reductionism vs. Macintosh simulation and surface: an icon of the modernist technological utopia vs. an icon of post-modern reverie. For years, avid loyalist on both sides fought private and not-so-private battles over which vision of computing was "best"."

Methods of bringing the computer closer to the user derive from opportunities for involving the end user through the design process. With specific task models in mind, it is likely the designer will further explore designing an interface that uses metaphors to represent function, thus developing the perceived affordances for the user. The designer employs the usual techniques for measuring usability e.g. heuristics, and other measures of usability provide information on the user's understanding and ability to use the system. The opportunity exists to influence the attitude and behaviour of the user towards the system, thus improving its usability. The designer needs to be involved in creative experimentation, replacing existing metaphors and exploring more appropriate representations for the user. Developing usability in a system design can be understood in terms of four components identified by Bennett [23] and later operationalised by Shackel [24] so that they could be tested. These are shown in Figure 2.

Learnability	The time and effort required to reach a specified level of use performance (also described as 'ease of learning').
Throughput	The tasks accomplished by experienced users, the speed of task execution and the errors made (also described as 'ease of use').
Flexibility	The extent to which the system can accommodate changes to the tasks and environments beyond those first specified.
Attitude	The positive attitude engendered in users by the system.

Fig. 2. Four Components of Usability [24]

4 Are Current Definitions of Usability Adequate?

Definitions of usability focus on the effectiveness of the software to provide functionality to the user and on measuring how well they perform. Within the four components in Figure 2, 'attitude' is alone in capturing the importance of the relationship of the system to the user, and based on the results of this research it is suggested that this may be insufficient. An evaluation of the positive attitude in response to the system is not necessarily capturing information on where the system performed less well, and there is no reference to a possible negative attitude engendered by the system. It is argued that the 'attitude' component needs to be broader to recognise the source of the stimulus on the user, so that an understanding of usability reflects the role of the user's needs when interacting with software, including recognition of user motivation and emotion. For this to be successful, the linkage between user's needs and the other components listed in Figure 2 should be clearly represented as all these components can substantially influence the behaviour of the user and ultimately the interaction experience.

The user tests designed to investigate the role of motivation and emotion in the user experience are based on the use of a basic online web site builder, Webomatic (see Figure 3). The web site builder was designed specifically for 'Small to Medium Enterprises' (SMEs) as part of a £3.5 million European funded project (1998–2001) to assist SMEs by helping them to get a basic web site up and running without the need for any specific knowledge of web site design and construction. Pilot research was carried out with the SMEs, exceeding 500 over a two-year period. The pilot research confirmed that reference to psychological theory would be required to establish an explanatory framework for the users' response and could be used to enhance data collected by the designer at the interface. An understanding of the relative importance of the differing and changing responses of users and how to address them in the design is derived from a theory of motivation, Motivation Systems Theory (MST) [25], that models this component of human behaviour as simple behavioural processes, delivering the potential for enabling the designer to attribute design features to components of motivated behaviour in the user. MST integrates the conceptual frameworks of 32 motivational theories around its core concepts. It was also found to compare well with models and theories already used to describe user interaction in HCI, for example, the Technology Acceptance Model (TAM) [2].

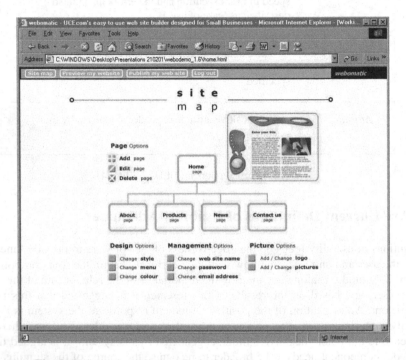

Fig. 3. Webomatic (A basic web site builder) was used for the tests

A user test was devised and twelve users, selected for their roles within SMEs (to have some involvement in web site design/content/construction and management) were introduced to Webomatic. All users had a demonstration of how to use the software before a timed test. Users completed a questionnaire that asked a series of questions about their experience, and linked design issues with motivational theory. The users were allowed thirty minutes to create a basic five page web site (this was easily achievable). During the test, the users were given keyword tables (emotions) with an intensity scale to record how they felt during the test. They were also asked to think out loud as the tests were recorded. Activity on-screen and a camera recording facial expression assisted in the interpretation and analysis of data collected via questionnaires. Reflective interviews were used to elicit further information about the user's experience, and in particular for comments on key events.

The descriptive terminology (for example, personal goals) used in MST required modification to improve semantic relevance to the HCI context. The application of the theory through the user tests provided a new 'lens' through which to view the users' experience, and this proved to be an effective tool during the user tests to gauge motivational responses. The applicability of MST to describe the interaction process in the HCI context was an important reason for its selection. The tests found that it was possible to gain further valuable information on the user that had implications for the design, particularly by tracking the user over time, highlighting the significance of each interaction the user has. The strengthening and waning of emotions is particularly evident and the results indicated that the opportunity to manage and capitalise on the interaction process is under-recognised. Using a theory of motivation for understanding and measuring the strength of the users' response was effective in providing a robust framework that detected measurable shifts in the user's response. These 'shifts' indicated a link to the qualities of the software, highlighting virtues and shortfalls of the software design. Post-demonstration and Post-use stages are comparative as 'before and after', so that perceptions the user established at the demonstration stage can be compared with their response when using the software and post-use. This was also found to be effective for identifying a shift in the users' response attributed to design characteristics of the interface. The tests established the importance for users of satisfying personal goals, and additionally this was recognised by the individuals, and was evident from user comments in interviews and questionnaires. This depended to a large extent on being successful with the software, but also on qualities of the design that improved the users' experience.

This research has utilised non-design literature (psychology and HCI), with the objective of extending the designers understanding of the user, as recent developments in HCI and the findings of this research, suggest that current tools (for example, user satisfaction surveys) may be inadequate to capture all information that has implications for design. Over recent years HCI literature has been increasingly recognising emotional aspects of the user experience where design has an important role and significant impact, for example, [12]; [26]; [27]; [28]; [29]; [30]; [31]; [32]. Recent work in HCI specifically examines aesthetics and design, beauty and user perceptions about ease of use, and usability. Other work explores different ways of capturing, recording and measuring the user's emotional response [5]; [7]; [33]; [34]; [35]; [36]. It could be argued that HCI research could benefit from a greater contribution from designers in response to these recent developments. The research highlights the fact that further work would be beneficial using interdisciplinary techniques to better understand the way the user 'thinks' at the interface, and that further review of current theories in psychology is required to assess opportunities for extending the scope of what we understand about the user. As computers become increasingly ubiquitous, in many forms, and begin to embed themselves into our lives and cultures, the need to match the interface design to an increasingly broad user base with differing (changing and evolving) needs and requirements becomes more important.

References

1. Picard, R.W., Klein, J.: Computers that Recognise and Respond to User Emotion: Theoretical and Practical Implications. Interacting with Computers 14(2), 141–169 (2002)
2. Davis, F.D.: Perceived Usefulness, Perceived Ease of Use, and User Acceptance of Information Technology. In: Venkatesh, V. (ed.) (2000) Determinants of Perceived Ease of Use: Integrating Control, Intrinsic Motivation, and Emotion into the Technology Acceptance Model, Information Systems Research, pp. 342–365 (1989)

3. Coffin, R.J., MacIntyre, P.D.: Motivational Influences on Computer-Related Affective States. Computers in Human Behaviour 15, 549–569 (1999)
4. Harbich, S., Hassenzahl, M.: Beyond Task Completion in the Workplace: Execute, Engage, Evolve, Expand. In: Peter, C., Beale, R. (eds.) Affect and Emotion in Human-Computer Interaction. LNCS, vol. 4868. Springer, Heidelberg (2008)
5. Picard, R.W.: Towards Computers that Recognize and Respond to User Emotion. IBM Systems Journal 39(3 & 4), 705–719 (2000)
6. Reeves, B., Nass, C.I.: The Media Equation: How People Treat Computers, Television and New Media Like Real People and Places. Cambridge University Press, Cambridge (1996)
7. Picard, R.W.: Affective Computing. The MIT Press, Cambridge (2000)
8. Norman, D.A.: Affordance, Conventions and Design. Interactions, 38–43 (May, June 1999)
9. Sweller, J.: Cognitive load during problem solving: Effects on learning. Cognitive Science 12, 257–285 (1988)
10. Paas, F., Renkl, A., Sweller, J.: Cognitive Load Theory and Instructional Design: Recent Developments. Educational Psychologist 38(1), 1–4 (2003)
11. Hooper, K.: Architectural Design: An Analogy. In: Norman, D., Draper, S.W. (eds.) User Centered System Design, pp. 9–23. Lawrence Erlbaum Associates, Hillsdale (1986)
12. Tractinsky, N., et al.: What is Beautiful is Usable. Interacting with Computers 13(2), 127–145 (2000)
13. Holtzblatt, K.: Customer Centred Design as Discipline. In: INTERACT 1999, pp. 3–17 (1999)
14. Hassenzahl, M.: Emotions Can Be Quite Ephemeral. We Cannot Design For Them, Interactions, 46–48 (September, October 2004)
15. Norman, D.A.: Human-Centred Design Considered Harmful. Interactions, 14–19 (July, August 2005)
16. Norman, D.A., Draper, S. (eds.): User Centred System Design: New Perspectives on Human-Computer Interaction. Lawrence Erlbaum Associates, Hillsdale (1986)
17. Shneiderman, B.: Designing for Fun: How Can We Design User Interfaces To Be More Fun? Interactions, September, October, pp. 48–50 (2004)
18. Porat, T., Tractinsky, N.: Affect as a Mediator between Web-Store Design and Consumers' Attitudes toward the Store. In: Peter, C., Beale, R. (eds.) Affect and Emotion in Human-Computer Interaction. LNCS, vol. 4868. Springer, Heidelberg (2008)
19. Nielsen, I., Pullin, G.: Simple Secret for Design, Interactions, 48–50 (July, August 2005)
20. Norman, D.A., et al.: Affect and Machine Design: Lessons for the Development of Autonomous Machines. IBM Systems Journal 42(1), 38–44 (2003)
21. Moran, T.: Interview with Tom Moran. In: Preece, J., et al. (eds.) Human Computer Interaction, p. 349. Addison-Wesley, Reading (1997)
22. Turkle, S.: Life on the Screen, Identity in the Age of the Internet. Phoenix, Orion Books Ltd, London (1997)
23. Bennett, J.L.: Managing to Meet Usability Requirements: Establishing and Meeting Software Development Goals. In: Bennett, J.L., et al. (eds.) Visual Display Terminals: Usability Issues and Health Concerns, pp. 161–184. Prentice-Hall, Englewood Cliffs (1984)
24. Shackel, B.: Human Factors and Usability. In: Preece, J., Keller, L. (eds.) Human Computer Interaction: Selected readings, pp. 27–41. Prentice Hall, Englewood Cliffs (1990)
25. Ford, M.E.: Motivating Humans, Goals, Emotions and Personal Agency Beliefs. Sage, London (1992)
26. Kim, J., Moon, J.: Designing Towards Emotional Usability in Customer Interfaces – Trustworthiness of Cyber-Banking System Interfaces. Interacting with Computers 10(1), 1–29 (1998)

27. Tractinsky, N., et al.: A Few Notes on the Study of Beauty in HCI. Human-Computer Interaction 19, 351–357 (2004)
28. Norman, D.A.: Emotional Design: Why we Love (or Hate) Everyday Things. Basic Books, New York (2004)
29. Norman, D.A.: Emotionally Centred Design. Interactions, 53–71 (May, June 2006)
30. Hassenzahl, M.: The Interplay of Beauty, Goodness, and Usability in Interactive Products. Human-Computer Interaction 19, 319–349 (2004)
31. Sklar, A., Gilmore, D.: Are you Positive? Interactions, 28–33 (May, June 2004)
32. Lindgaard, G., et al.: Attention Web Designers: You have 50 Milliseconds to make a Good First Impression! Behaviour & Information Technology. 25(2), 115–126 (2006)
33. Peter, C., Herbon, A.: Emotion Representation and Physiology Assignments in Digital Systems. Interacting with Computers 18, 139–170 (2006)
34. Partala, T., et al.: Real-Time Estimation of Emotional Experiences from Facial Expressions. Interacting with Computers 18, 208–226 (2006)
35. Light, A.: Adding Method to Meaning: A Technique for Exploring People's Experience with Technology. Behaviour & Information Technology 25(2), 175–187 (2006)
36. Axelrod, L., Hone, K.S.: Affectemes and Allaffects: A Novel Approach to Coding User Emotional Expression During Interactive Experiences. Behaviour and Information Technology 25(2), 159–173 (2006)

Affect as a Mediator between Web-Store Design and Consumers' Attitudes toward the Store

Talya Porat[1] and Noam Tractinsky[2]

[1] Industrial Engineering and Management, Ben-Gurion University of the Negev,
P.O. Box 653, Beer-Sheva 84105, Israel
[2] Information Systems Engineering, Ben-Gurion University of the Negev,
P.O. Box 653, Beer-Sheva 84105, Israel
{talya,noamt}@bgu.ac.il

Abstract. We propose a research model that focuses on the role of emotions in HCI in the context of e-retail. Based on the environmental psychology model of Mehrabian and Russell, the model suggests that design characteristics of the Web-store influence the emotional states of visitors to the store's site, which in turn affect the visitors' approach/avoidance response towards the store. The proposed model bridges the gaps between traditional and online retail research by demonstrating that HCI concepts such as perceptions of Web site aesthetics and usability constitute a psychological environment that influences the consumers' affective states.

Keywords: Emotions, aesthetics, usability, design, Web-store atmosphere.

1 Introduction

The introduction of e-commerce "is the most wide-ranging and significant area of current development in marketing" [1]. These developments increase the importance of how potential consumers view retail stores and how design features of the Web stores influence consumers' perceptions. The importance of Web-store design had generated considerable business interest in HCI concepts, practice, and design guidelines. The realm of store design can no longer rely on traditional marketing alone since the developing for the Web employs major aspects of information technology and HCI. One of the most intriguing challenges in the marriage of the marketing and the HCI disciplines is the apparent tension that exists in design that has to accommodate traditional marketing principles on the one hand and HCI goals and criteria on the other hand.

Thus, for example the field of marketing has been intensively involved in attempts to influence consumers' emotions through advertisements, and product and store design (e.g., [2], [3], [4]). Efficient and accurate information processing, navigation, and task execution by customers are not of major concern here. In fact, some marketing techniques attempt to make the information processing or the shopping process even less efficient for various reasons (e.g., [5], [6], [7], [8]).

The field of HCI, on the other hand, has traditionally been dedicated to the study and the practice of ease of use, and has emphasized accurate and fast task execution as its main success criteria. Until recently, the field has refrained from dealing with

C. Peter and R. Beale (Eds.): Affect and Emotion in HCI, LNCS 4868, pp.142–153, 2008.

the affective aspects of the interaction [9], [10]. Thus, the coupling of these contrasting disciplines in a new business model is challenging for both research and practice. Currently, research on the merger of marketing and HCI is scarce [1], [11]. Studies and design recommendations have mainly concentrated on the usability aspects of the Web store (cf. [12]), but not on the emotional aspects of the interaction. By far, studies of e-retail environments have not attempted to generate robust conceptual frameworks. Thus, there are only tentative explanations regarding how Web site design affects consumers' emotions, beliefs, attitudes and behavior *vis a vis* a particular vendor.

In this paper, we intend to help bridge the gaps between traditional and online retail research. For this purpose we integrate theoretical concepts and frameworks from both the field of Marketing and the field of HCI. The main objective of this paper is to propose a theoretical framework that puts the consumer emotions at center stage. The framework is based on the environmental psychology model of Mehrabian and Russell [13], which has been used to describe the atmospheric qualities of various environments and their effects on people's emotions and behavior.

2 Background

2.1 Emotions and Retail

The importance of affect, or emotion, in consumer behavior is widely accepted. In comprehensive reviews of the role of emotions in marketing, Bagozzi et al. [14] and Isen [15] enumerate various effects of emotional states in the retail environment. For example, emotions influence cognitive processes and evaluation and decision making; positive affect is positively correlated with customer satisfaction, which in turn increases the probability of repeat purchase. Marketers have also realized the importance of the shopping environment and product design in influencing the consumer's affective states [16], [17], [18], [2], [19], [20], [21].

Atmospherics, is the designing of space to create specific effects in buyers [17]. In marketing, it is the effort to design buying environments to produce certain emotional effects in the consumer that will enhance purchase probability. Atmospheric cues may include store layout and design, employee appearance, and musical and olfactory stimuli [22], [23], [24], [25]. Studies demonstrated that emotions experienced in the store environment trigger buying responses (e.g., [26], [27], [22]); influence price and value perceptions [28], [29]; impinge on shoppers' satisfaction and future shopping intentions [30], [31], [32], and on the quality of the transaction between the service provider and the customer [33]. The affective state of pleasure was found to be a significant predictor of extra time spent in the store and actual incremental spending [34]. Positive affect induced by store atmospherics increased perceptions of both hedonic and utilitarian value whereas negative affect decreased those perceptions [29].

In terms of the shopping experience, current e-stores are at a disadvantage relative to physical stores [35]. Tractinsky and Rao [36] speculate that online consumers value aesthetic designs that improve the shopping experience. In fact, to create a desired store atmosphere, e-retailers have to invest more in visual design in order to compensate for the medium's shortcomings: lack of olfactory and tactile information, limited auditory channel, and the lack of opportunity to use physical space to affect atmospherics. Recently, studies have begun to explore various aspects of the affective qualities of e-retail environments (e.g., [37], [38], [39]). Richard [40] examined the impact of Internet atmospheric cues on surfer behavior. One of the key findings was that entertainment cues (escapism, diversion, aesthetic enjoyment and emotional release) affected site involvement and site attitudes. Fiore et al. [41] tested linkages between emotion, hedonic value, consumer characteristics, and responses toward an online store. Their results revealed positive relations between hedonic value (image interactivity-feature in an apparel Web site) and emotional pleasure and arousal. Both arousal and pleasure enhanced willingness to patronize the on-line store. Mummalaneni [42] used the environmental psychology model [13] to demonstrate the importance of enhancing Web site navigation through the purchasing stages.

2.2 Web Site Design

Retailers of electronic stores rely on their Web sites to attract customers, present products, provide services and complete transactions. Over the last decade, a large number of studies evaluated e-commerce Web sites and their impact on customers' attitudes, shopping intentions, and satisfaction. In line with the traditional HCI approach, most of these studies have taken a cognitive perspective, emphasizing the Web-stores' functionality and usability (e.g., [43], [44], [12], [45]). Users' might consider other criteria, though, when shopping on the Web. For example, empirical evidence suggests that aesthetics is an important determinant of preferring a Web site [46], [47] or of influencing user satisfaction [48]. Consequently, recent studies have concentrated on understanding the relationships of Web site design with affective reactions [37], [38], [49], aesthetic perceptions [50], customers' beliefs [51], and site success [52].

3 Proposed Model

We propose a model that builds on the relation between perceived design qualities of the Web-store (i.e., e-store atmospherics), the emotions induced by those qualities, and consumer attitudes. The framework builds on two research streams. (1) An environmental psychology model of affective states [13], [53], which suggests that the affective reaction to environments influences diverse behaviors [54]. (2) HCI research on Web design. In particular we refer to usability, which had been the focus of research on Web site design [44], and to the aesthetics qualities of Web sites, a growing area of interest among HCI researchers [50].

3.1 Environmental Psychology Model – PAD

The basic environmental psychology model of Mehrabian and Russell (M-R) is depicted in Figure 1. It posits that all stimuli are perceived in terms of their affective qualities. Those emotional states can be reduced into a set of basic emotions or into underlying dimensions of emotions [55]. Mehrabian and Russell [13] proposed three such bipolar dimensions, abbreviated PAD: (1) *Pleasure*, referring to the degree to which a person feels happy or satisfied in a place; (2) *Arousal*, concerning the degree of stimulation caused by an atmosphere; and (3) *Dominance*, indicating the degree to which a person feels that he or she has influence over his/her surroundings and is in control of a situation. Subsequently, the person's emotional state influences her attitudes towards the environment, framed as an "approach avoidance" response.

Fig. 1. The Mehrabian-Russell model of environmental influence

This model and its derivatives have been used extensively in the study of physical retail environments [18], [56], [34], [57], [58], [29], [59]. However, only a few empirical studies (e.g. [60], [61], [41], [42]) have (partially) employed this model in a virtual shopping context. These studies have demonstrated the applicability of the model to the online environment in some concrete contexts. Yet, the relations between design attributes of online stores and consumers' affective states remain largely unexplored. The proposed model augments the above studies by offering a systematic and theory-driven treatment of HCI design variables that affect store atmospherics and emotions. In particular, it introduces perceived aesthetics as a major aspect of online retail environments. In addition, the model suggests that given the importance of usability in Web-store design all three aspects of the PAD model should be retained, as opposed to the tendency in past research to ignore the dominance dimension (see more detail in Section 3.2.2).

3.2 The Model

The model proposed in this study suggests that perceptions of the e-retail environment induce certain emotional states in the consumer, which in turn affect his/her attitudes toward the store (see Figure 2). In this model, perceptions of the environment (i.e., the internet store) are represented by perceptions of the two central design concepts: usability and aesthetics. The induced emotional states are based on the environmental psychology model of Mehrabian and Russell, and the approach-avoidance element of the M-R model is reflected in the users' attitudes towards the store.

3.2.1 The Environment – Web Site Design Characteristics

An interactive system can be characterized by many attributes (e.g., [62]). In this work we describe the e-store by two attributes: usability and aesthetics. We chose to concentrate on these two because they are central to the field of HCI; and because they are the most salient to the consumers when they interact with the e-store, and hence the most likely to influence the perceived atmosphere of the retail outlet and consumers' emotional states.

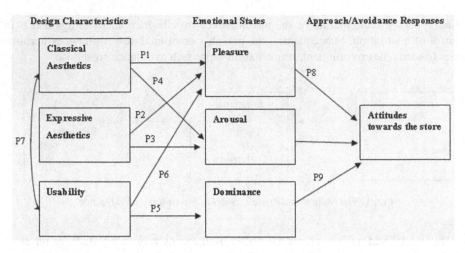

Fig. 2. The Proposed Model. Arrows indicate relations between constructs. The corresponding proposition numbers are indicated along the paths.

Usability has been the flagship concept of HCI for the last two decades [63]. It strives to focus the design and evaluation activities around users' ability to accomplish their tasks efficiently. It plays a central role in design recommendations for e-retail [44], [12]. While the usability of systems can be captured both objectively and subjectively (i.e., by self reports), the latter method appears more viable in practical settings. As such, usability can be viewed as the equivalence of the ease-of use construct in the technology acceptance model (TAM, cf. [64]) – a subjective measure that reflects users' perceptions of the degree to which the system facilitates easy interaction.

Recent HCI research, however, suggests that in addition to usability, aesthetics also serve a major role in affecting users' perceptions of Web sites. This argument goes hand in hand with a research tradition that regards aesthetics as a key factor in how people perceive their environment (cf. [10]). Lavie and Tractinsky [50] suggested that the aesthetic evaluation of Web pages can be divided into two dimensions: classical aesthetics and expressive aesthetics. Classical aesthetics represents the degree to which the design is clean and balanced. Expressive aesthetics relate to the creativity and innovativeness of the design. The advantage of this componential view is that it allows researchers to tease out finer details about how aesthetics relate to users' perceptions of other attributes of the Web site; how Web site design relates to users' emotions; and how it influences their attitudes towards the site. Thus, it was found that classical aesthetics is strongly correlated with evaluations of usability; that both aesthetic dimensions contributed to user satisfaction [50]; and that expressive aesthetics is a better determinant of immediate attractiveness impressions of Web sites [65].

Due to the documented role of emotions in consumer behavior, one of the important consequences of aesthetics in design is its effect on our emotions (e.g., [66], [67], [68]. There are several reasons for this effect, but perhaps the most obvious is that first aesthetic impressions are formed immediately (e.g., [69], [70], [68], [71], [65]. Those first impressions may linger and color subsequent evaluations of objects. Thus, to a large extent, aesthetics sets the tone for the rest of the interaction.

3.2.2 Emotional States

The major premise behind Mehrabian and Russell's model is that all stimuli are perceived in terms of their affective qualities. Those emotional states can be reduced into a set of basic underlying dimensions. Originally, Mehrabian and Russell [13] proposed three such bipolar dimensions: Pleasure, Arousal and Dominance (PAD). The original conceptualization underwent several modifications. Modern interpretations of the PAD model suggests that it is comprised of two dimensions: evaluation (also termed valence or pleasure) and activation (also termed arousal, energy or engagement) that together constitute "core affect" [72]. The affective quality of an object (e.g., a Web site) can be estimated by the dimensions of the core affect [72]. Recent studies have confirmed the bipolar nature of these dimensions and their independence of each other (e.g., [73], [74], [75], [76], [77]).

The third PAD dimension, dominance (or perceived control) has been neglected somehow over the years. The reasons for this may have been the fact that it represents a more cognitive reaction and less of an affective state [78] and that studies often failed to demonstrate its independence of the other two dimensions [79] or its effects on approach/avoidance variables [29]. Still, it is included in this model for two reasons. First, its lack of independence of the other two emotions in the M-R model might have been merely an artifact of limited stimulus sets in many studies (cf. [79]). Mehrabian demonstrated the independence of this dimension in a study featuring a more representative and comprehensive stimulus set [74]. Secondly, this dimension appears particularly relevant to situations such as e-retail where the consumer's interaction with the system is not as intuitive as in the physical world but rather mediated by a computerized system. In such environments, perceptions of control (or lack thereof) are very important [80], [81], [61].

In a study of representative everyday situations, [82] found that people preferred the most, situations that elicited positive pleasure and positive dominance. There were individual differences in people's preferences for arousal level in those situations that may be attributed to individual predispositions or to effects of the person's everyday life. The least preferred situations, were the ones that elicited negative pleasure and negative dominance (i.e., being controlled) coupled with positive arousal. Thus, the study demonstrated one of the interesting features of the PAD model − its contingent nature: the negative effects of unpleasant situations can be mitigated if users have more control over the situation or if they are perceived as low-intensity (i.e., not arousing).

3.2.3 Response: Approach or Avoidance

The original PAD model postulates that the environmental stimuli (e.g., store atmospheric) influence a person's affective states, which in turn will influence his or her response in terms of choosing to approach or to avoid the environment. In a retail context, approach responses might include the desire to stay longer in the store, to explore it, to be willing to return, and to communicate with salespeople. Avoidance responses might translate to a desire to leave the store, to remain inactive within it, and to avoid interaction with salespeople [18], [23]. Thus, in e-retail context an approach response would mean greater tendency to browse, search and interact with a store site for a longer period of time, greater willingness to buy from the store, and a better chance of actual purchase and loyalty. An avoidance response would mean just the opposite. Operationally, the literature refers to attitudes as a surrogate to approach/avoidance reactions (e.g., [83], [40]).

3.2.4 Propositions

Our model proposes a set of relationships between the model variables. These relationships are depicted in Figure 2 and are further described below. The results of a small-scale study [84] provided considerable support for the model.

Almost by definition, aesthetics entail pleasure (cf. The American Heritage Dictionary of the English Language). Indeed, [50] found strong positive correlations between both aesthetic dimensions and pleasure. Based on this, we propose that:

P1: *Web-stores perceived as having higher levels of classical aesthetics induce higher levels of pleasure.*
P2: *Web-stores perceived as having higher levels of expressive aesthetics induce higher levels of pleasure.*

Expressive aesthetics emphasize novel and creative designs [50], which are expected to correlate positively with arousal (e.g., [69]). Classical aesthetics, on the other hand, adheres to familiar and accepted notions of design, and is expected to have a calming effect on the senses. Hence, not only is it not expected to increase arousal - it might even reduce it.

P3: *Web-stores perceived as having higher levels of expressive aesthetics induce higher levels of arousal.*
P4: *Web-stores perceived as having higher levels of classical aesthetics induce lower levels of arousal.*

The HCI literature emphasizes the importance of allowing the user to be in control of the technological environment (e.g., [80], [81]). Users' perceptions of control over the interaction and of the likelihood of achieving their goals influence their affective states [85]. In addition, smoother interactions facilitated by better usability are likely to increase pleasure, whereas lower levels of usability increase frustration [85] and thus reduce pleasure. Hence, we hypothesize that:

P5: *Web-stores perceived as being more usable induce higher levels of perceived dominance.*
P6: *Web-stores perceived as more usable induce higher levels of pleasure.*

Previous studies have found that perceptions of systems' usability and aesthetics might be related [86], [48], [87]. This is especially the case concerning the relations between usability and classical aesthetics [50]. Thus:

P7: *Perceptions of Web-store's classical aesthetics and perceived usability will be positively correlated.*

Consumers who are more pleased and who feel more in control of their environment, are likely to exhibit greater approach, rather than avoidance, tendencies. For example, [88] findings show that perceived control and shopping enjoyment can increase the intention of new Web customers to return. The relations between arousal and approach/avoidance may be more complicated, reflecting the inverted U–shaped relations often observed between arousal and other attitudinal or behavioral measures (e.g., [69]). Research on store atmosphere provide evidence that more pleasurable store environments increase the consumers' approach responses (e.g., [22], [56], [34]). These studies, however, did not provide unequivocal support for the influence of arousal on approach responses. The lack of conclusive findings may be related to the nonlinear nature of the relations between arousal and positive affect [69], where a medium level of arousal produces a more positive attitude than very low or very high arousal.

Thus, the propositions concentrate only on the effects of pleasure and dominance on users' response.

P8: *Higher levels of pleasure increase users' approach response.*
P9: *Higher levels of dominance increase users' approach response.*

4 Summary

Donovan et al. [34] suggest that one of the most important directions in store environment research is to determine what constitutes a pleasant environment and how to implement such an environment. The retail world has changed considerably since then. HCI became a central discipline in reshaping much of the retail activity and in determining the affective consequences of store design. To account for these changes we have proposed a research model that focuses on the role of emotions in online shopping. The model suggests nine testable propositions regarding the antecedents and the consequences of emotions in the specific context of Web – based retail. The model argues that e-store atmospherics, which is described in terms of three design attributes – the site's usability, classical aesthetic and expressive aesthetic – influences users' emotional states. These states, then, influence approach/avoidance response towards the site. The model has theoretical and practical implications. Theoretically, it contributes to our understanding of virtual environments in general and in the e–retail domain in particular, and of the associations between design, emotion, and attitudes. Practically, it can help e-retailers and Web site designers in general to focus their efforts on concrete design objectives based on better understanding of the relations between design attributes and consumer behavior.

References

1. Barwise, P., Elberse, A., Hammond, K.: Marketing and the Internet. In: Weitz, B., Wensley, R. (eds.) Handbook of Marketing. Sage Publishing, London (2002)
2. Bloch, P.H.: Seeking the ideal form: product design and consumer response. Journal of Marketing 59, 16–29 (1995)
3. Kotler, P., Rath, A.G.: Design a powerful but neglected strategic tool. Journal of Business Strategy 5, 16–21 (1984)
4. Whitney, D.E.: Manufacturing by design. In: Harvard Business Review, July–August, pp. 83–91 (1988)
5. Russo, J.E.: The Value of Unit Price Information. Journal of Marketing Research 14, 193–201 (1977)
6. Levy, M., Weitz, B.A.: Retailing Management, 3rd edn. Irwin/McGraw-Hill, Boston (1998)

7. Hoyer, W.D., MacInnis, D.J.: Consumer Behavior, 2nd edn. Houghton Mifflin, Boston (2001)
8. Schroeder, J.E.: Visual Consumption. Routledge, London (2002)
9. Norman, D.A.: Emotion and design: attractive things work better. Interactions, 36–42 (July–August 2002)
10. Tractinsky, N.: Towards the Study of Aesthetics in Information Technology. In: Proceedings of the 25th Annual International Conference on Information Systems (ICIS), Washington, DC, December 12–15, pp. 771–780 (2004)
11. Vergo, J., Noronha, S., Kramer, J., Lechner, J., Cofino, T.: E-Commerce Interface Design. In: Jacko, J.A., Sears, A. (eds.) The Human-Computer Interaction Handbook, Lawrence Erlbaum Associates, New Jersey (2003)
12. Nah, F., Davis, S.A.: HCI Research Issues in Electronic Commerce. Journal of Electronic Commerce Research 3(3), 98–113 (2002)
13. Mehrabian, A., Russell, J.A.: An approach to Environmental Psychology. MIT Press, Cambridge (1974)
14. Bagozzi, R.P., Gopinath, M., Nyer, P.U.: The Role of Emotions in Marketing. Journal of the Academy of Marketing Science 27(2), 184–206 (1999)
15. Isen, A.M.: An influence of positive affect on decision making in complex situations: theoretical issues with practical implications. Journal of Consumer Psychology 11(2), 75–85 (2001)
16. Martineau, P.: The personality of the retail store. Harvard Business Review 36, 47–55 (1958)
17. Kotler, P.: Atmosphere as a marketing tool. Journal of Retailing 49(4), 48–64 (1973-1974)
18. Donovan, R.J., Rossiter, J.R.: Store atmosphere: An experimental psychology approach. Journal of Retailing 58, 34–57 (1982)
19. Nagamachi, M.: Kansei engineering as a powerful consumer-oriented technology for product development. Applied Ergonomics 33(3), 289–294 (2002)
20. Michon, R., Chebat, J.-C., Turley, L.W.: Mall Atmospherics: the Interaction Effects of the Mall Environment on Shopping Behavior. Journal of Business Research 58, 576–583 (2005)
21. Guiry, M., Magi, A.W., Lutz, R.J.: Defining and measuring recreational shopper identity. Journal of academy of Marketing Science 34, 74–83 (2006)
22. Baker, J., Grewal, D., Levy, M.: An Experimental Approach to Making Retail Store Environmental Decisions. Journal of Retailing 68, 445–460 (1992)
23. Bitner, M.J.: Servicescapes: The impact of the physical surroundings on customers and employees. Journal of Marketing 56, 57–71 (1992)
24. Darden, W.R., Babin, B.J.: Exploring the concept of affective quality: Expanding the concept of retail personality. Journal of Business Research 29, 101–109 (1994)
25. Spangenberg, E.R., Grohmann, B., Sprott, D.E.: It's beginning to smell (and sound) a lot like Christmas: the interactive effects of ambient scent and music in a retail setting. Journal of Business Research 58, 1583–1589 (2005)
26. Gardner, M.P.: Does Attitude Toward the Ad Affect Brand Attitude Under a Brand Evaluation Set? Journal of Marketing Research 22, 192–198 (1985)
27. Gardner, M.P., Hill, R.: The Buying Process: Effects Of and On Consumer Mood States. In: Wallendorf, M., Anderson, P. (eds.) Advances in Consumer Research, vol. 14, pp. 408–410. Association for Consumer Research, Ann Arbor (1987)
28. Grewal, D., Baker, J.: Do retail store environmental factors affect consumers' price acceptability? An empirical examination. International Journal of Research in Marketing 11, 107–115 (1994)
29. Babin, B.J., Attaway, J.S.: Atmospheric Affect as a Tool for Creating Value and Gaining Share of Customer. Journal of Business Research 49, 91–99 (2000)

30. Dawson, S., Bloch, P.H., Ridgway, N.M.: Shopping Motives, Emotional States and Retail Outcomes. Journal of Retailing 60, 408–427 (1990)
31. Swinyard, W.R.: The Effects of Mood, Involvement, and Quality of Store Experience on Shopping Intensions. Journal of Consumer Research 20, 271–280 (1993)
32. Yoo, C., Jonghee, P., MacInnis, D.J.: Effects of Store Characteristics and In-Store Emotional Experiences on Store Attitude. Journal of Business Research 42, 253–263 (1998)
33. Kluger, A.N., Rafaeli, A.: Affective Reactions to Physical Appearance. In: Ashkanasy, N., Hartel, C.E.J., Zerbe, W.J. (eds.) Emotions and organizational life, Greenwood Publishing Group, Westport (2000)
34. Donovan, R.J., Rossister, J.R., Marcoolyn, G., Nesdale, A.: Store Atmosphere and Purchasing Behavior. Journal of Retailing 70(3), 283–294 (1994)
35. Levin, A.M., Levin, I.R., Heath, C.E.: Product Category Dependent Consumer Preferences for Online and Offline Shopping Features and Their Influence on Multi-Channel Retail Alliances. Journal of Electronic Commerce Research 4(3), 85–93 (2003)
36. Tractinsky, N., Rao, V.S.: Social Dimensions of Internet Shopping: Theory-Based Arguments for Web-Store Design. Human Systems Management 20, 105–121 (2001)
37. Kim, J., Yoo, B.: Toward the optimal link structure of the cyber shopping mall. International Journal of Human-Computer Studies 52, 531–551 (2000)
38. Kim, J., Lee, J., Choi, D.: Designing Emotionally Evocative Homepages: An Empirical Study of the Quantitative Relations between Design Factors And Emotional Dimensions. International Journal of Human-Computer Studies 59, 899–940 (2003)
39. Menon, S., Kahn, B.: Cross-category effects of induced arousal and pleasure on the Internet shopping experience. Journal of Retailing 78, 31–40 (2002)
40. Richard, M.-O.: Modeling the impact of internet atmospherics on surfer behavior. Journal of Business Research 58, 1632–1642 (2005)
41. Fiore, A.N., Jin, H.-J., Kim, J.: For fun and profit: Hedonic value from image interactivity and responses toward an online store. Psychology and Marketing 22(8), 669–694 (1999)
42. Mummalaneni, V.: An empirical investigation of Web site characteristics, consumer emotional states and on-line shopping behaviors. Journal of Business Research 58, 526–532 (2005)
43. Spool, J.M., Scanlon, T., Schroeder, W., Snyder, C., DeAngelo, T.: Web Site Usability: A Designer's Guide. Morgan Kaufmann, San Francisco (1998)
44. Nielsen, J.: Designing Web Usability: The Practice of Simplicity. New Riders Publishing (2000)
45. Li, N., Zhang, P.: Toward E-Commerce Website Evaluation and Use: An Affective Perspective. In: Post-ICIS 2005 JAIS Theory Development Workshop, Las Vegas, NV (2005)
46. Schenkman, B.N., Jonsson, F.U.: Aesthetics and preferences of web pages. Behavior and Information Technology 19(5), 367–377 (2000)
47. van der Heijden, H.: Factors influencing the usage of websites: the case of a generic portal in the Netherlands. Information and Management 40, 541–549 (2003)
48. Lindgaard, G., Dudek, C.: What Is This Evasive Beast We Call User Satisfaction? Interacting with Computers 15, 429–452 (2003)
49. Gorn, G.J., Chattopadhyay, A., Sengupta, J., Tripathi, S.: Waiting for the Web: How screen color affects time perception. Journal of Marketing Research 41, 215–225 (2004)
50. Lavie, T., Tractinsky, N.: Assessing Dimensions of Perceived Visual Aesthetics of Web Sites. International Journal of Human-Computer Studies 60(3), 269–298 (2004)
51. Song, J., Zahedi, F.: A theoretical approach to Web design in e-commerce: A Belief Reinforcement Model. Management Science 51(8), 1219–1235 (2005)

52. Palmer, J.W.: Web Site Usability, Design, and Performance Metrics. Information Systems Research 13(2), 151–167 (2002)
53. Russell, J.A., Mehrabian, A.: Evidence for a three-factor theory of emotions. Journal of Research in Personality 11, 273–294 (1977)
54. Russell, J.A., Pratt, G.: A description of the affective quality attributed to environments. Journal of Personality and Social Psychology 38(2), 311–322 (1980)
55. Lichtenstein, A., Oehme, A., Kupschick, S., Jürgensohn, T.: Comparing Two Emotion Models for Deriving Affective States from Physiological Data. In: Peter, C., Beale, R. (eds.) Affect and Emotion in Human-Computer Interaction. LNCS, vol. 4868. Springer, Heidelberg (2008)
56. Bellizzi, J.A., Hite, R.E.: Environmental Color, Consumer Feelings and Purchase Likelihood. Psychology and Marketing 9, 347–363 (1992)
57. Chebat, J.C., Gelinas-Chebat, C., Vaninski, A., Filiatrault, P.: The Impact of Mood on Time Perception, Memorization, and Acceptance of Waiting. Genetic, Social, and General Psychology Monographs 121(4), 411–424 (1995)
58. Sherman, E., Mathur, A., Smith, R.B.: Store Environment and Consumer Purchase Behavior: Mediating Role of Consumer Emotions. Psychology & Marketing 14(4), 361–378 (1997)
59. Turley, L.W., Milliman, R.E.: Atmospherics effects on shopping behavior: a review of the experimental evidence. Journal of Business Research 49, 193–211 (2000)
60. Eroglu, S.A., Machleit, K.A., Davis, L.M.: Empirical Testing of a Model of Online Store Atmospherics and Shopper Responses. Psychology and Marketing 20(2), 139–150 (2003)
61. Huang, M.-H.: Modeling virtual exploratory and shopping dynamics: an environmental psychology approach. Information & Management 41, 39–47 (2003)
62. Lim, Y.-K., Donaldson, J., Jung, H., Kunz, B., Royer, D., Ramalingam, S., Thirumaran, S., Stolterman, E.: Emotional Experience and Interaction Design. In: Peter, C., Beale, R. (eds.) Affect and Emotion in Human-Computer Interaction. LNCS, vol. 4868. Springer, Heidelberg (2008)
63. Butler, K.A.: Usability engineering turns 10. Interactions 3(1), 59–75 (1996)
64. Davis, F.D.: Perceived usefulness, perceived ease-of-use, and user acceptance of information technology. MIS Quarterly, 319–340 (September 1989)
65. Tractinsky, N., Cokhavi, A., Kirschenbaum, M., Sharfi, T.: Evaluating the Consistency of Immediate Aesthetic Perceptions of Web Pages. International Journal of Human-Computer Studies 64(11), 1071–1083 (2006)
66. Desmet, P.M.A., Hekkert, P.P.M.: The basis of product emotions. In: Green, W.S., Jordan, P.W. (eds.) Pleasure with Products: Beyond Usability, Taylor and Francis, Abington (2002)
67. Rafaeli, A., Vilnai-Yavetz, I.: Discerning organizational boundaries through physical artifacts. In: Paulsen, N., Hernes, T. (eds.) Managing Boundaries in Organizations: Multiple Perspectives, Palgrave. Macmillan, Basingstoke, Hampshire, UK (2003)
68. Norman, D.A.: Emotional Design: Why We Love (or Hate) Everyday Things. Basic Books, New York (2004)
69. Berlyne, D.E.: Aesthetics and Psychobiology. Appleton-Century-Crofts, New York (1971)
70. Zajonc, R.B., Markus, H.: Affective and cognitive factors in preferences. Journal of Consumer Research 9(2), 123–131 (1982)
71. Lindgaard, G., Fernandes, G.J., Dudek, C., Brown, J.: Attention web designers: You have 50 milliseconds to make a good first impression! Behaviour and Information Technology 25(2), 115–126 (2006)
72. Russell, J.A.: Core affect and the psychological construction of emotion. Psychological Review 110(1), 145–172 (2003)

73. Green, D.P., Goldman, S.L., Salovey, P.: Measurement error masks bipolarity in affect ratings. Journal of Personality and Social Psychology 64, 1029–1041 (1993)
74. Mehrabian, A.: Framework for a comprehensive description and measurement of emotional states. Genetic, Social, and General Psychology Monographs 121, 339–361 (1995)
75. Reisenzein, R.: Pleasure-activation theory and the intensity of emotions. Journal of Personality and Social Psychology 67, 525–539 (1994)
76. Feldman Barrett, L., Russell, J.A.: Independence and bipolarity in the structure of affect. Journal of Personality and Social Psychology 74, 967–984 (1998)
77. Yik, M.S.M., Russell, J.A., Feldman Barrett, L.: Structure of self-reported current affect: Integration and Beyond. Journal of Personality and Social Psychology 77(3), 600–619 (1999)
78. Feldman Barrett, L., Russell, J.A.: Structure of current affect. Current Directions in Psychological Science 8, 10–14 (1999)
79. Brengman, M., Geuens, M.: The four dimensional impact of color on shoppers' emotions. Working Paper. Ghent University, Belgium (2003)
80. Brown, J.S.: From cognitive to social ergonomics and beyond. In: Norman, D.A., Draper, S.W. (eds.) User Centered System Design, Lawrence Erlbaum, London (1986)
81. Shneiderman, B.: Designing the User Interface: Strategies for Effective Human-Computer Interaction, 3rd edn. Addison Wesley Longman Inc., Amsterdam (1998)
82. Mehrabian, A., Wihardja, C., Ljunggren, E.: Emotional correlates of preferences for situation-activity combinations in everyday life. Genetic, Social, and General Psychology Monographs 123, 461–477 (1997)
83. Yalch, R.F., Spangenberg, E.: An Environmental Psychological Study of Foreground and Background Music as Retail Atmospheric Factors. In: Walle, A.W. (ed.) AMA Educators' Conference Proceedings, vol. 54, pp. 106–110. American Marketing Association, Chicago (1988)
84. Porat, T., Tractinsky, N.: The effects of perceived web-store characteristics on consumers' affective states and attitudes towards the store. In: Fifth Conference on Design&Emotion 2006, Gothenburg, Sweden, September 27-29 (2006)
85. Brave, S., Nass, C.: Emotion in human-computer interaction. In: Jacko, J., Sears, A. (eds.) Handbook of Human-Computer Interaction, Lawrence Erlbaum Associates, Mahwah (2003)
86. Tractinsky, N., Shoval-Katz, A., Ikar, D.: What is beautiful is usable. Interacting with Computers 13, 127–145 (2000)
87. Hartmann, J., Sutcliffe, A., DeAngeli, A.: Investigating attractiveness in web user interfaces. In: Proceedings of ACM CHI 2007 Conference on Human Factors in Computing Systems 2007, pp. 387–396 (2007)
88. Koufaris, M., Kambil, A., LaBarbera, P.A.: Consumer behavior in Web-based commerce: an empirical study. International Journal of Electronic Commerce 6(2), 115–138 (2002)

Beyond Task Completion in the Workplace: Execute, Engage, Evolve, Expand

Stefanie Harbich[1] and Marc Hassenzahl[2]

[1] Siemens AG, A&D MC RD, Frauenauracher Str. 80, 91056 Erlangen, Germany
stefanie.harbich@siemens.com
[2] Economic Psychology and Human-Computer Interaction, Department of Psychology,
University of Koblenz-Landau, Fortstraße 8, 76829 Landau, Germany
hassenzahl@uni-landau.de

Abstract. Research on user experience stresses the need to go beyond the mere accomplishment of behavioral goals, such as providing novelty and change, a compelling image, etc. Although it can be argued that the consideration of such non-instrumental aspects at the workplace will lead to joyous experiences, which in turn may be an important aspect of employee well-being, the offered link between current models of user experience and the work environment is rather weak. This paper presents a user experience model more closely linked to behavioral goals; that is tasks, their generation, and completion. We describe the e^4-model consisting of four groups of desired behavioral outcomes – execute, engage, evolve, expand – and its underlying motivation. e^4 does address not only task completion, but also persistence in task execution, modification of existing tasks, and the creation of novel tasks.

Keywords: User experience, motivation, workplace, goals.

1 Introduction

User experience (UX) research aims at extending the view on Human-Computer Interaction (HCI) beyond the mere focus on the effective and efficient accomplishment of behavioral goals, and thus the functionality and usability of interactive products [1]. Most available approaches (e.g., [2, 3]) emphasize the importance of taking *all* human needs and emotions into account when designing and evaluating technology use.

Industry got the message, too. Nokia [4], for example, explains: "Before mobility was about the delivery of products and services. Now it is about the delivery of personalized experiences", which add value and pleasure to daily lives. Their model of "Wow, flow, and show" acknowledges the importance of utility and usability (flow), but also emphasizes the need for novelty (wow) and self-expression (show). The latter are clearly non-utilitarian aspects. In other words, utility and usability is regarded as state of the art, a given, but no longer sufficient for an outstanding, positive, even joyous experience with a product [5, 6].

In the context of consumer products, such as mobile phones, the importance of addressing aspects beyond the mere functional is obvious. But how about the workplace?

C. Peter and R. Beale (Eds.): Affect and Emotion in HCI, LNCS 4868, pp. 154–162, 2008.
© Springer-Verlag Berlin Heidelberg 2008

From the employer's view, work is not primarily about satisfying human needs – there are jobs to be done. In contrast, one may argue that work performance will benefit from a more holistic consideration of human needs and that workplace technology can be a medium to facilitate this. However, in current approaches to user experience, effects on work or task performance are – if discussed – rather indirect (e.g., "attractive things work better", [7]). The present paper's objective is to take a closer look at user experience from a workplace perspective.

2 Experience at the Workplace

The most ubiquitous example for an enjoyable, motivating and appealing piece of interactive technology are computer games. The fact that there is no other reason to buy and play a computer game other than its positive experience [8, 9, 10] makes it a perfect model for studying the applied design principles. Playing computer games is challenging, trains new skills, and is able to enhance self-confidence by feelings of success and competence (personal) or by being involved in a gaming community (social). Wouldn't it be desirable to have the same qualities in a working environment? In other words, wouldn't it be desirable to have motivating, desirable, and enjoyable "tools"?

Often stark differences are made between work and entertainment use of software; i.e., between "tools" and "toys". We argue, however, that at least with respect to goal-directed behavior, work does not differ much from play, the home or the private context. In games, for example, clear tasks and goals exist and it seems irrelevant, whether these goals are work-related (writing an invoice) or fantasy-related (defeating a dragon) – in both cases goal-directed behavior has to be supported by the product. Take preparing a photo slideshow for the family celebration or working on the private club homepage as further examples – both is goal-directed behavior comparable to what people do at work.

One difference between work and home use of technology, however, is choice. If people do not want to fulfill a certain task or to use a specific piece of software, they simply do not have to. At work, personal choice appears to be more limited, although still plenty of opportunities to procrastinate, to alter or even reject particular tasks may exist. In addition, in a working environment, motivation to use a specific product for a given task is to a great extent *extrinsic*; that is, externally given and externally rewarded. However, it is the *intrinsic* motivation (i.e., the tendency to seek out novelty and challenges, to extend and exercise one's capacities, to explore, and to learn) that leads to well-being [11]. Thus, one objective in the working environment may be to provoke intrinsic motivation, to inspire employees to be curious, to explore tasks and given tools, to seek out new and better ways of getting things done, to master complex software in order to surprise and astonish boss and colleagues.

According to Ryan and Deci [11], intrinsic motivation can be elicited and sustained by the fulfillment of basic needs; i.e., need for competence, need for autonomy and need for relatedness, resembling Hassenzahl's "hedonic aspects" in the context of interactive products [12]. Intrinsic motivation is believed to enhance well-being in general, job satisfaction and even performance [13, 14]. In other words, in the working environment to foster and sustain intrinsic motivation seems key to a positive technology experience.

Being intrinsically motivated may have effects on performing at work in several ways: It may facilitate executing assigned tasks and pursuing the plans to accomplish these tasks, perfecting plans and even exceeding the task goals, and expanding the usually predefined subordinate goals to serve the overall working goal by generating new tasks:

- *Task Accomplishment.* First of all, motivation helps simply to get the work done. Parts of the daily work are recurring, routine tasks, which can be dealt with in the similar recurring manner. Usually, people develop fixed schemes for these tasks [15, 16], which renders them unchallenging, dull and monotonous at times.
- *Modification of Tasks.* For non-recurring tasks, fixed schemes can't be used, but a concept of the desired outcome (goals) and of the way to achieve this outcome (task, plan) has to be generated (e.g., [17, 15]). Even if the "main" goal is externally given, workers have to determine a plan to pursue the goal. The quality of this plan determines the required effort for its execution and the quality of the results [16, 18]. Devising a high-quality plan requires motivation and consideration of possible alternatives.
- *Creation of Novel Tasks.* Sometimes even the goal itself has to be specified [19]. Goals are considered to be hierarchically organized with a few higher-level goals unfolding in lower-level goals (e.g., [20, 15]). In the work context, people know their higher-level goal, i.e., the overall work goal. A marketing department is, for example, expected to see after the brand image and enhance sales figures, but the subordinate goals are not necessarily as specified. Occasionally, it is necessary to rethink previous methods to achieve the overall goal and create new methods and subordinate goals (e.g., [16]). This is where motivation is called for once again, as old routines are to be overcome and additional effort is required to constantly enhance the work quality.

To summarize, work does not only consist of the execution of given tasks in a specified way. The motivation to actually pursue goals, to modify existing goals, plans and tasks or to even create new ones could be facilitated by technology, too. In addition to merely providing functionality, interactive products for the workplace may attempt to motivate their users.

3   A Model: Execute, Engage, Evolve, Expand

One approach to formulate a model of user experience for work environments based on motivation is to look at desired behavioral outcomes. The advantage is the possible application to a broad range of workplace products. Desired behaviors, such as playing around with the interactive product given some free time, using the product even if the goal is already accomplished to make it even better, or finding novel uses not even intended by the product developers, hold for many software systems and interactive products. The disadvantage of this approach is that it merely defines desired behaviors, but does not actually prescribe the product attributes necessary to generate this behavior.

We nevertheless think it to be an adequate first step towards a systematic consideration of motivational aspects in interactive product evaluation and design.

In the remainder of the paper, we identify and discuss briefly four desired groups of behavioral outcomes a workplace interactive product should promote: execute, engage, evolve, and expand.

3.1 Execute

Execute subsumes the effective and efficient accomplishment of given behavioral (task) goals. Of course, people do not use workplace products for their enjoyment only. They've got work to do. Thus, as a category of behavioral outcomes *execute* relates to a product's utility and usability. This is not novel; however, any serious model attempting to disentangle user experience at the workplace must include this basic category (e.g., [21]).

3.2 Engage

However, besides the mere execution of tasks, a workplace product must *engage* its users. Being motivated facilitates good performance at work in several ways as pointed out above. Engagement will be a quality in itself and may additionally support the other aspects of e^4, *execute*, *evolve* and *expand*. The users should simply like to use their tools, and look forward to performing upcoming tasks. Engage – in our sense – summarizes situations, where people put additional effort into tasks, which would otherwise be avoided or finished with the least possible effort (and corresponding results (see [7])).

Some studies show that "perceived enjoyment" while working with a software can lead to more usage, often even in spite of usability problems (e.g., [22, 23]). With engaging products, users will more easily master their tools. In addition, employees might use their time more efficiently because of being harder to distract. They might engage less in alternative activities – a typical avoidance behavior, when being unmotivated.

Isen, Rosenzweig and Young [24], for example, found that positive affect let students perform as well as a neutral control group. Nevertheless, they reached their decision earlier and, thus, achieved their goal more efficiently. If arbitrarily induced affect can have such effects on task performance, the impact of affect deliberately induced by a product while being used might lead to similar effects on tasks.

3.3 Evolve

In addition to engagement, users should *evolve* their work itself; that is, modifying their tasks by discovering functions and possibilities they might not have been aware of so far. Putting those functions to use will inevitably alter tasks [25]. As tasks can be accomplished in several ways, the best way has to be found, in terms of efficiency and quality.

Interactive products are bloated with functions and users may have a hard time of becoming familiar with all of them. As a result, they will hardly ever use some of them, although they might be valuable for several tasks. But knowing those functions and the opportunities they provide is desirable, nonetheless. In a study of Baecker, Booth, Jovicic, McGrenere and Moore [26], the majority of users correspondingly expressed their desire for continually discovering new functions instead of entirely removing unused functions or having them tucked away. Paul [27] compared novice and expert users and found that the latter stand out due to their habit of exploring new systems freely in order to become acquainted with them. Facilitating exploration of a product's functions will lead users to tap the full potential of their products and therefore evolve their work quality. In other words, a workplace product, which supports evolvement, will suggest ways to restructure and modify tasks. Note that a product must present unknown functions as opportunities for action, without distracting from currently active tasks.

3.4 Expand

Knowing a workplace product well and interacting with it in a playful way can lead to a fourth outcome, namely to *expanding*.

In Isen et al's study [24], those subjects with positive affect not only were more efficient in executing their tasks, but even went beyond their assigned tasks and performed additional tasks as well. Going beyond the assigned task like this will add to the overall work goal. Users should be supported in defining new superordinate goals and expanding their scope in general to better accomplish their overall goal (see Erschließungsplanung, [16])[1].

This implies going beyond the product's original scope, using it for purposes not even intended by the developers. Take the VisiCalc, the first spreadsheet software as an example. In an interview with Dan Bricklin, one of the inventors of VisiCalc [28], he replies to the statement that early stories about VisiCalc had a hard time describing it with: "You can't describe some of these things. Until you're actually immersed in a certain technology and using it and seeing how the public uses it, you don't necessarily understand it. Some people don't understand why instant messaging has taken off so much among certain parts of the population. That was true for the spreadsheet, which seems so obvious now." Indeed, the spreadsheet is now used for a number of things, Bricklin hadn't thought about before. Expanding will surely be difficult to realize for many products, as some are designed to fulfill rather strict requirements, not offering the necessary "openness" for the invention of novel uses and tasks. Nevertheless, we argue that users should be able to use a product creatively, even if this means outwitting the software. This will lead to a feeling of autonomy and competence.

We believe that workplace products should be designed in a way to facilitate behaviors summarized by the four aspects of e[4]. People must be enabled to execute their daily tasks and must be engaged to show more persistence in executing even not so interesting tasks. In addition, a good workplace product will lend itself to modify tasks oneself or even to create completely novel tasks. See the following example for the expected effects of a well designed workplace product on the daily work and Table 1 for a summary of the four aspects of e[4]:

---

[1] Creation of new scopes of action (translated by the author).

"Mr. Smith got a new spreadsheet program three months ago. Compared to his old program, the weekly analysis of the sales figures was much quicker (*execute*). As he loves to work with this new tool, he even put extra effort in the already completed analysis to make it even more clearly and conveniently arranged (*engage*). For this purpose he used a lot of functions, he hadn't discovered in his former program (although they were available). This led to a general change in the way he approaches the analysis and what his boss expected from him (*evolve*). Being well versed, he even found a way to automatically remind sales representatives to send their figures in time (*expand*)."

Table 1. Execute, Engage, Evolve, Expand

Aspect	Desired behavior	Example Engineering	Example CT-Scanning
Execute	*Task completion* User accomplishes a given goal in an appropriate time	User is able to put her/his machine into operation in time	User is able to carry out an examination in a given time
Engage	*Persistence in task execution* User spends more effort on goals, s/he would normally avoid, e.g. exploring the product during lunch break	User concentrates on difficult error diagnostics until the error is found without giving up	User is more willing to do an examination on short notice close to leaving off work
Evolve	*Modification of tasks* User adjusts goals to produce better solutions by using an ever increasing basis of a product's functions	The production time per piece is reduced, because the user discovers new ways of programming her/his machine	User changes the way an examination is carried out, because of some functions s/he just discovered
Expand	*Creation of novel tasks* User creates novel usage scenarios for a given product	User contrives a new manufacturing method	User invents a new form of examination

4 Evaluation

To test the general idea of e^4, we constructed a questionnaire to actually measure, whether the desired behavioral outcomes occur at all, whether they can be grouped into the assumed four groups and whether they are positively valued. Preliminary results seem promising [29, 30]. From a set of items (i.e., descriptions of desired behavioral outcomes from each group) four scales emerged. A regression of the four scales on a general product evaluation (as "good") showed *execute* to explain 39% of the total variance. The inclusion of *engage*, *evolve* and *expand* added another significant 10%. Given "desirable" as product evaluation, *execute* explained only 18% and the remaining scales added another 22%. In other words, although execution of tasks is the primary source for a good product evaluation in the work context, motivational aspects as addressed by *engage*, *evolve* or *expand* add substantially to the product's appeal. Asked about desirability, task execution and motivational aspects were even seen as equal sources.

5   Conclusion

The formulation of a model of desired behavioral outcomes that go beyond mere task completion is a necessary first step towards the notion of user experience at the workplace and the corresponding desired qualities in interactive products. e^4 differs from available usability questionnaires and models by addressing not only the execution of tasks but also the modification and creation of plans – in short: motivation. We assume all four aspects of e^4 considered in a product to not only lead to a more enjoyable working experience – they comprise behaviors desired in any workplace that takes human capabilities seriously. In this sense, well-designed workplace products may not only be a source of employee subjective well-being, but will have broader effects on the quality of work itself.

To design for these qualities is challenging. It requires new approaches and empirical studies (see [31]). We are sure, however, that it can be done – and that HCI will be key in promoting more enjoyable, more motivating, more valuable interactive products for the workplace by addressing aspects beyond the mere utility and usability.

References

1. Hassenzahl, M., Tractinsky, N.: User Experience - a research agenda. Behaviour & Information Technology 25(2), 91–97 (2006)
2. Hassenzahl, M.: The Thing and I: Understanding the Relationship Between User and Product. In: Blythe, M.A., Overbeeke, K., Monk, A.F., Wright, P.C. (eds.) Funology: From Usability to Enjoyment, pp. 31–42. Kluwer Academic Publishers, Dordrecht (2003)
3. McCarthy, J., Wright, P., Wallace, J., Dearden, A.: The Experience of Enchantment in Human-Computer Interaction. In: Online Proceedings of CHI Fringe (2004), Retrieved 25 April 2006, http://www.shu.ac.uk/schools/cs/cri/adrc/research2/enchantment.pdf
4. Nokia Corporation. Inspired Human Technology (2005), http://www.nokia.com/NOKIA_COM_1/About_Nokia/Press/White_Papers/pdf_files/backgrounder_inspired_human_technology.pdf
5. Hassenzahl, M., Beu, A., Burmester, M.: Engineering Joy. IEEE Software 1&2, 70–76 (2001)
6. Jordan, P.: Designing pleasurable products. Taylor & Francis, London (2000)
7. Norman, D.A.: Emotional Design: Why We Love (or Hate) Everyday Things. Basic Books, New York (2004)

8. Draper, S.W.: Analysing fun as a candidate software requirement. Personal Technology 3(1), 1–6 (1999)
9. Heckhausen, H.: Entwurf einer Psychologie des Spielens. In: Flitner, A. (ed.) Das Kinderspiel. Piper, München, pp. 138–155 (1978)
10. Malone, T.W.: Heuristics for Designing Enjoyable User Interfaces: Lessons from Computer Games. In: Thomas, J.C., Schneider, M.L. (eds.) Human Factors in Computer Systems, Ablex, Norwood, NJ, pp. 1–12 (1982)
11. Ryan, R.M., Deci, E.L.: Self-Determination Theory and the Facilitation of Intrinsic Motivation, Social Development, and Well-Being. American Psychologist 55(1), 68–78 (2000)
12. Hassenzahl, M.: Hedonic, emotional, and experiential perspectives on product quality. In: Ghaoui, C. (ed.) Encyclopedia of Human Computer Interaction, pp. 266–272. Idea Group (2006)
13. Baard, P.P., Deci, E.L., Ryan, R.M.: Intrinsic Need Satisfaction: A Motivational Basis of Performance and Well-Being in Two Work Settings. Journal of Applied Social Psychology 34(10), 2045–2068 (2004)
14. Gagné, M., Deci, E.L.: Self-determination theory and work motivation. Journal of Organizational Behavior 26, 331–362 (2005)
15. Miller, G.A., Galanter, E., Pribram, K.H.: Plans and the structure of behavior, Holt, Rinehart and Winston, London (1970)
16. Oesterreich, R.: Handlungsregulation und Kontrolle. Urban & Schwarzenberg, München, Wien (1981)
17. Cropanzano, R., Citera, M., Howes, J.: Goal Hierarchies and Plan Revision. Motivation and Emotion 19(2), 77–98 (1995)
18. Stock, J., Cervone, D.: Proximal goal-setting and self-regulatory processes. Cognitive Therapy and Research 14(5), 483–498 (1990)
19. Hacker, W.: Arbeitspsychologie. Psychische Regulation von Arbeitstätigkeiten, Huber, Bern, Stuttgart, Toronto (1986)
20. Carver, C.S., Scheier, M.F.: On the Self-Regulation of Behavior. Cambridge University Press, Cambridge (1998)
21. International Organization for Standardization ISO 9241: Ergonomic requirements for office work with visual display terminals (VDTs) – Part 11: Guidance on usability (1998)
22. Davis, F.D., Bagozzi, R.P., Warshaw, P.R.: Extrinsic and Intrinsic Motivation to Use Computers in the Workplace. Journal of Applied Social Psychology 22(14), 1111–1132 (1992)
23. Igbaria, M., Schiffman, S.J., Wieckowski, T.J.: The respective roles of perceived usefulness and perceived fun in the acceptance of microcomputer technology. Behaviour & Information Technology 13(6), 349–361 (1994)
24. Isen, A.M., Rosenzweig, A.S., Young, M.J.: The Influence of Positive Affect on Clinical Problem Solving. Medical Decision Making 11, 221–227 (1991)
25. Carroll, J.M., Kellogg, W.A., Rosson, M.B.: The Task-Artifact Cycle. In: Carroll, J.M. (ed.) Designing Interaction: Psychology at the Human-Computer Interface, pp. 74–102. Cambridge University Press, Cambridge (1991)
26. Baecker, R., Booth, K., Jovicic, S., McGrenere, J., Moore, G.: Reducing the gap between what users know and what they need to know. In: Proceedings on the 2000 conference on Universal Usability, Arlington, Virginia, United States, pp. 17–23. ACM Press, New York (2000)
27. Paul, H.: Exploratives Agieren. Ein Beitrag zur ergonomischen Gestaltung interaktiver Systeme. Verlag Peter Lang, Frankfurt am Main (1995)
28. Bender, E.: Three Minutes: Godfathers of the Spreadsheet (2004), Retrieved 9/13/2007, http://www.pcworld.com/article/id,116166-page,1/article.html

29. Harbich, S., Hassenzahl, M.: Messung der Qualität von interaktiven Produkten für den Arbeitskontext: Ergebnisse zur Reliabilität und Validität des e^4-Fragebogens. In: Prospektive Gestaltung von Mensch-Technik-Interaktion. 7. Berliner Werkstatt Mensch-Maschine-Systeme, VDI-Verlag, Düsseldorf (2007)
30. Harbich, S., Hassenzahl, M., Kinzel, K.: e^4 – Ein neuer Ansatz zur Messung der Qualität interaktiver Produkte für den Arbeitskontext. In: Gross, T. (ed.) Mensch & Computer 2007, pp. 39–48. Oldenbourg Wissenschaftsverlag, München (2007)
31. Kohler, K., Hassenzahl, M., Niebuhr, S.: Stay on the ball! An interaction pattern approach to the engineering of motivation. In: Baranauskas, C., Palanque, P., Abascal, J., Barbosa, S.D.J. (eds.) INTERACT 2007. LNCS, vol. 4663. Springer, Heidelberg (2007)

Simulated Emotion in Affective Embodied Agents

Chris Creed and Russell Beale

School of Computer Science, University of Birmingham, Birmingham, B15 2TT, UK
{cpc,r.beale}@cs.bham.ac.uk

Abstract. An important strand of research that is often neglected in the field of affective computing is that of how users respond to simulated displays of emotion. We present an overview of the few studies that have explicitly investigated this space and discuss a number of issues related to simulated emotion research. An overview of our own work in this area is then provided, along with forthcoming studies that we plan to conduct. We conclude with a number of suggestions of where future research in this space should focus.

1 Introduction

An important strand of research that is often neglected in the field of affective computing is that of how users respond to simulated displays of emotion. How do we respond to synthetic displays of happiness, sadness, anger, frustration and fear? Can we catch emotions from users? How do we respond to computer empathy and sympathy? With interface designers increasingly incorporating emotion into their interfaces through a variety of modalities (e.g. textual content, speech, video and facial expressions in embodied agents), it is imperative that we understand in detail the impact of simulated emotion on computer users.

A number of recent studies have investigated user responses to simulated emotion through the use of embodied agents – screen-based entities that attempt to closely simulate humans to make interactions with computers more natural and engaging [6]. Recent research into embodied agents has predominantly focused on their use in situations where human-human relationships are important, such as teaching [5], exercise and nutritional advisors [2, 7] and simulations [11]. Such agents have also been used in computer games for a number of years [15] and are now widely utilized in online virtual environments such as Second Life [20] and There.com [21].

Research into online virtual environments and games that utilize embodied entities suggests that the social rules and norms that apply in human-human interaction also apply in human-computer interactions (e.g. [23]). Therefore, our interactions with embodied entities in virtual environments appear, to some extent, to mirror our social interactions with others in the physical world. Numerous studies conducted in the last decade within other computing domains also support this reported effect – that is, interactions in both physical and virtual worlds are governed by similar social rules and norms [19]. As emotional expression plays a pivotal role in human-human interactions, the social nature of virtual environments and our interactions with embodied agents strongly suggests that emotion will likely be of importance in HCI. As such,

C. Peter and R. Beale (Eds.): Affect and Emotion in HCI, LNCS 4868, pp. 163–174, 2008.

designers of embodied agents have been investigating how to incorporate emotional capabilities into agents to enable them to express simulated human emotions and have been examining the effects it has on user attitudes and behavior.

Several recent studies have suggested that we respond to simulated emotion in a similar way to human emotion (e.g. [2, 4]) – this is unsurprising considering our reactions to the computer generated characters developed by Disney and Pixar. Whilst these characters cannot dynamically interact with their audience during the film, they still have the potential to rouse strong emotional and social responses. However, while it is clear that users may respond to simulated emotion in a similar way to expressions of human emotion, it is less clear which emotions are best utilized in which domains and how best they should be expressed. For example, how do users respond to more cognitive emotions such as frustration, humiliation and guilt? How important is it to simulate mixed emotions – sometimes we are a bit happy and a bit sad at the same time – how do we simulate this and is it even necessary to do so in HCI? Is the simulation of so-called "negative" displays (e.g. frustration, fear and anger) of emotion necessary in HCI? There are many important questions such as these to which we currently have little understanding and very few answers.

This paper will discuss the main issues involved in studying the effects of emotion simulation on users. We start with an overview of the main studies in this area and describe many of the issues when attempting to make comparisons between related research. We also focus on issues that generally apply to the majority of studies that have investigated the effects of emotion simulation that need to be addressed in future research. We then provide an overview of our research in this space and conclude with suggestions for future research areas that will help to take this important and often neglected aspect of affective computing forward.

2 Related Work

While there have been many studies that have focused on the simulation of emotion in artificial intelligence (e.g. developing computational models of emotion) computer graphics (e.g. real-time rendering of emotions), and HCI (e.g. examining the impact of affective embodied agents), very few studies have explicitly investigated how we respond to simulated displays of emotion. There have been a large number of studies over last decade that involve an interaction with an affective agent, but emotion is often not the primary area of investigation of such studies. In this section, we start with an overview of more recent studies that have primarily focused on the effects of simulated emotion on users. We then move on to identify and discuss a number of general issues with research in this space.

2.1 Emotion Simulation Studies

A number of recent studies have suggested that we respond to simulated emotion in a similar way to human emotion. For example, Brave et al. [4] examined our responses to simulated emotion by asking subjects to play a casino-style blackjack game with an agent that exhibited either self oriented or other-oriented empathic emotion. The agent was essentially a static photograph of a human that communicated with the user

through the use of speech bubbles. Results from the study found that subjects perceived the agent which was empathetic toward them as more likeable, trustworthy,
supportive and caring than the agent which was not empathetic toward them.

Bickmore and Picard [2] found a similar effect when evaluating their embodied
exercise advisor "Laura" which attempted to build and maintain a relationship
with users over the period of a month. Laura used a number of relational strategies
that humans use to establish and maintain relationships, including expressions of
empathy, politeness, humor, appropriate forms of address, and discussion about the
relationship. Results from this study found that subjects generally perceived Laura
more positively when they interacted with the relational version as opposed to the
non-relational version (i.e. the condition where no relational strategies were used).

Fabri [10] examined the impact of simulated emotion by asking subjects to discuss
a moon survival scenario through the use of a "Virtual Messenger." When using the
virtual messenger, subjects were represented by three dimensional animated avatars
and could see both their partner's representation on the screen, and a small image of
their own representation. Subjects were represented by either an emotionally expressive or unemotional avatar - results found that subjects who interacted with the emotionally expressive avatar felt more involved in the task than those who interacted
with the unemotional avatar. However, in contrast to the studies above, subjects appeared to enjoy the interaction with non-expressive avatar more.

Prendinger et al. [18] investigated the effect of simulated empathy on users through
measuring their galvanic skin response and blood pressure whilst playing a mathematical game. One group of subjects interacted with an empathetic agent during the
game while another group interacted with a non-empathetic agent. In a number of the
questions asked during the game, a short delay was experienced by subjects – in
the empathy condition, the agent would be empathetic toward the user when this happened, while the other agent would do nothing. It was found that the incorporation of
empathy helped reduce galvanic skin response in subjects, but did not significantly
reduce how frustrated subjects felt whilst playing the game.

These studies illustrate that simulated emotion can influence user attitudes and perceptions - however, our understanding of exactly how they influence users and how
simulated emotion can best be utilised to enhance HCI is still relatively superficial.

2.2 Issues with Emotion Simulation Research

One of the primary issues with emotion simulation research is the lack of studies that
have explicitly compared an emotional agent against an unemotional one. Numerous
studies have made use of emotionally expressive agents in their experimental systems,
but emotion is often not the main focus of the study (e.g. [17], [16], [22], [2]). Attempting to compare and analyse such studies from an emotion simulation perspective
becomes problematic as inferences have to be made and this can lead to uncertainty
about whether or not reported effects were down to the manipulation of emotion. For
example, Van Mulken et al. [22] conducted an experiment with two different conditions – one that made use of an animated agent to present information and one where
an arrow was used instead of the agent to present the information. This is most likely
a fair comparison from the author's point of view, but when attempting to evaluate
such a study from an emotion simulation angle it becomes an unfair comparison.

Emotional expression is not the only variable that has been manipulated here – the functionality of the two conditions is also significantly different. Therefore, while many studies have utilised affective embodied agents for experimental purposes, it is problematic when attempting to compare the majority of these studies from an emotion simulation perspective. More studies that explicitly compare an emotional and unemotional agent are required to further our understanding of the effects of simulated emotion.

Another issue with emotion simulation research is that many of these studies do not check the emotional expressions of their agent prior to conducting their primary experiment. Failure to take this essential step before testing the effects of simulated emotion can cause problems as it is not clear whether or not subjects perceive the emotional expressions as expected. For example, consider the difference between a genuine smile and a social smile – the primary difference between the two is that a *genuine* smile (i.e. a duchenne smile) involves the movement of the orbicularis oculi muscle near the eyes, while a *social* smile does not [9]. We have found from own studies (described in next section) that users put a great deal of emphasis on the eyes when interacting with affective embodied agents. The application we used to develop our embodied agent did not allow us to manipulate the muscle around the eye – therefore, when we wanted the agent to simulate being genuinely pleased to see the user, we found that subjects often perceived these *welcoming* smiles more as social ones, and therefore perceived them as slightly false and patronising. This highlights how small details can easily alter perceptions of emotion and the amount of attention to detail that researchers need to pay when simulating human emotion – it should not be assumed that emotions will be perceived as expected. As Hook argues [13], they should be checked and tested before conducting primary experiments.

Another issue is the importance of researchers being explicit about what constitutes emotional expression in their study, and where, when and how it was expressed. Even in studies where emotion is main component being examined, researchers often do not include sufficient detail regarding this. Important information includes detailing exactly which emotions were expressed, at what times they were expressed, which model of emotion was used, and how the emotions were displayed (i.e. through textual content, speech, animated bodily and facial expressions, or combinations of these). The majority of studies where emotion has been incorporated into embodied agents tends to focus predominantly on basic emotions such happiness, sadness, joy, fear, surprise and anger [8]. Very few studies have investigated the impact of more cognitive emotions such as frustration, humiliation and guilt. The main reason for this is most likely down to the fact that these emotions are more difficult to simulate – all basic emotions have a unique facial expression associated with them, while cognitive emotions tend not to.

A further issue that has rarely been discussed in the field is that of mismatched emotional expressions. For example, many studies that use embodied agents equip them with the ability to express emotion through bodily and facial expressions, but also provide them with a synthetic and monotone voice. As we discuss in the following section, this can result in a mismatched emotional expression – for example, you may have a happy facial expression with a monotone synthetic voice. This mismatch has occurred in a number of studies, yet very few researchers have discussed the impact of it or the influence it may potentially have on their results. From our own investigations, we have found that users have very strong reactions to mismatches in emotional expressions and find them to be particularly tedious, frustrating and annoying.

An important question that is related to this research is whether or not all emotions are of interest to HCI. For instance, why would a computer ever need to express fear, frustration, or disappointment? Perhaps frustration or disappointment might be used by a sports coaching agent as a means for motivating an individual who has not adhered to their strict fitness regime, by attempting to make them feel guilty. An expression or statement of fear might be used by a security agent to add urgency in getting the user to patch software that has vulnerable holes located within it. Emotions which are typically perceived as being more negative should not be ignored and thought of as harmful to HCI, but instead, should be utilized by interface designers (along with other more positive emotions) to produce a desired or beneficial outcome for the user.

How do users respond to simulated emotion in embodied agents over multiple and extended interactions? This is another area that has been neglected and aside from Bickmore and Picard's work [2], there have been no other major longitudinal studies with affective embodied agents. The majority of experimental studies that utilize embodied agents often require a single short interaction that typically lasts less than an hour. These short interactions often result in agents expressing one emotion at a time – for example, they are either happy or sad at any one time, but never a mixture of the two. This approach misses the main point about how emotions arise and are expressed – as Boehner et al. state [3]:

"...emotions are constructed and experienced as individuals act in and through their culture and social interactions. So what we feel is not simply a pre-existing fact, but something that develops over the course of conversations and interactions with one another. We work out what we feel through expressing it and through seeing how others react. We negotiate our feelings with ourselves and with others, over time crystallizing meanings for us of what may initially be vague, confusing, and ambiguous sensations."

Emotions, therefore, are often constructed through interactions and conversations with others over time and are shaped by culture. This suggests that for users to have meaningful social and emotional interactions and relationships with agents, they must have the opportunity to interact with each other over time. There is a real need for more longitudinal studies in this space to help us understand this further – how should emotional expression adapt over time? How can agents "co-construct" emotional experiences with users? How do users respond to simulated emotion over time – does it remain novel and engaging, or does it become tedious and tiresome for users?

3 Using Affective Agents for Behavior Change

As highlighted in section 2, a number of recent studies have suggested that we perceive emotionally expressive agents as more likeable, trustworthy, supportive and caring than unemotional agents. But how strong are effects such as these? Do they remain consistent over two, three, four or fifty interactions? In human-human interaction, we are more likely to act of the advice of people we like and trust rather than people we dislike and distrust. Does the same principle apply in HCI? That is, if we perceive emotionally expressive agents to be more likeable, trustworthy and caring than unemotional agents, can they potentially influence user attitudes and habitual behavior more effectively over extended periods of interaction? To investigate this we have built an embodied agent (Fig. 1.) that simulates the role of a human nutritional coach and are currently investigating the following questions: (1) are emotionally expressive agents perceived more positively than unemotional agents? (2) can emotional agents help motivate people to change unhealthy habits more effectively than unemotional agents over extended periods of interaction? (3) how do our perceptions of emotional agents change over multiple and extended interactions?

Fig. 1. Rachael – Our embodied agent

3.1 Experiment 1

We recently conducted a study that examined subjects' perceptions of the agent's emotional expressions. Additionally, were also interested in how people perceive mismatched expressions – for example, if the agent has a happy face and a concerned voice, what do users perceive? Does the visual or audio channel dominate user's perception of emotion? Does inconsistency lead to confusion and extra cognitive load? We tested for four different emotions: happiness, warmth, neutral, and concern – we chose these emotions as a number of studies have found these to be the ones most frequently displayed in therapist-client interactions [1, 12]. The experiment had a within-subjects repeated measures design with twenty-four different conditions. There were four static facial expressions (happy face, warm face, neutral face, concern face), four audio only expressions (happy audio, warm audio, neutral audio, concern audio, and sixteen animations (four where the face and audio matched, and twelve where they were mismatched). We used a measure from [1] to assess how subjects perceived the emotional expressions (see Fig. 2). Subjects were also asked to answer three questions related to their general opinions of the agent.

Sixty eight subjects participated in the experiment and we found that they could correctly recognize the emotions in the static facial expressions, but had difficulty with the audio only expressions. With regard to the matched emotions, subjects were able to recognize happy and warm animations, but the neutral animation was rated a little low on all scales, while the concerned emotion appeared to be rated more as sadness than concern. Mismatching of faces and voices in the animations significantly influenced subjects' perceptions. While neither channel (visual nor audio) seems to dominant when identifying emotional expressions, it appears that with this particular set of animations, subjects rated them higher on all measures when a happy or warm face was in the animation, or when a happy or warm voice was used. Surprisingly, this was also true of the of the "concern" measure: subjects rated animations with happy or warm dimensions as more concerned than animations with neutral and concern dimensions. There were some strong responses to the mismatched facial expressions with many subjects venting their frustration. Also, subjects put a lot of emphasis on the eyes when rating the emotional expressions. Some thought that smiles were false and patronizing as the orbicularis oculi muscle around the eye did not move, while others stated that they liked how the eyes were used to emphasize emotions (even though we did not intentionally use the eyes to express emotion).

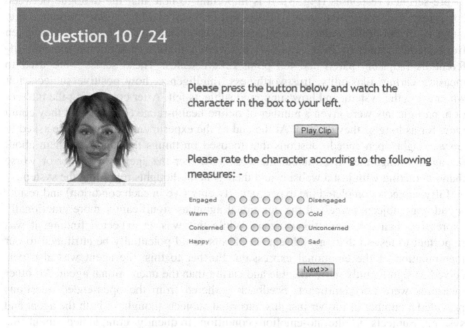

Fig. 2. Screenshot of first experimental system

3.2 Experiment 2

After gathering feedback on the embodied agent and confirming that subjects could correctly recognize the emotional expressions of the agent, we conducted another web-based experiment that involved around a ten minute interaction with the agent. The experiment had a between-subjects design with two different conditions – emotion and no-emotion. Emotion was manipulated through facial and vocal expressions – for example, in the emotion condition, the facial expressions alternated between happiness, warmth, concern, and neutral facial expressions, depending on the context of the conversation, while in the no-emotion condition, the facial expressions always remained neutral. Also, in the emotion condition, the speech rate, pitch average and pitch range were faster, higher and wider than in the no-emotion condition.

The interaction with the agent attempted to simulate a 'first session' with a human health professional [14] – the interaction started with the agent introducing itself and attempting to build rapport with the subject through the use of small talk. The agent then clarified both its own role and the role of the subject during the interaction, and followed this by asking subjects about their dieting history and current eating habits. The agent then moved on to discuss the pros and cons of both the subject's current diet and in changing their diet, and then talked about options the subject has for improving their dietary habits. The interaction concluded with the agent attempting to get an initial commitment for change and then terminating the interaction appropriately. Subjects were able to respond to the agent's utterances by selecting from a list of pre-scripted responses (Fig. 3). It is important to note that the dialogue between conditions was exactly the same – it was just the way in which it was presented (i.e. either in an emotional or unemotional manner) that differed. The measures were taken from a similar study by Brave et al. [4] and were a mixture of ten point semantic differentials (adjacent pairs) and ten point Likert scales. These scales were used to measure caring, likeability, trustworthiness, intelligence, how positive subjects felt when using the system, and how supported subjects felt. After completing the interaction, participants were given a number of online health-related articles that they could view for as long as they desired. At the end of the experiment, subjects were asked to answer eight open-ended questions that focused on things that annoyed them about the agent, things they liked about the agent, whether the agent was better or worse than interacting with just a website, and their general thoughts regarding the system.

Fifty subjects completed the experiment (twenty five in each condition) and results found that subjects perceived the emotional agent as significantly more emotionally expressive than the unemotional agent. While this was an expected finding, it was important to test so that any subsequent effects could potentially be attributed to our manipulation of the emotional expression. Further to this, the agent was also perceived as significantly more likeable and caring than the unemotional agent. All other measures were not significant. Feedback gathered from the open-ended questions provided a number of further insights into what subjects thought of both the agent and system. Subjects in the no-emotion condition frequently complained about the unemotional nature of the agent – they described its voice as "slow", "boring", "monotonous", and "unenthusiastic." On the other hand, the comments regarding the emotional agent were generally more positive – subjects liked the "realism" of the agent and often cited the agent's ability to express emotion as something they liked. Others commented on the "pleasant" and "friendly" voice and stated how they liked the general appearance of the agent. However, a few subjects commented on how they did not like the "fake perkiness" of the agent. In both conditions, subjects stated that they would have liked more options to choose from answering the agent's questions and also would have liked an option to skip answering certain questions. Subjects also wanted further feedback after the interaction with Rachael had been completed, as well as more health-based resources to use.

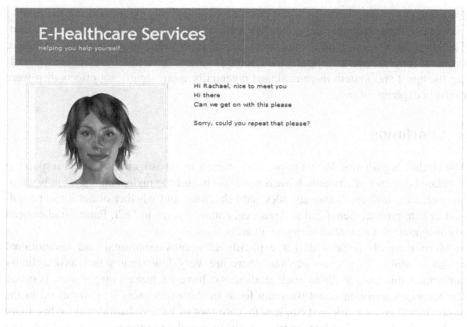

E-Healthcare Services
Helping you help yourself.

Hi Rachael, nice to meet you
Hi there
Can we get on with this please

Sorry, could you repeat that please?

Fig. 3. Screenshot of second experimental system

3.3 Future Experiments

We are currently working on a longitudinal study that will investigate whether simulated emotion has any influence on an agent's ability to help motivate people to change poor dietary habits over multiple and extended interactions. The experiment will be eleven weeks in length and will involve subjects logging into the system daily to record how many portions of fruit and vegetables they have consumed the previous day. Once they have provided this information, they will be able to access a resource area where they will be able to view their progress over time (through the use of graphs) and to make use of a number of other resources such as a BMI calculator, a calorie counter, a weight monitor, and other tools. At the end of every week, they will have an interaction with the agent to discuss their progress and to set goals for the next week. These interactions will last around 5 minutes. The first phase of the experiment will last seven weeks and will involve eight interactions with the agent. Subjects will then be requested not to use the system for another four weeks – after these four weeks have elapsed, subjects will be asked to provide information about their current fruit and vegetable consumption. This data will be used to assess if any changes that occurred during the interaction with the character have remained.

In conjunction with the longitudinal study, we also plan to run another experiment – this will focus on recording the dialogue with a human actress and then replacing the current agent with this. The main motivation for this is related to comments regarding lip synchronisation from the first two experiments – feedback collected from subjects suggests that they find inaccurate lip synchronisation to be particularly annoying and frustrating to interact with. Such responses could potentially be influencing the finding of subtle effects that were expected, but not found in previous experiment explained. Therefore, by recording an actress, the issue of lip synchronisation will be removed. From this experiment, we expect to see more positive comments from subjects regarding the agent and system in general, and potentially more significant effects than were found in experiment two.

4 Conclusion

The studies highlighted in this paper have started to investigate how users respond to simulated displays of emotion, however, we still have little understanding of how simulated emotion influences user attitudes and behaviour, and whether or not it can be utilised to help produce beneficial and practical enhancements to HCI. Future studies need to concentrate on a number of important areas.

More research is needed that explicitly compares emotional and unemotional agents – while this appears obvious, there are very few studies that have actually performed this test. Without such studies, we have to make comparisons between studies where emotion is not the main focus of the experiment – as discussed in the paper, this is problematic and can lead to a number of issues. In addition to this, more studies need to examine how users respond to simulated emotion over multiple and extended periods of interaction. The majority of studies conducted in this area to date require subjects to have a single and short interaction with an affective embodied agent – as result, it is unclear how we respond to affective agents over time. How do users respond to simulated displays of emotion over multiple interactions? Does it keep them engaged, or do they find it false and patronising? Are emotional agents more effective than unemotional agents at motivating change in user attitudes and behaviour over extended lengths of time? Further to this, there also needs to be a change of focus from that of whether or not emotional agents are better than unemotional agents, to one where we concentrate on which emotions, used at which times, and expressed in which ways, enhance (or hinder) HCI. Too many studies have focused purely on the so-called basic emotions of anger, disgust, fear, happiness, sadness and surprise. More focus needs to be given to cognitive emotions – both in how to effectively simulate them and in how users respond to them. These emotions play an important role in our lives and should not be neglected.

Understanding user responses to simulated emotion is an important research area that has received little attention to date. As more and more users become familiar with using embodied entities as a means for collaboration and interaction with others in virtual spaces, it is imperative that we understand in detail how simulated emotion influences user attitudes and behaviour. Early studies in this area have illustrated that simulated emotion can influence users in a number of ways, but research now needs to move beyond this, so that we can understand more clearly how affective agents can build effective social and emotional experiences with users that can be utilised for beneficial and practical purposes.

References

1. Bickmore, T.: Relational Agents: Effecting Change through Human-Computer Relationships. PhD Thesis, Department of Media Arts and Sciences, Massachusetts Institute of Technology (2003)
2. Bickmore, T., Picard, R.: Establishing and Maintaining Long-Term Human-Computer Relationships. ACM Transactions on Computer-Human Interaction (TOCHI) 12, 293–327 (2005)
3. Boehner, K., DePaula, R., Dourish, P., Sengers, P.: How emotion is made and measured. International Journal of Human Computer Studies 65, 275–291 (2007)
4. Brave, S., Nass, C., Hutchinson, K.: Computers that care: investigating the effects of orientation of emotion exhibited by an embodied computer agent. International Journal of Human-Computer Studies 62, 161–178 (2005)
5. Burleson, W., Picard, R.: Affective agents: sustaining motivation to learn through failure and a state of stuck. In: Social and Emotional intelligence in learning environments workshop, in conjunction with the 7th International Conference on Intelligent Tutoring Systems, August 31, 2004, (24th August 2007)
   http://affect.media.mit.edu/ pdfs/04.burleson-picard.pdf
6. Cassell, J., Sullivan, J., Prevost, S., Churchill, E. (eds.): Embodied Conversational Agents. The MIT Press, Cambridge (2000)
7. Creed, C.: Using Computational Agents to Motivate Diet Change. In: IJsselsteijn, W., de Kort, Y., Midden, C., van den Hoven, E. (eds.) First international conference on Persuasive Technology for human well-being, Eindhoven University of Technology, the Netherlands, pp. 100–103. Springer, Heidelberg (2006)
8. Ekman, P.: Emotions Revealed: Recognizing Faces and Feelings to Improve Communication and Emotional Life. Henry Holt & Co. (2004)
9. Ekman, P., Davidson, R.J., Friesen, W.V.: The Duchenne smile: emotional expression and brain physiology. Journal of Personality and Social Psychology 58, 342–353 (1990)
10. Fabri, M., Moore, D.J., Hobbs, D.J.: Empathy and Enjoyment in Instant Messaging. In: McKinnon, L., Bertlesen, O., Bryan-Kinns, N. (eds.) Proceedings of 19th British HCI Group Annual Conference (HCI 2005), Edinburgh, UK, pp. 4–9 (2005)
11. Gratch, J., Marsella, S.: A domain-independent framework for modeling emotion. Journal of Cognitive Systems Research 5, 269–306 (2004)
12. Grolleman, J., van Dijk, B., Nijolt, A., van Emst, A.: Break the habit! Designing an e-therapy intervention using a virtual coach aid of smoking cessation. In: IJsselsteijn, W., de Kort, Y., Midden, C., Eggen, B., van den Hoven, E. (eds.) PERSUASIVE 2006. LNCS, vol. 3962, pp. 133–141. Springer, Heidelberg (2006)
13. Hook, K.: User-Centred Design and Evaluation of Affective Interfaces. In: Ruttkay, Z., Pelachaud, C. (eds.) From Brows to Trust: Evaluating Embodied Conversational Agents, vol. 7, pp. 127–160. Kluwer, Dordrecht (2004)
14. Hunt, P., Hillsdon, M.: Changing Eating and Exercise Behaviour: A Handbook for Professionals. Blackwell Science, London (1996)
15. Isbister, K.: Better Game Characters by Design: A Psychological Approach. Morgan Kaufmann, San Francisco (2006)
16. Lester, J., Converse, S., Kahler, S., Barlow, T., Stone, B., Bhogal, R.: The persona effect: affective impact of animated pedagogical agents. In: Pemberton, S. (ed.) CHI 1997: Proceedings of the SIGCHI conference on Human factors in computing systems, pp. 359–366. ACM Press, Georgia (1997)
17. Okonkwo, C., Vassileva, J.: Affective Pedagogical Agents and User Persuasion. In: Stephanidis, C. (ed.) Universal Access in Human - Computer Interaction (UAHCI), pp. 5–10 (2001)

18. Prendinger, H., Mayer, S., Mori, J., Ishizuka, M.: Persona Effect Revisited. Using Bio-signals to Measure and Reflect the Impact of Character-based Interfaces. In: Fourth International Working Conference On Intelligent Virtual Agents (IVA 2003), pp. 283–291. Springer, Heidelberg (2003)
19. Reeves, B., Nass, C.: The media equation: How people treat computers, televisions, and new media like real people and places. Cambridge University Press, New York (1996)
20. Second Life: Second Life: Basic Overview (August 24, 2007), http://secondlife.com/whatis/
21. There.com: A Basic Overview of There.com (August 24, 2007), http://www.there.com/whatIsThere.html
22. Van Mulken, S., Andrè, E., Muller, J.: The Persona Effect: How Substantial Is It? In: Johnson, H., Laurence, N., Roast, C. (eds.) HCI 1998: Proceedings of HCI on People and Computers XIII, Sheffield, UK, pp. 53–66. Springer, Heidelberg (1998)
23. Yee, N.: The Psychology of MMORPGs: Emotional Investment, Motivations, Relationship Formation, and Problematic Usage. In: Scroeder, R., Axelsson, A. (eds.) Social Life of Avatars II, pp. 187–207. Springer, London (2006)

Affective Human-Robotic Interaction

Christian Jones[1] and Andrew Deeming[2]

[1] University of the Sunshine Coast, Queensland, 4558 Australia
cmjones@usc.edu.au
[2] Heriot-Watt University, Edinburgh, EH14 4AS, United Kingdom

Abstract. Entertainment robots are becoming commonplace in the home. Users are less fearful of interacting with robotic systems however these interactions are often limited to performing pre-recording sequences of actions. The next generation of consumer-level entertainment robots should offer more natural interfacing and more engaging interaction. This paper reports on the development and evaluation of a consumer-level robotic dog with acoustic emotion recognition capabilities. The dog can recognise the emotional state of it's owner from affective cues in the owner's speech and respond with appropriate actions. The evaluation study shows that users can recognise the new robotic dog to be emotionally intelligent and report that this makes the dog appear more 'alive'.

Keywords: Entertainment Robots, Sony AIBO, Affective computing, Acoustic emotion recognition, Human-Robotic interaction.

1 Introduction

In the 2004 film version of Isaac Asimov's I, Robot, an android interrupts a row between the hero Police Detective Del Spooner's played by Will Smith, and heroine psychologist Dr. Susan Calvin played by Bridget Moynahan to prevent violence. 'Excuse me. I note there are elevated stress patterns in your speech,' Sonny (the robot) announces, recognising the anger in their voices. Set in 2035, having consumer robots with autonomous intelligence and the facility for complex communications seems well beyond what researchers can achieve, however recognising stress and emotion in the human voice is becoming not only possible but more commonplace. Voice stress analysis [1] or acoustic emotion recognition [2] remains of interest to the research community however solutions are finding their way into products and the lives of consumers. Call centres are tracking the conversations between callers and agents for emotive events to help agents better support caller frustrations, aid agent training and detect fraudulent insurance claims [3]. In-car systems are not only voice controlled but can recognise driver emotion and react to drowsy or angry drivers to help them drive more safely [4-5]. Computer games can recognise player emotion and adapt game play to maintain active engagement and interest of the player without stressing the player with over challenging game play [6-7].

Humanoid robots in the home may be decades away however 'entertainment' robots have arrived. Robotic systems are sold as toys which can be controlled remotely

C. Peter and R. Beale (Eds.): Affect and Emotion in HCI, LNCS 4868, pp. 175–185, 2008.

or programmed to perform a sequence of actions [8]. These entertainment robots can be robotic dinosaurs, cats, dogs or of humanoid form [9]. To support the longevity of interest of consumers, developers of these consumer-level robotics must consider ways in which to support natural and engaging interactions. One way is to provide emotion recognition and response (affective computing solutions) such that robots can respond to human emotion with empathy and compassion.

2 Project Outline

The project aims to develop a consumer level emotionally responsive home robot and to evaluate the emotive interaction between the robot and it's owner. Emotionally responsive technologies in the home are uncommon. To aid the participants in their understanding of how a device could react with emotional intelligence we have built emotion recognition and response into a robotic dog. This simplifies the interaction for the participant as they expect the dog to react to emotion but to not fully understand the context of what the owner says. In fact 'real' dogs react more to the emotion of the owner than learned commands, and the request 'Go away' said in a happy friendly manner will have a dog excited, whilst 'Come here' said with anger and aggressive will see a dog retreat.

To facilitate natural interaction between the owner and the robotic dog, speech will be used to detect and recognise emotion in the owner. Rather than recognising the emotion of the owner by the words spoken and transcribed using speech recognition software, the project will determine owner emotion from the acoustic cues of emotion in speech, in a similar way to emotion recognition of a 'real' dog.

The robotic dog will recognise the emotional state of the owner and then react to the emotion with an appropriate response or action, e.g. if the owner is angry the robotic dog will whimper and cower in fear. We will assess using participants if, and how, the emotionally responsive robotic dog can enhance the interaction between the owner and their home robot. We will evaluate whether the new robotic dog is believed be participants to be reacting intelligently to their voice.

3 Implementation

The project implementation involves the development and integration of a consumer level robotic dog and emotion recognition technologies. The robotic dog used in the project is Sony's *AIBO* model ERS7-M3 with MIND 2 software [10]. The model incorporates features of autonomy, object detection/recognition, tactile sensing, obstacle avoidance and wireless LAN, a short term memory, and communication through speech, Fig. 1.

Our previous research considered the use of the AIBO's camera to recognise facial expressions and to infer owner emotional state [11]. However limited image resolution, focusing, and dependency on lighting conditions prevents accurate and robust face detection and expression recognition. Instead, the project uses AIBO's built in stereo microphone to record the owner's speech. In this way the owner does not need to be close to and in front of the AIBO, and lighting conditions can be ignored. The speech is processed for emotional cues using an acoustic emotion recognition systemdescribed in the article 'Acoustic Emotion Recognition for Affective Computer Gaming'.

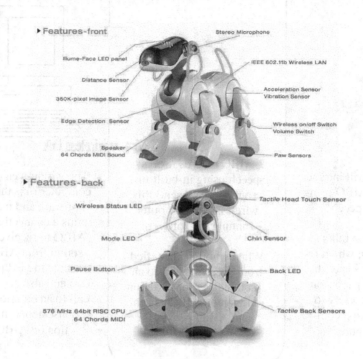

Fig. 1. Sensor hardware on Sony AIBO ERS7 [10]

3.1 Integrated System

The AIBO has a 64 bit RISC CPU operating at 576 MHz with 64MB of RAM. However the acoustic emotion recognition system (ER) is computationally intensive and on board processing would incur lengthy latency delays. Instead the ER system resides on a laptop which communicates wirelessly with the AIBO to retrieve the owner's speech, process the speech for emotional cues, and return the recognition result to the AIBO, Fig. 2. On receipt of the emotional classification, the AIBO performs the appropriate action.

3.2 AIBO Actions

The actions performed by the AIBO, together with the code to stream speech and communicate wireless, is built around Sony's MIND 2 software (*'aiboware'*). Sony has a *Software Development Environment (SDE)* for the AIBO series, known as *Open R SDE* [12]. This contains various *Software Development Kits (SDK)s* which range

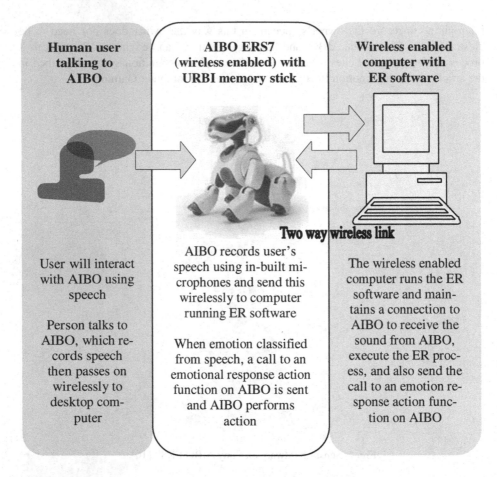

Human user talking to AIBO	AIBO ERS7 (wireless enabled) with URBI memory stick	Wireless enabled computer with ER software
	Two way wireless link	
User will interact with AIBO using speech

Person talks to AIBO, which records speech then passes on wirelessly to desktop computer | AIBO records user's speech using in-built microphones and send this wirelessly to computer running ER software

When emotion classified from speech, a call to an emotional response action function on AIBO is sent and AIBO performs action | The wireless enabled computer runs the ER software and maintains a connection to AIBO to receive the sound from AIBO, execute the ER process, and also send the call to an emotion response action function on AIBO |

Fig. 2. System configuration for AIBO with integrated acoustic emotion recognition

from simple scripting (in R-Code) of actions, to providing control of individual joints or wireless remote control. Other development languages exist including *Tekkotsu* [13] (a C++ based framework to create a level of abstraction above Open R SDE); *Universal Real-time Behavior Interface (URBI)* [14] (similar to Tekkotsu's abstraction from Open R, but is based on a client/server model and supports other languages like Java and Matlab as well as C++); and *YART (Yet Another RCode Tool)* [15] (a small program to aid users in creating R-Code scripts for AIBO to perform simple actions such as dancing). In this project we use the URBI environment to code the actions, data capture and streaming. We have developed responses for AIBO to perform triggered by the owner's emotional speech, Table 1.

The AIBO constantly listens for owner speech however the actions are performed fully before the dog can change it's emotive response thereby preventing confusing actions being exhibited.

Table 1. AIBO performed action in response to owner detected emotion

Owner emotion recognized	Noise playback from AIBO	Action performed by AIBO
Anger	Whimper	Cower in fear by moving its front legs forward to its face, while keeping its rear legs in the same position as well as moving its head and neck downwards
Sadness	Howling	"Howl" by arching up and raising its head, while opening and closing mouth
Happiness	Bark (playful)	Wag tail then bark again
Boredom	Yawn	Stretch and open its mouth as if it were yawning.
Surprise	Bark (surprise) and then sniffs	Move its head up and then move it from side to side, while making a sniffing noise as if to see what caused a 'surprise'

4 Published Studies

Previous studies have considered the human-robot relationship, and in particular interactions between users and the AIBO robotic dog [16-18]. Surveys of visitors to an online AIBO forum investigated the relationship between owner and robotic dog with aspects of technological essences, Life-like essences, Mental states, Social rapport and Moral standing [16]. It was reported that most (75%) respondents surveyed had comments which regarded AIBO as "a cool piece of technology", 47% referred to AIBO biologically and 14% attributed *animism* (in that it has some form of 'spirit'). In terms of mental states and emotion itself, 42% said that AIBO appeared to do things purposely, while 38% reported it having real feelings (e.g. being angry when the owner's boyfriend talked to the AIBO). Some 27% of those surveyed also engaged in a reciprocal exchange of information, where the AIBO responded in a particular way each time it was asked about something. We infer that although owners of AIBO understand that the dog is mechanical and not alive they attribute real-life characteristics of personality and intelligence to the AIBO.

The child-robot relationship was studied where preschool children compared the AIBO with a stuffed toy dog [17]. Children were allowed to play equally with both dogs and then asked questions relating to categories created in the online forum study [16]. Results showed that the children played/behaved the same way with the AIBO as they did with the stuffed dog. However the children interacted more with the AIBO *"as if it were a live dog"* and engaged in more shared action (e.g. one child noticed AIBO looking for its pink ball, brought the ball to the AIBO and expects AIBO to kick it).

A third study involved children from ages 7 to 15 comparing the AIBO with a real dog (a female Australian Shepherd called "Canis") [18]. The result reported that the children generally spent more time with the Australian Shepherd than with AIBO. However interestingly interviews with the children showed that although they knew

AIBO was a machine, they would attribute it with life-like qualities and treat AIBO as if it were real. When asked whether the AIBO or Canis *"could know how you re feeling?"*, the child study rated 68% to Canis and AIBO 22%.

We proposed that by integrated emotion recognition capabilities into the AIBO we can enhance the human-robot interaction and improve the sense that the AIBO is alive.

5   Evaluation Method

The study evaluated whether the addition of acoustic emotion recognition technology for the AIBO can enhance the human-robotic interaction and relationship and allow the AIBO to appear more 'alive', with the ability to 'feel' and respond to the owner in an emotionally intelligent manner.

16 participants completed the evaluation study (5 female, 11 male, aged between 19 and 34). All were aware of consumer-level robotics and entertainment robotic dogs however none of the participants had previously interacted with an AIBO.

The evaluation involved participants interacting with two different AIBOs:

- AIBO 1: a non-emotionally intelligent AIBO. The AIBO will listen to the owner's speech and perform the same actions however the ER system is disengaged and the actions are performed randomly
- AIBO 2: an emotionally-intelligent AIBO. The AIBO will listen to the owner's speech, pass to the ER system which will recognise the owner's emotional state and trigger the AIBO to perform the emotionally appropriate action.

The participants were split into two groups where the first group interacted with AIBO 1 first and then AIBO 2, whereas the group 2 interacted with AIBO 2 first and then AIBO 1. Participants were not told that the two AIBOs were different. Participants were informed that they could only interact with the AIBO using speech. They were also told that the AIBOs could detect boredom, sadness/grief, frustration/extreme anger, happiness and surprise but not told how the AIBOs would respond. Participants were not constrained in how they could interact with the AIBO and what they could say.

Participants spent on average 15 minutes interacting with each AIBO during which their actions were observed and recorded, together with their speech, the ER output and the AIBO responses. After interaction with both AIBOs participants were requested to complete a questionnaire in which they scored using a 5-point Likert scale how well each AIBO recognised each of the 5 emotional states, and how effective each AIBO was at dealing with the emotional stimulus. The participant was then told the difference between the two AIBOs and which of the two responded using the emotion recognition technology. They were then asked additional questions about how well the ER AIBO had performed and whether the ER system made the AIBO appear more alive.

6   Results

The AIBO would only appear emotionally-intelligent if the emotion recognition technology performed accurately and robustly. The observations of interactions and recorded speech files showed that the ER system correctly recognised the emotional state with greater than 75% frequency, averaged over the 16 participants. This is in line with the stated performance of the acoustic emotion recognition system for speaker independent and utterance independent speech (see article 'Acoustic Emotion Recognition for Affective Computer Gaming').

Results were gained from responses to the questionnaires. Firstly participants were asked to rate how well each dog responded to their (owner) emotion using a 5-point Likert scale where 1 represented poor and 5 excellent. Participants were not told which dog was using emotion recognition. Results in Fig. 3 are compiled for non-ER against ER AIBOs.

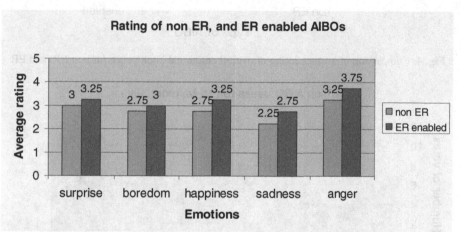

Fig. 3. Comparison of average rating of emotional responses for non ER, and ER AIBOs

With the non ER AIBO, most emotions are rated around average, with happiness and anger being (on average) considered to be most effective responses (although it should be noted that the responses for the non-ER AIBO were performed randomly), Fig. 3.

With the ER AIBO, the emotional response rates are higher for all emotions, most noticeably for anger. This is corroborated by evidence given by participants saying that anger was the easiest emotion for them to portray, Fig. 3. The ratings indicate that the ER AIBO is performing with more emotional-intelligence than the non-ER AIBO. We may also presume that the ER AIBO rates would be higher still if the ER technology itself performed with 100% accuracy.

Before being informed which AIBO used the ER system, participants were asked to rate, using a 5-point Likert scale where 1 represented poor and 5 excellent, each dog for overall emotional intelligence, Fig. 4. The ER enabled AIBO is rated more highly than the non-ER AIBO, however the lower than expected ER AIBO result may be caused by the error rate of the ER system, noise in the testing environment and inability of participants to portray emotions on demand.

Participants were informed that one of the AIBOs was using an automated emotion recognition system but not told which one. They were then asked to state which of the two AIBOs they believed to be more 'alive', Fig. 5.

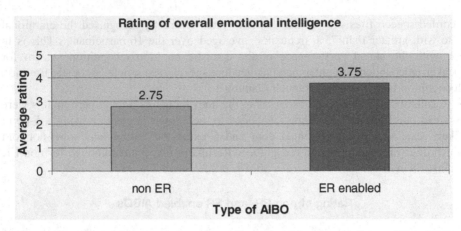

Fig. 4. Comparison of average rating of overall emotional intelligence for non ER, and ER

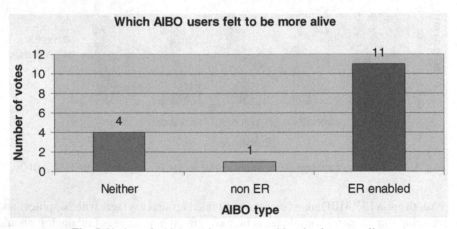

Fig. 5. Voting of which version users considered to be more alive

The results show that although the participants did not significantly rate the ER AIBO responses for each emotion, they could easily recognise which of the two AIBOs was more emotionally-intelligent and more 'alive', Fig. 5. Comments from participants echoed the statistical results with one participant saying about the ER enabled AIBO 'better responses, seemed to respond accurately to what I said', and another participant said 'able to react how a real dog would and convey such things as empathy when needed'.

Participants were asked about their feelings towards interacting with robots able to detect and act upon human emotion. Most participants were enthusiastic about the future of emotionally-intelligent robotics, indicating that users can see the benefits of affective computing for practical applications, Fig. 6. However the technology requires further refining before it will be widely adopted.

When asked whether the ER enabled AIBO is a substitute for a real dog, 60% of participants responded that it could not. Many comments related to the mechanical aesthetics and feel which prevented full emotional engagement between the owner

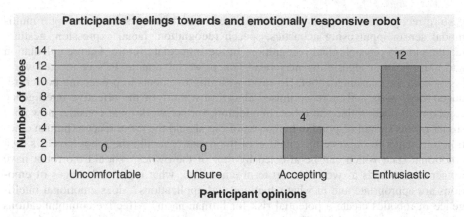

Fig. 6. Participants' feelings towards robots able to detect and act upon human emotion

and AIBO rather than the ER technology and intelligence itself. Encouragingly 40% of participants believe the ER enabled AIBO could provide significant emotional engagement. In particular, participants considered the use of the ER AIBO with patients in hospital settings where real pets would not be allowed. Additionally, the ER AIBO could be used to help develop social and emotional interaction skills for children or given to children with allergies.

7 Conclusion

The research considers the integration of acoustic emotion recognition technologies into a consumer robot (AIBO) and evaluates the impact on the human-robotic interaction and relationship. By comparing two AIBO configurations (one with random responses to human emotion, the other with automatic emotion recognition triggering responses), we have been able to show that users can recognise which of the two robots is more emotionally intelligent. The addition of emotion recognition capabilities to the robotic dog provides an intuitive and natural interaction mechanism. Participants were able to talk to the ER robotic dog and the dog respond to emotion in their voice. Consumer robotics of today offer considerable technology capabilities (such as videocam, reading websites, reading RSS news feeds and mp3 music playback). However, we believe that consumer robotics should offer more affective interactions rather than technology convergence. In this way robotic dogs can act like real dogs and offer the owner empathy, compassion and companionship.

8 Future Work

The integration and evaluation of affective technologies with consumer level robotics is in its infancy. The Science fiction of today may become the reality of tomorrow, when we will have consumer robots which can recognise human emotion and respond appropriately. Recognising emotion from acoustic cues in speech overcomes limitations in camera resolution and dependencies on lighting required for expression and gesture recognition. However future affective consumer robots should adopt a multi-modal sensor input using acoustics, speech recognition, facial expression, gesture, tactile and bio-physiological recognition. In the immediate future, feature calculation and classification algorithms may reside on powerful remote PCs connected wirelessly with the consumer robot. However with improvements in processing power, reduced CPU costs and more optimised algorithms, more of the affective intelligence can be embedded within the robot. In addition, further work must consider how consumer robots should respond to human emotion: should the robot react to human emotion or attempt to improve the emotion of the owner?, should the robot have it's own emotional state which can be affected by that of the owner?, should the robot have longer-term moods as well as short-term emotions?, what types and ranges of emotions are appropriate and in what situations and applications?, does emotional intelligence in robotics create a potential risk for human harm? Affective communications with consumer robots will offer the missing natural interaction which can make mechanical inanimate robot appear alive.

References

1. Digilog, Voice Analysis Insurance, Banking Fraud Internal Audit,
   http://www.digilog.org/
2. Jones, C.M., Jonsson, I.-M.: Detecting Emotions in Conversations Between Driver and In-car Information Systems. In: Proceedings of the International Conference on Affective Computing and Intelligent Interaction, Beijing, China (2005)
3. MIT Media Lab: Affective Computing Group, http://affect.media.mit.edu/
4. Fernandez, R., Picard, R.W.: Modeling Driver's Speech under Stress. Speech Communication 40, 145–159 (2003)
5. Jones, C.M., Jonsson, I.-M.: Automatic Recognition of Affective Cues in the Speech of Car Drivers to Allow Appropriate Responses. In: Proceedings of OZCHI Canberra, Australia (2005)
6. Kaiser, S., Wehrle, T., Edwards, P.: Multi-Modal Emotion Measurement in an Interactive Computer Game: A Pilot-Study. In: Frijda, N.H. (ed.) Proc Conf International Society of Research on Emotions, pp. 275–279. ISRE Publications, Storrs (1994)
7. Jones, C.M., Sutherland, J.: Creating an Emotionally Reactive Computer Game Responding to Affective Cues in Speech. In: Proceedings of British HCI Group Annual Conference, Edinburgh, UK (2005)
8. LEGO.com Mindstorms, http://mindstorms.lego.com/
9. Official Robosapien site,
   http://www.wowwee.com/robosapien/robo1/robomain.html
10. Sony AIBO Europe, Sony Entertainment,
    http://www.sonydigital-link.com/AIBO/
11. Roux, J.: Pursuit Ability of a Robotic Pet, MSc Dissertation. Heriot-Watt University (2005)
12. Sony Corporation: AIBO SDE Official web site, Open R Development Platform for AIBO robots, http://openr.aibo.com/
13. Carnegie Mellon University: Tekkotsu: Homepage, Open Source Development Environment for Sony's AIBO, http://www.cs.cmu.edu/~tekkotsu/
14. Baillie J-C/ENSTA/URBI/Goasti, S.A.S.: URBI – Universal Real-Time Behavior Interface, Robot Control Using the URBI Scripting Language,
    http://www.urbiforge.com

15. AiboPet: AiboHack Main Page - AiboPet and other 'Pets, Information Regarding Programming in AIBO R-Code Scripting Language Including R-Code Tool YART (Yet Another RCode Tool), http://www.aibohack.com/
16. Friedman, B., Kahn, P.H., Hagman, J.: Hardware Companions?: What On-line AIBO Discussion Forums Reveal About the Human-Robotic Relationship. In: Proc. SIGCHI Conference on Human Factors in Computing Systems, Florida, USA, pp. 273–280 (2003)
17. Kahn, P.H., Friedman, B., Freier, N.G., Perez-Granados, D.R.: Robotic Pets in the Lives of Preschool Children. In: CHI 2004 Extended Abstracts on Human Factors in Computing Systems, Vienna, Austria, pp. 1449–1452 (2004)
18. Kahn, P.H., Friedman, B., Melson, G.F., Beck, A.M., Roberts, T., Garrett, E.: Robots as Dogs?: Children's Interactions with the Robotic Dog AIBO and a Live Australian Shepherd. In: CHI 2005 Extended Abstracts on Human Factors in Computing Systems, pp. 1649–1652 (2005)

In the Moodie: Using 'Affective Widgets' to Help Contact Centre Advisors Fight Stress

Nicola Millard[1] and Linda Hole[2]

[1] British Telecommunications PLC, Adastral Park, Martlesham Heath, Ipswich, UK
nicola.millard@bt.com
[2] Bournemouth University, Wallisdown, Bournemouth, UK
lhole@bournemouth.ac.uk

Abstract. This paper describes an user experience study of a particular 'affective widget' – called a 'moodie'. This onscreen device helps to paint an emotional picture of the day of a contact centre employee. These users undertake work that can be classified as 'emotional labour' [10] – in other words they may have to express emotions whilst on a customer telephone call that they may not necessarily feel, both about the customer and the technology that they are using to mediate the conversation. This often leads to user stress, a poor customer experience and high staff churn. Moodies were designed as part of a prototype interface called a Motivational User Interface (MUI). They were created as a way of expressing and self reporting the emotional responses that users feel throughout the day. These prototype affective widgets were then evaluated by contact centre employees and their managers.

Keywords: Affective computing, emotion, HCI.

1 Emotional Labour and the Challenges of the Contact Centre

Until the new millennium, one of the primary aims of Human-Computer Interaction was the design and implementation of usable systems to support either work-force productivity or leisure choices. Extrinsically motivated, captive users in the workplace [1] needed to be able to work efficiently, effectively and with a certain amount of satisfaction.

One particularly technology-driven job is that of the high volume work in contact centres, where the captive users' time is focused on the number and length of calls they handle. Techno-stress [2] in customer service advisors can result both from using the computer as a work tool and via the automatic call distribution technology (ACD), which allows easy measurement of such things as talk time [3]. At the customer interface, the call management technologies drive their pace of work and monitor and measure their performance. Within the organisation, the database technologies may present either help or hindrance at the system interface. Customer service advisors have been found to experience work overload, insufficient time between calls and computer failures which further add to the workload and long hours in front of a computer screen leading to irritability and eye strain [3]. This can result in a far from positive user (or customer) experience and high levels of employee churn.

This study was part of a wider research study investigating the causes of stress and demotivation in contact centres. It was designed as a user experience study of a customer

C. Peter and R. Beale (Eds.): Affect and Emotion in HCI, LNCS 4868, pp. 186–193, 2008.

service advisors' day and investigated how they could record their 'emotional weather' as the hours ticked past.

2 Introducing the 'Moodie': Methods and Design

Designed as part of an innovative prototype interface to be used by contact centre advisors (called the MUI – see [4, 5, 6, 7]), the 'moodie' was created as a reaction to a difficult customer where advisors are experiencing moments of emotional dissonance [8] after completion of a call.

MUI (and moodie) design was done with an opportunistic sample of customer service advisors as they passed through the contact centre coffee area. Rapid prototyping and continual informal user evaluation was used in conjunction with an observational approach that involved sitting next to advisors and listening to them taking calls. This gave the design team a real insight into the challenges of the advisors' working day.

After initial (politically incorrect) discussions around the use of a gun to shoot customers, the design team and the advisors settled on a more animated way of expressing frustration. The advisor could use the mouse to physically throw the call (represented by a spherical customer capsule) into the on screen waste bin (see figure 1).

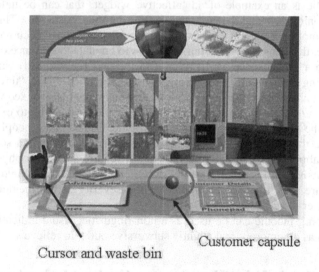

Cursor and waste bin   Customer capsule

Fig. 1. The MUI Desktop

Fig. 2. 'Moodies'

This action releases a 'moodie' (see Figure 2), an animated stick figure that struts up and down the screen with an exaggerated stride and body inclination. This posture is designed to express a certain amount of frustration and personality [9].

Advisors may be feeling 'undesired' emotions that they cannot express to the customer. However, they may feel the need to release these emotions in some way. This was usually observed in the call centre in the form of (unseen) gestures and (unheard) comments to the customer during or after the call.

Frustration and anger can be a vicious circle because advisors have to deal with both the source of their frustration (usually either the customer or feelings of helplessness relating to company process and policy), but also the emotional reaction itself. This is an aversive state that people tend to try and avoid or escape and is positively linked with emotional exhaustion and job dissatisfaction [8].

Klein *et al.* [10] found that allowing systems to actively acknowledge and support user frustration and anger helped the user's ability to manage and recover from negative emotional states. This could be a kind of symbolic game allowing a kind of belated emotional mastery over the event. Reynolds and Picard [11] suggest that "user interface widgets", e.g. a 'frustrometer' or thumbs up/down, can be used to actively express user frustration through direct user manipulation. The computer then needs to respond in a socially appropriate manner [9, 12].

The moodie is an example of an 'affective widget' that can be unleashed by the physical action of throwing the customer capsule into the waste bin. This physical expression of emotion is akin to the kind of reaction that may have occurred in the physical world (i.e. throwing paper in a bin). It seeks to emulate the essence of that physical experience in a virtual space whilst tying it to the task (i.e. the call) via the customer capsule. During evaluation of the prototype, users described this as "throwing the customer in the bin" and described a visceral, feeling of "naughtiness mixed with triumph".

Wensveen *et al.* [13] have supported the use of physical action to express emotion rather than the more common use of physiological data. Since people express and communicate their emotions through behaviour, this behaviour is a source of direct information about the emotions. It also does not require any direct physical intervention or expensive hardware, as with physiological data capture techniques. The disadvantages are that it cannot communicate the severity of the incident and it does require the user to actively apply effort [11].

The resulting moodie can be used as a non-linguistic, visual indication of state of mind as well as a humorous and slightly subversive outlet to relieve stress [14].

3 Fun at Work: Using Humour as a Coping Mechanism

There seems to be very little research on the design of applications to support informal communication or task related "messing around" which is often needed to relieve the pressures of the workplace [15].

Research on humour itself suggests that it can often be the result of opposing (or incongruent) emotions (Joubert's Ambivalence Theory (1980); [16, 17]) or can be used as a release mechanism after a stressful incident (e.g. [18]). Although the popular claim that laughter releases endorphins (e.g. [19]) enjoys no scientific support whatsoever, it has been shown to have a positive effect on the immune system [20].

The ability of humour to build a sense of community in the workplace has also been demonstrated [21, 22]. Understanding humour presupposes a shared context and this shared context can be reinforced within many groups by the use of humour [23]. However, the workplace is different from other places in two ways. There is a task to be done and that task has been assigned to, rather than selected by, those who are undertaking it. Because of the task focus, there is somewhat less tolerance in a work-place for "distractions" like humour. However, Venkatesh notes that the concept of playfulness can be divided into unproductive play (something that is unproductive, pleasant and involving) and playful work (something that is productive, pleasant and involving) [24]. The latter can be used to enhance employees' job experience and, as a result, positively influence the resulting customer experience that they deliver [25].

Braverman claims that humour at work can add to the bottom line [19]. Goodman and Gorkin write that humour can relieve tension, enhance relationships and motivate people [26]. Feigelson claims that employees who have fun at work are less likely to be late or absent and job turnover improves while motivation and productivity climb [27].

Morkes, Kernal and Nass found that humour, where used appropriately on an inter-face, did not result in task distraction and could add to likeability and acceptance [28]. However, Reeves and Nass warn against adding additional cognitive load to the advisor by drawing attention to an animation and taking concentration from the task at hand [9]. Moodies can, therefore, be deleted, shared or stored by the advisors at any point.

One point of discussion about the moodie is around how long it remains effective. There are opposing views about the effect of novelty on humour. On one hand, Des-cartes' theory of surprise in humour would posit that multiple uses of the moodie would mean that its novelty would soon wear off [29]. However, whilst surprise is a ubiquitous quality in jokes (especially in the punch line of a joke) it does not seem essential, based around the enduring quality of comedy routines [30]. Assuming the former is true, the moodie may need to incorporate some element of unpredictability, e.g. not always having a stick man as a response to throwing the call into the bin.

4 Unleashing a 'Moodie': Emotional Self-report

Moodies can also be used to paint a picture of an advisor's day. Macdonald and Sir-ianni point out that the advisor's daily work experience is "often one of a series of minor complaints assuming major proportions for the customer" [31]. Suppression of these feelings can then cause stress problems for the advisor [10]. If the advisor has had a tough day, they can choose to send moodies to their buddies or to their man-ager. This is a similar device to the 'affective awareness GUI widgets' that have been used by Garcia et al. to support emotional awareness in computer supported collabo-rative work [32].

Self-disclosure and privacy could also be an issue here [33]. This is especially since stress at work is still somewhat stigmatised. To facilitate this, the advisor is in control of who sees the moodie. They can choose to reveal their emotional state to their buddies or to their manager. This allows users to control what sort of emotional data is collected on them rather than invading their privacy [11] and prevents emo-tional data from becoming another element of call centre monitoring. They are also only likely to use this as a channel of communication where they perceive there to be a benefit to them [12]. Earley found that the greater extent that the employee has control over the type of performance data collected and presented, the greater the impact on employee motivation and performance [34].

In terms of this form of emotional self-report, there is an argument that self-rating of stress is too subjective to be of use and that self-ratings can be over inflated and inaccurate, particularly via electronic communication [35]. The biggest problem is associated with the basic nature of the question (i.e. "how do I feel?") and the vagaries of self-insight.

Extreme and moderacy response styles describe a respondent's possible tendency to consistently respond at the extremes of the scale. Culture, education and age can also exert an influence on this response bias. Another distortion is response sets, i.e. a conscious or unconscious attempt on the part of the respondent to create a certain socially desirable impression [36]. In some circumstances, respondents may be tempted to give the socially desirable response rather than describe what they actually think, believe or do. A distinction can be made between social desirable responding being either a function of attempting to present oneself in a favourable light to others (impression management) and/or a self-esteem preservation function (self-deception or ego defense [37]). Fundamental to this is the assumption that the management culture of the call centre is not one of fear since, as Pfeffer and Sutton say, "fear causes people to cheat, conceal the truth, focus on the short term and focus on the individual" [38]. This would not be conducive to moodie usage.

Self-report tools may provide users with the means to say how they are feeling, but the onus lies with the advisor to both label and disclose the emotion. A large body of research has detected significant direct and indirect effects of Negative Affectivity (NA: [39]) on job stress and stress related coping mechanisms. It is a logical extrapolation that those people with high NA rating would be prone to report their current emotional state in a more negative manner. This suggests that if traditional self-report measures were used it may be prudent to determine an individual's 'base-line' NA and determine the current emotional state as a deviation from that base. Conversely, the issue is circumvented if the assessment method is objective in the sense that there is no readily discernable connection between the items or input with the emotions being measured.

This is why the data needs to be interpreted by a team manager who knows the individual and can use the emotional information in constructive ways. Rather than just using call handling statistics that may not paint a true picture of the advisors' day, this provides an "information enriched environment" [40] allowing the use of job and social resources to manage job demands and reduce stress.

5   Moodie Alternatives: The 'Splatty'

As part of the original MUI prototype, the moodie was a way to make advisor stress more transparent to both themselves and their peers and managers. One of the intentions for the prototype was to simply highlight the importance of emotional wellbeing and motivation in the contact centre environment. It succeeded in this task and subsequent incarnations of MUIs have investigated other ways of using the user inter-face to express stress and emotion.

In an attempt to recreate the popularity of the moodie design amongst users, other emotional widgets were prototyped in these new MUI designs. One such device was a 'splatty' - a pump action 'splat gun' (see figure 3). This involved using the mouse as a frustration release device to shoot paint balls at the screen. Again, the option was given to send these splats to colleagues or managers, who could, if necessary, provide support, sympathy or advice.

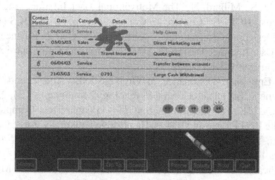

Fig. 3. The 'Splatty'

However, users seemed to find this less of an emotional release than the moodie. The manager's feedback mechanism was received well, with the proviso that "man-agement don't use it to penalise me for getting stressed". In terms of the splat gun, the users liked the emotional release of shooting the paint. However, they felt somewhat disconnected with what they were shooting at. One explanation for this was that users found it easier to anthropomorphise the moodie and empathise with it [41].

6 Results and Ways Forward

The moodie, and the MUI as a whole, resulted in many user experience studies inves-tigating the emotional behaviour and wellbeing of customer service advisors. Al-though the moodie has yet to be incorporated into an operational contact centre interface, it has raised the issue of emotional labour and coping mechanisms for con-tact centre advisors with both the designers of contact centre systems and also the managers of contact centre operations. The concept is being taken forward into fur-ther research into contact centre emotion and fun at work.

References

1. Adams, D., Nelson, P., Todd, P.: Perceived usefulness, ease of use, and usage of information technology: a replication. MIS Quarterly, 227–247 (June 1992)
2. Gignac, A., Appelbaum, S.: The impact of stress on customer service representatives: a com-parative study. Journal of Workplace Learning 9(1), 20–33 (1997)

3. Feinberg, R., Kim, I., Hokama, L., De Ruyter, K., Keen, C.: Operational determinants of call satisfaction in the call center. International Journal of Service Industry Management 11(2), 131–141 (2000)

4. Millard, N., Hole, L., Crowle, S.: From Command to Control: Interface Design for Customer Handling Systems. In: Howard, S., Hammond, J., Lindgaard, G. (eds.) Human-Computer Interaction: INTERACT 1997, pp. 294–300. Chapman & Hall/ IFIP (1997)

5. Millard, N., Hole, L., Crowle, S.: Smiling Through: Motivation At The User Interface. In: Bullinger, H., Ziegler, J. (eds.) Human-Computer Interaction: Ergonomics and User Interfaces, pp. 824–828. LEA, London (1999)

6. Hole, L., Crowle, S., Millard, N.: The Motivational User Interface. In: May, J., Siddiqi, J., Wilkinson, J. (eds.) HCI 1998 Conference Companion, pp. 68–69. BCS (1998)

7. Millard, N.J.: Designing Motivational User Interfaces: Can A Balance Between Effective And Affective User Interface Design Be Used To Motivate Call Centre Advisors? PhD Thesis, Lancaster University, UK (2005)

8. Abraham, R.: Emotional Dissonance in Organisations: Antecedents, Consequences and Moderators. Genetic, Social and General Psychology Monographs 124, 229–246 (1998)

9. Reeves, B., Nass, C.I.: The Media Equation: How People Treat Computers, Television and New Media Like Real People and Places. Cambridge University Press, Cambridge (1996)

10. Klein, J., Moon, Y., Picard, R.W.: This Computer Responds to User Frustration. Interacting with Computers 14, 119–140 (2002)

11. Reynolds, C., Picard, R.W.: Designing for Affective Interactions. MIT Media Lab (2001)

12. Picard, R.W., Klein, J.: Computers that Recognise and Respond to User Emotion: Theoretical and Practical Implications. MIT Media Lab Tech Report No 538 (2001)

13. Wensveen, S., Overbeeke, K., Djajadiningrat, T.: Touch Me, Hit Me and I Know How You Feel: A Design Approach to Emotionally Rich Interaction. ID Studio Lab, Delft University of Technology, Netherlands (2000)

14. Taylor, P., Bain, P.: Subterranean Worksick Blues: Humour as Subversion in Two Call Centres. Organization Studies (November 2003)

15. Abramis, D.J.: Play at Work: Childish Hedonism or Adult Enthusiam? American Behavioural Scientist 33(3), 353–373 (1990)

16. Koestler, A.: The Act of Creation: A Study of the Conscious and Unconscious Processes of Humour. Scientific Discovery and Art. Hutchison Press, London (1964)

17. Minsky, M.: Jokes and their Relation to the Cognitive Unconscious. In: Vaina, L., Hintikka, J. (eds.) Cognitive Constraints on Communication: Representations and Processes, Reidel, Hingham (1984)

18. Spencer, H.: The Physiology of Laughter. Macmillan's Magazine 1, 395–402 (1860)

19. Braverman, T.: Enhance Your Sense of Self Mirth: Fun in the Workplace: Philosophies Keep Firms Laughing All the Way to the Bank. Training and Development 47(7), 9–11 (1993)

20. Burns, C.A.: Comparative Analysis of Humour Versus Relaxation Training for the Enhancement of Immunocompetence. Dissertation Abstracts International 57(08-B), 5319 (1996)

21. Hayworth, D.: The Social Origin and Function of Laughter. Psychological Review 35, 367–385 (1928)

22. Meyer, J.C.: Humour in Member Narratives: Uniting and Dividing at Work. Western Journal of Communication 61, 188–208 (1997)

23. Zilberg, N.: In-group Humour of Immigrants from the Former Soviet Union to Israel. Israel Social Science Research 10(1), 1–22 (1995)

24. Venkatesh, V.: Creation of Favorable User Perceptions: Exploring the Role of Intrinsic Motivation. MIS Quarterly 23(2), 239–260 (1999)

25. Heskett, J.L., Sasser, W.E., Schlesinger, J.L.: The Value Profit Chain: Treat Employees Like Customers and Customers Like Employees. Free Press (2003)
26. Goodman, J.B.: Laughing matters: Taking your job seriously and yourself lightly. Journal of the American Medical Association 13, 267 (1992)
27. Feigelson, S.: Energize Your Meetings With Laughter. Association for Supervision and Curriculum Development (1998)
28. Morkes, J., Kernal, H., Nass, C.: Effects of Humour in Computer-Mediated Communication and Human-Computer Interaction. In: Proceedings of the Conference of Human Factors in Computer Systems (CHI 1998). ACM Press, Los Angeles (1998)
29. Descartes, R.: Les Passions de L'Ame, Paris (1649)
30. van Thriel, C., Ruch, W.: The Role of Surprise in Humour Appreciation. In: Eleventh International Conference on Humour, Grand-Duche de Luxembourg (September 1993)
31. Macdonald, C.L., Sirianni, C.: Working in the Service Society. Temple University Press, Philadephia (1996)
32. Garcia, O., Favela, J., Licea, G., Machorro, R.: Extending a Collaborative Architecture to Support Emotional Awareness. CICESE, Mexico (1999)
33. Howard, S., Vetere, F., Gibbs, M., Kjeldskov, J., Pedell, S., Mecoles, K., Bunyan, M., Murphy, J.: Mediating Intimacy: Digital Kisses and Cut and Paste Hugs. In: Proceedings of HCI 2004: Design for Life, 2, Leeds. British Computer Society (2004)
34. Earley, P.C.: Computer Generated Performance Feedback in the Magazine Subscription Industry. Organisational Behaviour and Human Decision Processes 41, 50–64 (1988)
35. Weisband, S., Atwater, L.: Evaluating Self and Others in Electronic and Face-to-face Groups. Journal of Applied Psychology 84, 632–639 (1999)
36. Knapp, H., Kirk, S.: Using pencil and paper, Internet and touch-tone phones for self-administered surveys: does methodology matter? Computers in Human Behaviour 19, 117–134 (2003)
37. Fox, S., Schwartz, D.: Social desirability and controllability in computerized and paper-and-pencil personality questionnaires. Computers in Human Behaviour 18, 389–410 (2002)
38. Pfeffer, J., Sutton, R.: The Knowing-Doing Gap. Harvard Business School Press (November 1999)
39. Watson, D., Clark, L.: Negative Affectivity: The disposition to experience unpleasant emotional states. Psychological Bulletin 95, 465–490 (1984)
40. Amick, B.C., Smith, M.J.: Stress, Computer Based Work Monitoring and Measurement Systems: A Conceptual Overview. Applied Ergonomics 23, 6–16 (1992)
41. Nowak, K.L., Biocca, F.: The Effect of the Agency and Anthropomorphism on Users' Sense of Telepresence and Social Presence in Virtual Environments. Presence: Teleoperators and Virtual Environments 12(5) (2003)

Feasibility of Personalized Affective Video Summaries

Arthur G. Money and Harry Agius

Brunel University, School of Information Systems, Computing and Mathematics,
St John's, Uxbridge, Middlesex, UB8 3PH, UK
arthurmoney@yahoo.com, harryagius@acm.org

Abstract. Video summaries present the content of a video stream concisely while trying to preserve its original, essential message. By means of a feasibility study, this article investigates whether users' physiological responses to video content can adequately serve as a basis for the creation of affective video summaries that are personalized for an individual user.

Keywords: Video summaries, multimedia, affect, emotion, physiological responses, personalization.

1 Introduction

Video summaries are sequences of still or moving images, optionally with accompanying audio, which present the content of a video stream in such a way that the respective target user group is rapidly provided with concise information about the content, while the essential message of the original stream is preserved [1]. The demand for video summaries originates primarily from users' viewing time constraints [2], typically when users need to assess a set of candidate video streams, e.g. when presented with a set of search results. Video streams often have a lengthy duration; hence there is a need to reduce user effort by providing a concise version of each stream. Traditionally, video summaries are produced by analyzing the underlying semantic content of the original video stream to determine what segments of the stream should be included and excluded in the summary; however, recent approaches have sought to look outside of the video stream, particularly to context and user as potential sources for determining content significance. Video frequently invokes certain emotions, attitudes or moods in the viewer and such responses are likely to be heightened in proportion to the significance of the content to the viewer at the time. Consequently, if these responses could be captured and analyzed sufficiently, could they be used to form the basis of a video summarization technique that personalized the video summary for an individual user? To answer this question, we have undertaken a feasibility study that collected and analyzed data representing a user's physiological responses to video content. The organization of this article is as follows. Section 2 provides an overview of video summarization techniques. Section 3 discusses the relevance of affective data for video summarization. Sections 4–6 present the design, analysis method and results of the feasibility study. Section 7 discusses the research implications. Section 8 makes some concluding remarks.

C. Peter and R. Beale (Eds.): Affect and Emotion in HCI, LNCS 4868, pp. 194–208, 2008.

2 Creating Video Summaries

Previously [3], we have surveyed video summarization research and identified three types of techniques that can be used to generate video summaries (see Fig. 1). *Internal video summarization techniques* identify video segments for inclusion in the summary by analyzing information internal to the video stream; that is, low-level *image* (e.g. colour, texture, object motion), *audio* (e.g. speech, crowd noise, background noise), and *text* (e.g. subtitles, captions) features, using conventional computer vision techniques [4-6]. After analysis, internal information is associated with the video content to produce the video summary. For example, Shao et al. [7] summarize music videos automatically by using music features, an adaptive clustering algorithm and music domain knowledge to analyze content in the music track, while detecting and clustering shots in the video track. In contrast, motion activity, cut density and sound energy have been used to produce content-based excitement curves [8] and affect curves that probabilistically infer how the user's affective state might be changed by the video content [9].

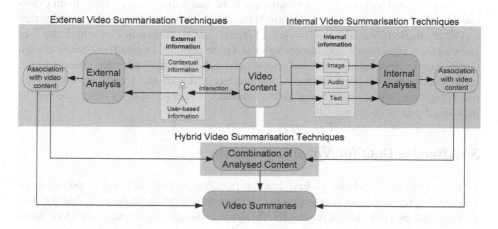

Fig. 1. Internal, external and hybrid video summarization techniques

External video summarization techniques use information external to the video stream for the creation of the video summary in the form of *contextual information*, e.g. time and location of a video's recording and user interactions and movements [10], and/or *user-based information*, e.g. user descriptions of content and user browsing and viewing activity. For instance, Jaimes et al. [11] employ a high-level semantic analysis of basic manual annotations created by users, in conjunction with a supervised learning algorithm that determines a user's preference for particular content events based on their prior expressions of importance. Takahashi et al. [12] also use manual annotations to generate summaries of baseball videos, which include player information, key event information, e.g. 'plays of the ball', and information about the extent to which the user enjoyed specific events. Annotations are linked temporally to the original video to indicate significant events and individual players.

Hybrid video summarization techniques use a combination of internal and external summarization techniques. For example, external techniques can compliment internal techniques by providing additional levels of detail to reduce semantic ambiguity. In one hybrid approach [13], a worn video camera captures video content, while contextual information such as location, speed and acceleration is captured from worn GPS receivers and daily weather and news information is provided via wireless Internet access. Spoken voice annotations and SMS textual annotations can be provided by the user to tag key events. A conversation scene detection algorithm carries out low-level analysis on the video's audio track to identify interesting segments within the captured video content for inclusion in the summary. In contrast, Rui et al. [14] automatically produce video summaries by using a training set of manually annotated videos which are then propagated to unannotated video content through similarity matching of internal information. Likewise, Zimmerman et al. [15] produce video summaries by initially analyzing internal information through shot and scene segmentation applied to news video content. Contextual information about the video content is then sourced from the Web, while user-based information is provided by user profiles and zip codes (providing geographical relevance for the user).

While internal summarization techniques have had some success, their main drawback is in overcoming the *semantic gap* [16], which is the gap between semantics that can be abstracted by analyzing low-level features and the semantics by which the user associates, comprehends and remembers the video content. In addition, because such techniques exclude contextual and user-based information, internally-created video summaries cannot be personalized. Consequently, external and hybrid techniques are receiving more attention as being able to produce video summaries more relevant to individual users.

3 Affective Data for Video Summaries

Advances in sensor technology have made it possible for physiological responses to be measured in real time, without requiring any conscious input from the user, and are well documented as providing a means for measuring changes in a user's *affective state*, which is the user's underlying emotion, attitude or mood at a given point in time [17]. Affective state is made up of: *valence*, the level of attraction or aversion the user feels toward a specific stimulus, and *arousal*, the intensity to which an emotion elicited by a specific stimulus is felt. Several physiological responses have been used to infer a user's affective state. *Electro-dermal response (EDR)* and *respiration rate (RR)* have been used as indicators of arousal [18], while *blood volume pulse (BVP)* and *heart rate (HR)* can serve as measures of valence [19, 20]. *Respiration amplitude (RA)* can indicate both arousal and valence levels [21].

It is becoming increasingly viable for users' physiological responses to be sourced by means of wireless wearable sensors such as the SenseWear armband from Body-Media. Furthermore, video content is known to elicit the above physiological responses in the user [22-24]. As a result, some multimedia metadata standards now allow for some limited affective description [25, 26] and, as was seen in Section 2, some internal video summarization techniques have been developed that summarize video streams based on their affective content. However, to the best of our knowledge, no research work has been undertaken to produce affective video summaries from sources external to the video stream; namely from users' physiological responses.

Consequently, we consider if users' physiological responses may serve as a suitable external source of information for producing individually-personalized affective video summaries (via an external or hybrid technique). User responses are likely to be most significant during the segments of a video stream that have most relevance to that user, since these will tend to be the segments that have the most impact and are the most memorable; hence, it is these segments that are the foremost candidates for inclusion within a summarized version of the video stream.

Fig. 2 shows how physiological responses may be used to achieve personalized affective video summaries. Initially, the user views the full video stream while physiological responses are captured and measured and the most significant responses identified. After viewing the video content, the temporal locations of these significant video segments are then associated with the viewed video content and the video summary is created. The result is personalized affective video summaries; that is, video summaries that incorporate the video segments that elicited the most significant physiological responses in the user during viewing. This approach is specifically formulated to be applicable within the context of real-time viewing of video content, where analysis of user physiological responses is taken to directly reflect the user's personal experience of the video content at the time of viewing. When considering one individual user viewing the same video content on more than one occasion, it is likely that their physiological responses to the same content may be different on each viewing occasion and this would be reflected in any further video summaries produced. Therefore, considerations of a user's overall mood and long-term affective state at the time of viewing are inherently taken into account as they are reflected in the user's physiological responses to the video content at the time of viewing, and thus the video content selected for inclusion in a video summary also reflects this. Since users generally recall video content based on their overall mood and long-term affective state at the time of viewing video content, this approach is naturally in-step with a user's holistic experience of the video content.

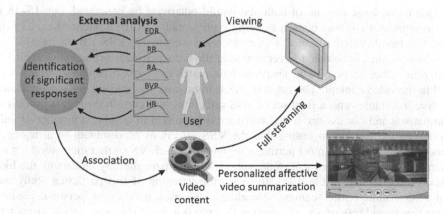

Fig. 2. Utilization of a user's affective data for personalized video summaries

4 Experiment Design

To investigate the use of physiological response data for determining candidate video segments for inclusion in a video summary, we undertook a feasibility study in the form of a laboratory experiment with ten users (6 males, 4 females). All users reported good eyesight and hearing, were non-smokers, and considered themselves to be experienced viewers of film and TV. To ensure a wide range of video content was utilized, popular films and TV shows were chosen from five different genres: action/sci-fi, horror/thriller, comedy, drama/action, and drama/comedy. This was desirable since it was possible that specific video genres would not be suited to eliciting physiological responses in the user sufficiently for discerning candidate video segments for inclusion in a video summary. This could not be known in advance and, consequently, the use of a range of genres provided the potential for gaining some indicative understanding. To this end, three films were chosen from the IMDb Top 250 Films together with two award-winning TV shows (see Table 1).

Table 1. Video content used in the feasibility study

VS	Title	Genre	Dur.	VSS1	VSS2	VSS3
1	The Matrix	Action/ Sci-fi	15:33	Building 06:12-06:42	Bug in 10:53-11:23	Bug out 14:20-14:35
2	The Exorcist	Horror/ Thriller	18:06	Hospital 07:44-08:14	Bedroom 10:20-10:50	Stairs 17:25-17:40
3	Only Fools and Horses (5×04)	Comedy	15:15	Sunbed 03:30-03:45	Dinner 03:57-04:27	Hang gliding 13:58-14:13
4	Lost (1×08)	Drama/ Action	15:06	Peanuts 03:10-03:40	Torture 06:50-07:20	Kissing 11:10-11:40
5	Lost in Translation	Drama/ Comedy	16:02	First meet 01:20-01:50	Restaurant 08:03-08:33	BB gun 14:48-15:18

Due to the large amount of data that would otherwise be generated, one 15–18 m video segment (VS) was chosen as being representative of the content of each of the five full length video streams. Three video sub-segments (VSSs) from each of the VSs were manually selected as representing the most pertinent segments of each VS, and were either 15 or 30 s in length to best match the most pertinent content found within the video content. The manual selection process was carried out independently by five individuals and a final set of VSS selections was chosen through a process of comparison and discussion. It was considered important to involve a number of individuals in the process to ensure that the VSS selections represented, to a degree, a generalized view of the most pertinent segments of each VS so that they stood a good chance of also being pertinent to the subjects taking part, thereby increasing the likelihood of obtaining usable data. However, the intention of this particular study was not to determine if the segments correlated with each user's own personal choices, since that would rely on the assumption that physiological responses could already be used to determine the significance of segments, for which there is no precedence in the research literature. The focus of this study was instead on whether physiological responses may be suitable for video summarization at all, that is, whether they are even sensitive enough to distinguish between video segments, so that this could be established as a valid assumption for future research.

To control for order effects, VSs were allocated randomly to each user in a way that ensured each of the five VSs had a reasonable number of viewings once all ten experimental sessions had been completed, i.e. a minimum of five and maximum of six viewings per VSS. Thus, each user viewed three of the five VSs in their entirety. Each VS was preceded by a 4 m interval during which relaxing music was played to control for the possible effects of pre-experimental nerves and previously viewed video content. Users were given 40 s to read a textual synopsis of the story so far before the VS commenced, to ensure understanding of the VS storyline by all.

A video viewing room and observation room were set up (see Fig. 3), separated by a one-way mirror which allowed unobtrusive observation of the user during the session. All VSs were played back via a laptop connected to a projector which displayed the image on a 42" screen. Clear viewing was ensured by switching off all lights, with the exception of a small, low-intensity lamp near the user, which provided sufficient illumination for observation throughout the session.

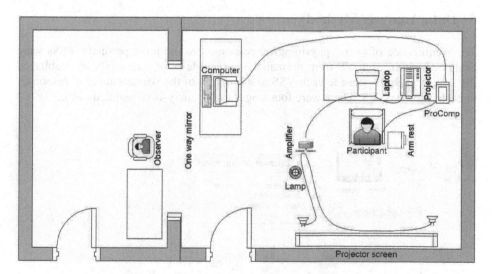

Fig. 3. Layout of the experiment rooms

Physiological data were captured using the ProComp Infiniti system and BioGraph Infiniti software from Thought Technology. Users' BVP and HR were recorded by measuring levels of light absorption of blood through capillary beds in the finger, using the HR/BVP-Flex/Pro sensor (SA9308M) connected to the peripheral phalanx of the middle finger. EDR was measured with the SC-Flex/Pro Sensor (SA9309M) connected to the middle phalanxes of the index and ring fingers. The sensor passes a small electrical charge between electrodes, measuring the level of electrical conductivity in the skin. RR and RA was measured with the Resp-Flex/Pro Sensor (SA9311M) which is an elasticized band connected around the thorax. The band expands and contracts as the user breathes in and out. Physiological measures were captured at the standard sampling rates for each sensor, which was 256 Hz for EDR and 2048 Hz for the respiration and BVP/HR sensors. Fig. 4 shows how the respective sensors were attached to the user.

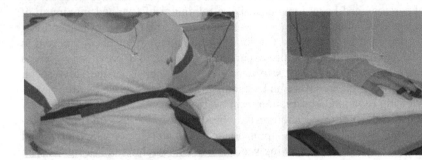

Fig. 4. Respiration sensor (left), BVP/HR and EDR sensors (right)

5   Data Analysis Method

The significance of users' physiological responses to the most pertinent VSSs were evaluated within each VS from normalized percentile rank values. These established the rank of each response to each VSS as a function of the whole sample of responses to each respective VS. There were four stages to the analysis (illustrated in Fig. 5):

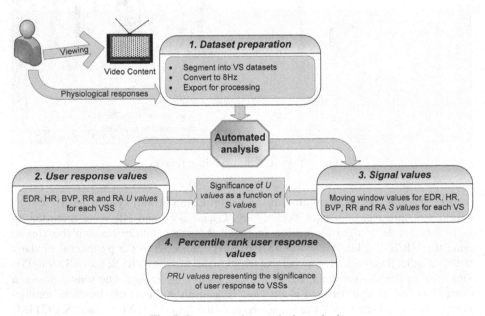

Fig. 5. Four-stage data analysis method

1. *Dataset preparation:* Each set of experiment session data was temporally segmented into VS datasets using the 'set event marker' option within the BioGraph Infiniti application, so that each user's viewing of each VS was represented by a physiological response dataset. These were then interpolated and converted into an 8Hz format to reduce processing overhead, and exported in CSV format to allow for analysis outside of the Infiniti application. At the considerably reduced 8Hz sampling rate, each physiological response measure produced a substantial amount of data. For example, a 15 m experimental session would produce 7,200 observations per physiological measure; therefore with five physiological measures a total of 36,000 observations per 15 m session were collected. Given the significant number of observations, it was necessary to automate the analysis process as much as possible. In this instance, customized scripts were developed to carry out the remaining stages.

2. *User response values:* For each VSS within each VS, the user's average responses for HR, BVP, RA and RR were calculated. This was achieved by calculating, for each respective physiological response measure, the average of all observations corresponding with the temporal location of each respective VSS. The VSS temporal locations were also used for EDR; however, the signal was detrended using an approach similar to that of van Reekum et al. [27]. The reading at the start of the time period was subtracted from the highest value within the time period, which then represented the maximum level of deflection the stimuli elicited within the specified time period. This constitutes a method for evaluating local fluctuations in the EDR signal regardless of unpredictable baseline variations. The output of this stage was a set of user response values (*U values*).

3. *Signal values:* 15 and 30 s moving average windows for HR, BVP, RA and RR and detrended moving time windows for EDR were then constructed. This was achieved in a similar fashion to Stage 2, but applied to all observations of each individual physiological measure within the dataset. The output of this procedure produces additional signal values (*S values*) for each user's physiological response measure for each VS dataset, which serve as a baseline from which the significance of user responses to individual VSSs could be calculated.

4. *Percentile rank user response values:* Percentile rank U values (*PRU values*) were then derived by calculating percentile rank values for the corresponding U values as a function of the constructed S values. Therefore, S values served as the population against which U values could be ranked, thereby facilitating the calculation of the significance of user responses to respective VSSs as a function of the users' overall responses to respective VSs.

While any proportion of the sample could be used, for the purposes of this study, we used 30% of the sample since this was found to provide a range of responses sufficient for discerning significant candidate video segments. Thus, we considered significant responses to VSSs as those equal to or greater than the 85th percentile or equal to or less than the 15th percentile for RA, RR, BVP and HR, and those equal to or greater than the 70th percentile for EDR. This reflects the fact that EDR percentile rank values represent the level of positive deflection of the signal, and hence values less than or equal to the 15th percentile do not necessarily represent significant responses, but rather reflect little or no significant response.

6 Results

This section presents the individual and aggregate results of applying the data analysis method from the previous section to the subject data. At an individual user level, physiological responses to VSSs varied widely. For example, VS1:VSS3 (action/sci-fi content) elicited significant RA, BVP and HR responses in User #2, but only elicited a significant HR response in User #6. Similarly, VS2:VSS1 (horror/thriller content) elicited significant EDR, RR and HR responses in User #4 and significant EDR and RA responses in Users #2 and #10, but elicited no significant responses in Users #5 and #9. VS3:VSS1 (comedy content) elicited no significant responses in User #1, but elicited significant EDR, RA, RR and BVP responses in User #10. VS4:VSS2 (drama/action content) elicited a significant EDR response only in User #7, but elicited significant EDR, RA, RR and HR responses in User #2 and significant EDR, RA and RR responses in Users #4 and #9. VS5:VSS1 (drama/comedy content) elicited significant EDR and RR responses in User #8, but did not elicit any significant responses in Users #9 and #10. Given this wide range of responses, we now review in more detail the VSS from each content genre that has the highest overall percentage of significant responses:

- *Action/sci-fi (VS1:VSS1):* All VSSs in *The Matrix* elicited similar overall percentages of significant response (36%), thus VSS1 is selected for review here. EDR produced the most marked response, which was significant in all five users. Four responses were well in excess of 0.85, the lowest of which was 0.801 and the remaining four were 0.958 and above. RA was not significant for any of the users, while RR was significant for two of the five users. User #1 took significantly less breaths during this VSS with 0.104. The other user, #7, took significantly more breaths in this period with a PRU response value of 0.939. BVP was significant for one out of five cases, with a reading of 0.990, which indicates very significant increased blood volume to the body's peripherals. HR was only significant for one user with a response of 0.915. However, all five users appeared to have raised HR in this VSS.
- *Horror/thriller (VS2:VSS2):* EDR was significantly raised for four of the five users. User #10 had the highest significant rise in EDR with a value of 0.991. RA was reduced in all five cases; however, User #2 was the only significant RR response with a value of 0.004, indicating that they took significantly faster breaths during this VSS. RR was significantly high in two of the five cases: User #2 increased RR by 0.876 percent rank significance and User #9 by 0.860. BVP was significant in four of the five cases. The general trend was a reduced BVP, with three of the four significant cases showing lowered BVP, indicating a constriction of blood to the peripherals. Interestingly, User #4 experienced significantly increased blood flow to the peripherals with a percent rank of 0.884. Users #5 and #9 showed significant increases in HR with 0.929 and 0.940 respectively. 52% of all the physiological responses elicited by this VSS were found to be significant. This was the third highest percentage of all VSSs evaluated in the experiment.
- *Comedy (VS3:VSS3):* Although VSS3 elicited several significant responses, no EDR values were significant. User #3 took significantly shorter breaths during this VSS with a PRU value of 0.099. User #6 showed the most significant increase in

RA with a value of 0.943 and User #8 showed the next most significant value of 0.932. RR was varied with three significant response values, two showing significantly faster breaths: User #3 had the highest significance with a value of 0.949, User #1 had the next highest value with 0.911, and User #6 took significantly slower breaths during this VSS with a value of 0.120. BVP tended to be significantly reduced with four of the six users experiencing significantly constricted blood volume in their peripherals. User #3 showed the most significant constriction with a value of 0.035. HR tended to increase during this VSS with five of the six users showing some increase in HR. User #8 showed the most significant increase with 0.991. User #10 was the only user to show a significantly reduced HR with a value of 0.091. A total of 53.34% of all the physiological responses elicited by this VSS were found to be significant. This was the second highest proportion of significant responses of all VSSs evaluated in this experiment.

− *Drama/action (VS4:VSS2):* All six users experienced significantly raised EDR. User #9 had the lowest significant response with a value of 0.848, and the highest response was elicited in User #2 with a response value of 0.999. RA increased for four of the six users, of which User #9 showed the most significant increase with 0.899. User #2 appeared to take shorter breaths with a significant response in the lower 50th percentile of 0.035. Users #9 and #4 showed a marked decrease in RR with response values of 0.40 and 0.122 respectively. User #2 showed a marked increase in RR with a value of 0.993. BVP was not significant for any user, while HR was significant for three users; User #6 had the most significant increase in HR with 0.984 and User #8 had the most significant decrease in HR with 0.056.

− *Drama/comedy (VS5:VSS3):* EDR was significantly elevated for four of the six users. User #8 had the most significant response with 0.931 and User #10 was next with 0.871. RA was lowered for four of the six users, three of which experienced significantly lowered amplitude. User #8's breaths were most significantly reduced with a value of 0.102. RR was elevated in four of the six cases, but none were significant rises. User #4 had the only significant response indicating reduced RR at 0.15. Four of the six responses for BVP were in the lower 50th percentile, two of which were significant reductions in peripheral blood volume: these were User #10 with 0.125 and User #8 with 0.133. User #5 responded with increased blood volume to the peripherals with a value of 0.923. HR was in the lower 50th percentile for five of the six cases, four of which were significantly low. User #10 was the lowest of these with 0.043.

From the above, it seems that user physiological responses to video content varied significantly for individual users and that this may reflect individual user's personal experiences of video content. In turn, this may suggest that physiological responses may serve as a usable source of external (user-based) information and show potential as an aid for personalized affective video summaries.

To examine the overall user physiological responses to the VSSs, EDR, RA, RR, BVP and HR response measures were aggregated for each VSS and compared. To see how each physiological response measure relates to each content genre, the number of significant user response values observed in each of the three VSSs within each content genre were added together and presented as a percentage of significant responses as a function of the total responses observed for each VS. As discussed in Section 4, since this study was concerned with the feasibility of using physiological responses to video content as a means for developing video summaries, the primary purpose of analyzing the data in this way was to establish whether user physiological response measures were sufficiently sensitive, and thus could be deemed significant for, the content of specific VSSs. It is therefore important to note that aggregated response values were not calculated with the primary aim of ascertaining general population trends. Nevertheless, since the VSS selections may be taken to be an approximation of the most pertinent video content, as agreed by the group of five individuals that selected them, the results may provide an approximate indication of whether user physiological responses match pertinent video content.

Our results indicated that, in general, users responded significantly to VSSs, therefore indicating that physiological response measures seem to be sensitive enough to identify significant VSSs based on the user responses. In particular, horror/thriller content seemed to elicit relatively high numbers of significant EDR, RA, RR and BVP responses. Fig. 6 illustrates all physiological responses grouped by video genre. Since significant responses are considered to be those that are in the 15th percentile and below or in the 85th percentile and above for RA, RR, BVP and HR (totalling 30% of the whole sample), and those that are in the 70th percentile and above for EDR (totalling 30% of the sample), the proportion of significant responses that can be expected is at least 30%. In other words, regardless of the elicitation effects of a given VSS, 30% of RA, RR, BVP and HR user responses would be expected to fall either within the 15th percentile or below or within the 85th percentile and above; and likewise 30% of significant responses for EDR would be expected to fall within the 70th percentile and above. Therefore, a higher proportion than 30% of physiological responses falling within these limits indicate that users responded in excess of what would normally be expected, thus indicating that these VSSs elicited higher than normal levels of physiological response in the user. To give an indication of the extent to which the proportion of physiological responses exceeded this 30% limit, Fig. 6 includes a normal response level line.

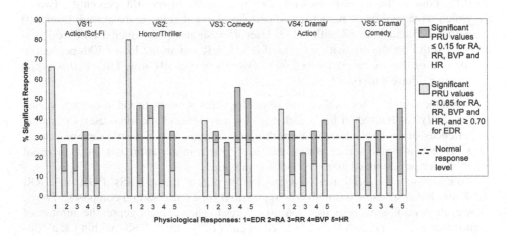

Fig. 6. Significant physiological responses grouped by video genre

The results show that the percentages of significant responses for EDR, RA and RR to horror/thriller content are higher than any other video genre with 80.00%, 46.67% and 46.67% significant responses respectively. A relatively high percentage of significant response (46.67%) was also observed for BVP; this was the second highest percentage observed for this measure. Comedy content elicited a relatively low number of significant EDR and RA responses (only 38.89% and 33.33% of all responses were significant, respectively) and a low proportion of significant RR responses (27.78%, which is below the normal response level). However, comedy did elicit a higher percentage of significant BVP (55.56%) and HR (50.00%) responses than any other genre. In comparison, action/sci-fi and drama/action content elicited generally lower levels of response, with less significant differences being observed between the respective physiological measures. The highest percentage of significant response observed in either of these genres was the EDR response for action/sci-fi with a response of 66.67%, which was the second highest EDR response out of the five genres. Finally, the drama/comedy content elicited the lowest percentage of significant responses overall at 33.33%. However, this video genre elicited the second highest percentage of significant HR response (44.44%) and the second least amount of significant EDR responses (38.89%). Interestingly this indicates that both video genres with a comedy element elicited relatively high levels of significant HR response and relatively low levels of significant EDR response.

From these results, we may therefore reasonably conclude that there is good potential for developing personalized affective video summaries based on user physiological responses to video content for all genres, although certain video genres appear to elicit significant physiological responses more consistently than others, which is discussed in the next section.

7 Implications for Video Summarization

Our findings suggest that new external or hybrid video summarization techniques can be developed by using physiological response data as a user-based source of information for analysis. Physiological response data seems to vary considerably between individual users; hence its unique nature indicates that video summaries based on this data have the potential for being highly personalized.

The fact that external information in the form of physiological responses can be collected automatically, without requiring any conscious input from the user, whilst potentially providing detailed information about the user's personal experience of the content, is of significant benefit since no additional effort is required from the user to collect this information. This is a valuable departure from the majority of current video summarization techniques that achieve personalized summaries through requiring the user to manually input information relating to their experience of video content, which is costly in terms of the time and effort required.

Our research also appears to indicate that certain video genres may elicit significant physiological responses more consistently than others. This would have implications for how physiological responses may be automatically interpreted and video summaries automatically generated. Specifically, the following conclusions can be drawn regarding the nature of user responses to video sub-segments:

- Horror/thriller content tends to elicit substantially higher levels of EDR compared with other content genres.
- User response to horror/thriller content tends to result in constricted BVP flow to the peripherals, as may be expected. This suggests the user is under duress or fearful during the viewing of VSSs of this content genre.
- Horror/thriller content tends to elicit increased respiration rates and decreased respiration amplitudes in VSSs, eliciting significantly different responses to comedy content (which tends to cause increased respiration amplitudes in VSSs).
- Comedy content elicits a comparatively low percentage of EDR responses to pertinent video sub-segments (apparent in both genres containing comedy).
- Comedy content also seem to elicit the most significant BVP and HR responses, both of which seem to be evenly distributed between increased and decreased levels of BVP and HR responses.
- In general, drama/action content elicits physiological responses evenly; that is, no single physiological response seems to stand out as the most appropriate measure for content in these genres.
- Drama/comedy content elicits the lowest amount of significant responses, perhaps reflecting the subtle and slow paced nature of this content. However, VSSs of this content do seem to elicit significant changes in HR and only a small number of significant EDR responses, a pattern paralleled in comedy content.

Since responses appeared to be more consistent in the horror/thriller and comedy genres, this suggests that these genres might lend themselves more easily to automated video summarization. Specific VSSs within the action/sci-fi, drama/action and drama/comedy genres elicited high percentages of significant responses; however the nature of the users' responses was mixed and less consistent resulting in the overall significant response percentages being generally lower and more evenly spread than in the horror/thriller and comedy genres. Automated interpretation of the responses for these genres could therefore prove more difficult.

8 Concluding Remarks

This article has examined whether affective data can be used as a potential information source that is external to the video stream for producing personalized affective video summaries. Through a feasibility study that collected and analyzed data representing a user's physiological responses to video content, it has been shown that physiological responses are potentially a valuable source of external user-based information. Future research will formally develop a framework so that video sub-segments can be identified automatically from physiological response data. In addition, mapping users' physiological response data onto valence and arousal is likely to further assist in identifying candidate video sub-segments for inclusion in the video summary. This will also offer the user the option of viewing video summaries that consist of specific affective qualities, an approach that has already proven useful for music media [28]. In the longer term, further research into other content genres, such as sports, news and reality TV shows, will help develop a robust and in-depth understanding of how users respond to all video content genres.

References

1. Zhu, X., Wu, X., Fan, J., Elmagarmid, A.K., Aref, W.G.: Exploring Video Content Structure for Hierarchical Summarization. Multimedia Systems 10(2), 98–115 (2004)
2. Li, Z., Schuster, G.M., Katsaggelos, A.K.: MINMAX Optimal Video Summarization. IEEE Transactions on Circuits and Systems for Video Technology 15(10), 1245–1256 (2005)
3. Money, A.G., Agius, H.: Video Summarisation: A Conceptual Framework and Survey of the State of the Art. Journal of Visual Communication and Image Representation 19(2), 121–143 (2008)
4. Everingham, M., Sivic, J., Zisserman, A.: Hello! My name is.. Buffy. In: 17th British Machine Vision Conference, vol. III, pp. 899–908 (2006), http://www.macs.hw.ac.uk/bmvc2006/BMVC06%20Proceedings%20III.pdf
5. Sivic, J., Schaffalitzky, F., Zisserman, A.: Object Level Grouping for Video Shots. International Journal of Computer Vision 67(2), 189–210 (2006)
6. Wang, Y., Liu, Z., Huang, J.: Multimedia Content Analysis: Using Both Audio and Visual Clues. IEEE Signal Processing Magazine 17(6), 12–36 (2000)
7. Shao, X., Xu, C., Maddage, N.C., Tian, Q., Kankanhalli, M.S., Jin, J.S.: Automatic Summarization of Music Videos. ACM Transactions on Multimedia Computing, Communications, and Applications 2(2), 127–148 (2006)
8. Hanjalic, A.: Adaptive Extraction of Highlights from a Sport Video Based on Excitement Modeling. IEEE Transactions on Multimedia 7(6), 1114–1122 (2005)
9. Hanjalic, A., Xu, L.: User-Oriented Affective Video Content Analysis. In: IEEE Workshop on Content-Based Access of Image and Video Libraries, pp. 50–57. IEEE Computer Society, Los Alamitos (2001)
10. de Silva, G., Yamasaki, T., Aizawa, K.: Evaluation of Video Summarization for a Large Number of Cameras in Ubiquitous Home. In: 13th Annual ACM International Conference on Multimedia, pp. 820–828. ACM Press, New York (2005)
11. Jaimes, A., Echigo, T., Teraguchi, M., Satoh, F.: Learning Personalized Video Highlights from Detailed MPEG-7 Metadata. In: IEEE International Conference on Image Processing, vol. I, pp. 133–136. IEEE, Piscataway (2002)
12. Takahashi, Y., Nitta, N., Babaguchi, N.: Video Summarization for Large Sports Video Archives. In: IEEE International Conference on Multimedia and Expo., pp. 1170–1173. IEEE, Piscataway (2005)
13. Aizawa, K., Tancharoen, D., Kawasaki, S., Yamasaki, T.: Efficient Retrieval of Life Log Based on Context to Content. In: 1st ACM Workshop on Continuous Archival and Retrieval of Personal Experiences, pp. 22–31. ACM Press, New York (2004)
14. Rui, Y., Zhou, S.X., Huang, T.S.: Efficient Access to Video Content in a Unified Framework. In: IEEE International Conference on Multimedia Computing and Systems, vol. 2, pp. 735–740. IEEE Computer Society, Los Alamitos (1999)
15. Zimmerman, J., Dimitrova, N., Agnihotri, L., Janevski, A., Nikolovska, L.: Interface Design for MyInfo: A Personal News Demonstrator Combining Web and TV Content. In: IFIP TC13 International Conference on Human-Computer Interaction (INTERACT), pp. 41–48. IOS Press, Amsterdam (2003)
16. Smeulders, A.W.M., Worring, M., Santini, S., Gupta, A., Jain, R.: Content-Based Image Retrieval at the End of the Early Years. IEEE Transactions on Pattern Analysis and Machine Intelligence 22(12), 1349–1380 (2000)
17. Simon, H.A.: Comments. In: Sydnor Clark, M., Fiske, S.T. (eds.) Affect and Cognition, pp. 333–342. Erlbaum, Hillsdale (1982)

18. Gomez, P., Danuser, B.: Affective and Physiological Responses to Environmental Noises and Music. International Journal of Psychophysiology 53(2), 91–103 (2004)
19. Cacioppo, J.T., Berntson, G.G., Klein, D.J., Poehlmann, K.M.: The Psychophysiology of Emotion Across the Lifespan. Annual Review of Gerontology and Geriatrics 17, 27–74 (1997)
20. Carlson, N.R.: Psychology of Behaviour. Allyn and Bacon, Boston (2001)
21. Philippot, P., Chapelle, C., Blairy, S.: Respiratory Feedback in the Generation of Emotion. Cognition & Emotion 16(5), 605–627 (2002)
22. Brown, W.A., Corriveau, D.P., Monti, P.M.: Anger Arousal by a Motion Picture: A Methodological Note. American Journal of Psychiatry 134, 930–931 (1977)
23. Detenber, B.H., Simons, R.F., Bennett, G.: Roll 'Em!: The Effects of Picture Motion on Emotional Responses. Journal of Broadcasting & Electronic Media 42(1), 113–127 (1998)
24. Lang, A., Bolls, P., Potter, R., Kawahara, K.: The effects of Production Pacing and Arousing Content on the Information Processing of Television Messages. Journal of Broadcasting and Electronic Media 43(4), 451–476 (1999)
25. Agius, H., Crockford, C., Money, A.G.: Emotion and Multimedia Content. In: Furht, B. (ed.) Encyclopedia of Multimedia, pp. 222–223. Springer, New York (2006)
26. McIntyre, G., Göcke, R.: The Composite Sensing of Affect. In: Peter, C., Beale, R. (eds.) Affect and Emotion in Human-Computer Interaction. LNCS, vol. 4868. Springer, Heidelberg (2008)
27. van Reekum, C., Johnstone, T., Banse, R., Etter, A., Wehrle, T., Scherer, K.R.: Psychophysiological Responses to Appraisal Dimensions in a Computer Game. Cognition and Emotion 18(5), 663–688 (2004)
28. Loviscach, J., Oswald, D.: In the Mood: Tagging Music with Affects. In: Peter, C., Beale, R. (eds.) Affect and Emotion in Human-Computer Interaction. LNCS, vol. 4868. Springer, Heidelberg (2008)

Acoustic Emotion Recognition for Affective Computer Gaming

Christian Jones[1] and Jamie Sutherland[2]

[1] University of the Sunshine Coast, Queensland, 4558 Australia
cmjones@usc.edu.au
[2] Heriot-Watt University, Edinburgh, EH14 4AS, United Kingdom

Abstract. Computer games are becoming visually realistic, and coupled with more violent storylines and characters there is concern among parents and parts of the media that violent games could encourage aggressive behaviour in those who play them. There have been links made between a number of murders and the violent games played by the murderers. To stimulate other emotions in game players we have developed an emotionally responsive computer game. Based on a traditionally aggressive role-playing environment, we have removed the violent elements and replaced with a goal to navigate obstacles using both positive and negative emotions. Affective cues in the speech of the player are analysed automatically using an emotion recognition system and these affect the physical and behavioural attributes of the gaming character. The character is better able to overcome obstacles based on the emotional state of the player.

Keywords: Affective computing, Emotion recognition, Computer games.

1 Introduction

Violence in computer games has been criticised by parents and lobby groups who believe that violent games can invoke violent behaviour. The Grand Theft Auto series developed by Rockstar North has been criticised in the US where the games has been blamed for killings by youngsters shooting at passing cars. Activision's Doom was linked to the Columbine high school shootings. The prosecution of 17 year old Warren Leblanc for the murder of 14 year old Stefan Pakerrah in February 2004 reinvigorated the debate of possible association between violent behaviour and violence in computer games.

The depiction of violence in games has become more extreme over recent years. Today all games developers can create highly realistic and believable visuals using lighting and sound effects seen in the film industry. It can appear that developers are turning to more violent scenarios and game play in order to differentiate their game from others. However there are more ways to engage with game players than simply more extreme violence, and there are many more emotions that games could stimulate rather than feelings of anger, rage and aggression [1].

This paper reports on a feasibility study to invoke different emotions (rather than anger) from game players and automatically recognising these emotions using affective cues in the speech of the player. Characters in the game can then respond to the game player's emotional state.

C. Peter and R. Beale (Eds.): Affect and Emotion in HCI, LNCS 4868, pp. 209–219, 2008.

2 Emotionally Responsive Computer Game

The new emotionally responsive computer game is built on the traditional first person shooter game Half-Life developed by Sierra Entertainment for the PC. Half-life places the player in the role of Gordon Freeman a research associate in a decommissioned missile base of a top secret project. Here the player must fight off a range of inhuman monsters and government assassins in the attempt to escape the base. The games contains the common elements of a shooter game including a range of weapons, violent creatures which must be killed and levels which have to be navigated. Modifying the Half-life game using software development kits we have been able to eliminate the need for aggression to fight and kill and replace this with other human emotions such as happiness and sadness. We have developed a new world for Gordon Freeman where the player must navigate levels using not only mouse and keyboard controls but also emotional feelings. These emotional feelings are recognised from affective cues in the speech of the player and which similarly alter the behavioural characteristics of Gordon Freeman in the game. For example, if the game player is happy then Dr. Freeman's behaviour in the game is more energetic whereas if the game player is bored Dr. Freeman becomes slow and lethargic. Dr. Freeman's behaviour in the game affects the ease at which the game player can complete the level. The paper reports on work to develop the speech-based emotion recognition system to determine the player emotional state together with initial developments and testing of the emotionally responsive computer game.

3 Acoustic Emotion Recognition

There is continued research interest in detecting and recognising human emotions automatically [2], [3]. Emotional information can be obtained by tracking facial motion, gestures and body language using image capture and processing; monitoring physiological changes using biometric measurements; and also analysing the acoustic cues contained in speech [4]. Sony has had significant success with the EyeToy for the PlayStation 2. Essentially a webcam, EyeToy allows computer game developers to create games which can be controlled by head and arms movement using image capture and processing techniques. However EyeToy suits small-scale games such as heading a ball and swatting flies rather than large-scale multiplayer virtual worlds. Instead, game platforms such as Sony's PlayStation 2 and Microsoft's X-box have *live* versions and PC's have microphones and soundcards allowing easy access to the speech of game players without the need for additional hardware. This project makes use of voice-based affective cues to determine the emotional state of the game player.

We have developed an acoustic emotion recognition system to recognise emotion in human speech. The system is speaker independent and utterance independent, ignoring the content of speech and instead calculating acoustic cues representative of emotion.

The system is based on Banse and Scherer's research into the vocal portrayal of emotion [5]. We were able to confirm their findings which associate acoustic cues of pitch, intonation, rate of speech and volume to emotion in speech, however the range and number of emotions in their study is limited. We have extended the Banse and Scherer study to consider a larger range of acoustic features and sixteen emotional categories including subtle and extreme emotion of hot anger (extreme anger), cold anger (frustration), interest (upbeat), despair, disgust, happiness, boredom, surprise, sadness, grief, troubled, excitement, fear, love, sexy and natural.

3.1 Acoustic Features for Human Emotion

The system can currently calculate 40 acoustic features including pitch, intonation, gain, spectral energies, speaking rates, voicing ratios and pronunciation affects. Using statistical analysis we then define an optimal sub-set of acoustic features which are speaker and utterance independent whilst representative of the required emotions. Depending on the range, number and type of emotions to be recognised, the optimum number of acoustic features can vary. If emotions are acostically similar (e.g. sadness and boredom), or a larger number of emotions must be recognised, we require additional acoustic features to distinguish between the emotional categories. For our research studies we have coupled similar subtle and extreme emotions together to form emotional groups. For example, to recognise 5 emotional groups of happiness, surprise, sadness/grief, hot anger/cold anger, and boredom needs 10 acoustic features, whilst to recognise 3 emotional groups of natural/sadness/grief, happiness/surprise, and hot anger/cold anger requires only 7 acoustic features.

3.2 Compilation and Validation of the Emotional Speech Databases

The calculated acoustic features are processed using neutral network classification algorithms to provide the emotion recognition result. These are trained in supervised mode using example emotive speech. We have compiled 4 emotional speech databases using different collection methods including voice actors reading scripts; drama actors playing out emotive scenarios; scripted emotional conversations between every-day people on mobile phones; and real-life recordings of emotive conversations obtained from call centres and mobile operators. All recordings are in English and contain both native and non-native English speakers. The databases include both North American and British speech. The speech recognition system ignores the words spoken and therefore offers approximate emotion recognition for other non-English speech. An online version of the 5 emotional group system has been used by many non-English speakers including German, Italian, and Chinese users, and trialed by French and Spanish telecommunications companies. The system can easily be retrained to recognise emotion in the other languages by compiling language specific emotional samples.

The emotion speech database for voice and drama actors, and scripted conversations, contain fixed and context-independent utterances, both emotionally independent (e.g. 'Yes') and dependent (e.g. surprise – 'Wow I've won a prize'). The fixed utterances contain data phrase examples from Liberman et al emotive database (e.g. 'April fifthteeth' and 'two thousand two') [6] as well as new fixed utterances aligned to our applications (e.g. 'Good morning', 'Can I set up a meeting'). The utterances also vary in length from single words (e.g. 'No', Really') to longer multi-sentence utterances. The context-independent utterances are generated by requesting participants to provide information about themselves (e.g. 'Tell me where you lived as a child up to present day?').

The voice actors were recorded in a professional audio studio at 48kHz, 16bit stereo using high quality condenser microphones. The drama actors were recorded in a drama studio using 16kHz, 16bit mono and performance dynamic directional microphones. The scripted every day conversations and commercial recordings were recorded on voice servers at 8kHz, 16bit from speakers on mobile phones. Our research shows that higher quality recordings provide more acoustic resolution allowing better discrimination between emotions, however are not practical for commercial settings. Additionally, voice actors tend to over emphasis the presentation of emotion which can improve acoustic recognition in the studio but create emotion models which are not representative of the general population and every day speech. Instead the emotion recognition systems are trained on emotional speech compiled from the scripted mobile phone conversations and tested on the real-life commercial recordings.

All recordings are manually segmented by the research team into separate speech files and labeled with an utterance and emotion file tag. These speech files are analysed by human evaluators in a blind listener study to determine those samples representative of each emotion. The human evaluators are researchers in the team and have at least 3 years experience working in acoustic affective computing. They are presented with unlabelled emotional speech samples in a randomized order and must rate each recording for emotional category and confidence of classification, which are then averaged across all listeners. We then create sub-corpus of emotional speech from each database containing i) samples which were recognised correctly and with 100% confidence level, ii) samples which were recognised correctly and with 75% confidence level, and iii) samples which were recognised correctly but with 50% confidence level. By including more, or less, samples with lower confidence levels increases the amount of data on which to train the classifiers and also provides wider variation of emotional portrayal to support greater speaker variability.

3.3 Recognition Performance of the System

Using a test set of previously unseen emotive speech, the overall performance of the emotion recognition system is greater than 70% for five emotional groups: boredom, sadness/grief, frustration/extreme anger, and happiness and surprise; over 80% for four emotional groups: natural, sadness/grief, frustration/extreme anger, and happiness/surprise; and over 90% for three emotional groups: natural/sadness/grief, frustration/extreme anger, and happiness/surprise.

The emotion recogniser can track changes in emotional state over time and present its emotion decisions as a numerical indicator of the degree of emotional cues present in the speech, Table 1.

Table 1. Emotion tracking using acoustic emotion recognition. Output is numerical and results returned every 2 seconds with a one second overlapping window for example.wav.

Segment start/end (secs)	0 – 2	1 – 3	2 – 4	3 – 5	4 – 6	5 – 7	6 - 8
Boredom	0.0000	0.0000	0.0000	0.0000	0.0000	0.0000	0.0000
Happiness	0.0000	0.0000	0.9997	0.0000	0.0000	0.0000	0.0000
Surprise	0.0000	0.0779	0.0000	0.0000	1.0000	0.7566	1.0000
Cold/Hot anger	1.0000	0.9540	1.0000	0.0000	0.0000	0.0000	0.0000
Sadness/Grief	0.0000	0.0000	0.0000	1.0000	0.0000	0.0000	0.0000

Additionally the information can be displayed graphically, Fig. 1. The frequency of recognition can easily be altered to offer results every second or for longer time intervals, with overlapping windows to smooth recognition outputs.

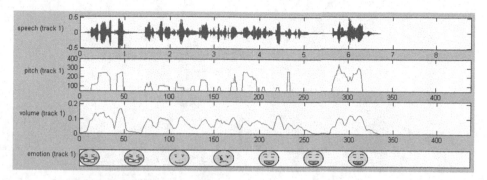

Fig. 1. Graphical output of acoustic emotion recognition showing speech waveform, pitch track, volume, and representation of emotional classification for *example.wav*

4 The Emotive Computer Game Project

The aim of a player in the new emotional responsive computer game is to help Gordon Freeman to escape from a prison. There are traditional obstacles hindering the escape such as damaged bridges, high ravines, cliffs with small ledges, minefields etc., Fig. 2. The player must guide the character through the level using traditional control devices such as keyboard and mouse control. However whether the character can overcome an obstacle depends not only on player's dexterity but also the emotion the player portrays. Thus in order to jump over the large ravine from one cliff to another the player must portray an upbeat, energetic emotional state. Conversely, it is easier for the character to slowly walk along a narrow pipe if the player portrays and downbeat, sad emotion.

During the game the player requests the character to listen by pressing a key on the keyboard. The player can then speak to the character and the speech is recorded. The game does not recognise what is said but instead recognises the emotion portrayed from affective cues using the emotion recognition system. The character then adopts the same emotional state and behaviour as portrayed by the game player. For this initial study of emotional gaming we have considered two emotional states of upbeat and downbeat. We map the 7 emotions from the emotion recognition system into these two states such that upbeat includes happiness, surprise, frustration and anger, and downbeat contains boredom, sadness and grief. We wish to consider more positive emotions of happiness than have traditionally been associated with first person shooter games however have included frustration and anger in the upbeat state for completion. In the future we could create an additional behavioural state for anger or ignore anger completely thus promoting the use of other emotions.

The game recognises the emotion portrayed in the speech of the player and alters the physical and behavioural characteristics of Gordon Freeman. These characteristics then affect the way the character can overcome obstacles in the level. The association between player emotion and character behaviour is presented in Table 2 and Fig. 3.

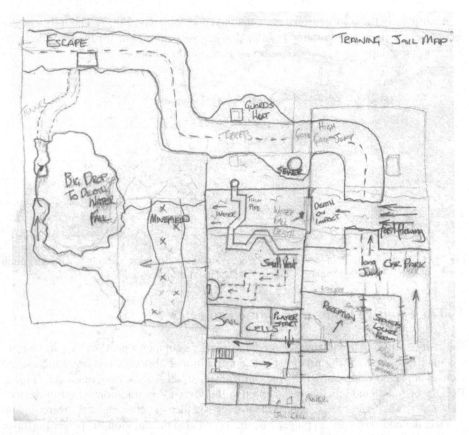

Fig. 2. Level map of obstacles and escape route for emotional responsive computer game

Table 2. Link between player emotional cues and physical and behaviour attributes

Emotion	Physical attributes	Behavioural attributes	Gaming advantages
Upbeat (happy, surprise, frustration, anger)	Larger	Faster	Can jump higher, longer and move faster
Downbeat (sadness, grief, boredom)	Smaller	Slower	Fit through small gaps, walk slowly and carefully

The first person view height is adjusted depending on emotional state. The viewing height is the height from the ground which the view camera sits at. This is altered to give the impression that the character height level has changed, Fig. 4. When moving from upbeat to downbeat the game player has the sensation that they are getting smaller by lowering the first person view height.

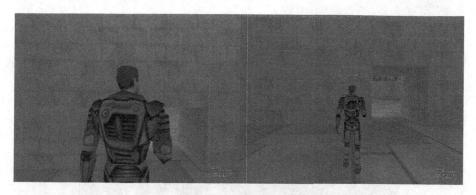

Fig. 3. Large and small in-game physical stages. Note the hole in the wall is the same size in the left and right screenshots however the player character size is large (left) and small (right).

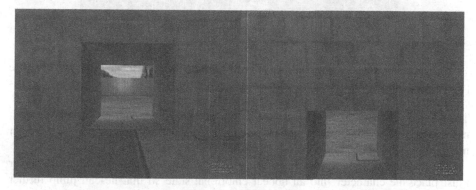

Fig. 4. First person view height for small character (left) and large character (right)

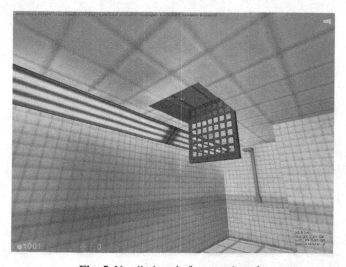

Fig. 5. Ventilation shaft game obstacle

Fig. 6. Thin pipe game obstacle

The game commences with the player realising that they are locked in a jail cell. The player must portray an upbeat emotion in their voice in order that Gordon Freeman becomes upbeat, more energetic and able to jump high into the ventilation system, Fig. 5. The second obstacle is a narrow walk along a winding pipe, Fig. 6. The player must make Gordon Freeman downbeat by portraying a downbeat emotion so that the character moves more slowly and is more easily controllable along the pipe.

The third obstacle is a drawbridge over a fast following river in which the player must place the character into an upbeat emotional state so that he can jump further and able to clear the gap, Fig. 7. The fourth obstacle is a minefield where Dr. Freeman

Fig. 7. Broken bridge game obstacle

Fig. 8. Minefield game obstacle

must be in a downbeat state to be able to walk slowly through the maze of mines without detonating them, Fig. 8. The level continues through a series of obstacles each requiring an emotional response by the player in order to select the emotional behaviour in the game character.

5   Evaluation of the Emotive Computer Game

The emotive computer game is evaluated using user trials. 10 computer game players aged 16 to 24 and experienced with first-person shooter games are given a short demonstration of the speech interface and the affect of the emotion in their voice (the player emotion) on the physical and behavioural attributes of the game character. Each player then commences the level in the cell and must navigate the character to freedom. The players do not have access to the level map however are familiar with the type of obstacles and gaming environment. The participants are timed to reach the end goal, recording when and where the player invokes changes in the emotional behaviour of the character, any occasions when the player feels the game has not correctly recognised their emotional state, recording the speech of the player (to validate the emotion recognition system performance), and counting the number of times the character perished. Death of the game character results in a 1 second delay and then reinstates the character at the end of the last obstacle accomplished.

The results show that the system is capable of recognising the emotion portrayed by the player adequately. The minimum number of emotional state changes required to complete the level starting from the sad state is eight. The game players averaged eighteen attempts at changing state when testing out different strategies to complete the map. On average the number of errors in the detection of the emotion of the player by the game is four (e.g. the observer considered the player to sound happy but the software detected the emotion as sad). Therefore a correct decision is made 78% of the time. Those occasions when the player must repeat the speech due to erroneous recognition appears not to frustrate the player or hinder the game play, however users suggest that it would be unacceptable for more frequent errors when attempting to complete a full length computer game.

Results from user questionnaires show that the game players believe the emotionally interactive computer game is novel and interesting and can help to engage the player in the story and characters. The mappings of emotion to character behaviour and physical attributes were learned quickly and were easily remembered by the gamers with the player having greater speed and size in the happy state, and less size and speed for the sad state. However there was some concern regarding potential repetition in the game play if the player has only two emotional states and repeatedly has to switch from one to another to overcome obstacles. In response we wish to increase the number and range of emotions which are detected from the player and the range of physical and behavioural attributes of the gaming character. More control and more subtle control using different emotions will eliminate repetition and allow players to control the character more naturally using emotion.

Furthermore, the players suggest that the ability to scale the character physics and bahaviour proportionally to the degree of the emotion expressed would provide more subtle game play. Also modifying the level such that selecting the 'wrong' state only hinders the ability to overcome the obstacle rather than completely blocking the path would provide more freedom and flexibility in how to complete the game.

Although feedback shows that the game players enjoyed the emotional interaction with the game and agreed that emotion recognition technologies can enhance gaming, half of those who took part in the study reported that they felt uncomfortable talking to the game simply in order to change the characters emotional state. They suggested that emotional interaction could be used more naturally in multiplayer gaming where the technology could recognise the reactions of the player to events such as being shot at, or collecting a good item in the game. In addition the players suggest that they would feel more comfortable interacting with other characters in the game both computer controlled avatars and other player characters.

All participants reported that they would like to see anger used in the game as an individual physical and behavioural characteristic. Furthermore, half of the players wanting a fear element included and a quarter would like to have frustration and extreme anger separated and the game play to respond differently for each. A consideration of this initial research was to develop an emotional game without the more traditional aggressive and violent game play. However our findings suggest that game players want to be able to interact with their games using their full range of emotional states including anger and aggression.

6 Future Research

The project will address the desire of game players for an extended range of emotional states to be recognised by the game and develop physical and behavioural responses of the game characters to these new emotions such that the game does not become repetitive. We wish to extend the study to consider additional uses of emotion recognition for computer games. These include automatically controlling the expressions of game characters in multiple player roll-playing environments thereby allowing players to know the emotional state of each other; allowing players to interact with game characters emotionally so that game characters respond with different information depending on the way the player talks to them; and creating acting games where the player must use emotion to act out scripts with a director awarding points on how well they perform. Building emotional interaction into computer games may provide a new genre of game play which is not wholly reliant on aggression and violence but instead rewards positive feelings and emotional interaction. However as we see currently within the computer game community the desire for violence and aggression may result in emotion recognition technologies becoming integrated into the next generation of games and used in the main to recognise anger and frustration.

Acknowledgments. We thank Affective Media Limited [www.affectivemedia.com] for their assistance in compiling the emotional speech databases and in the development and testing of the acoustic emotion recognition systems.

References

1. Freeman, D.: Creating Emotion in Games. New Riders Publishing (2004)
2. Cowie, R., et al.: Emotion Recognition in Human-Computer Interaction. IEEE Signal Processing Magazine, 32–80 (January 2001)
3. Picard, R.W.: Affective Computing. MIT Press, Cambridge (1997)
4. The Humaine Portal.: Research on Emotion and Human-Machine Interaction (2004), http://www.emotion-research.net/
5. Banse, R., Scherer, K.R.: Acoustic Profiles in Vocal Emotion Expression. Journal of Personality and Social Psychology 70, 614–636 (1996)
6. Liberman, M., et al.: Emotional Prosody Speech and Transcripts, Linguistic Data Consortium, Philadelphia (2002)

In the Mood:
Tagging Music with Affects

Jörn Loviscach and David Oswald

Hochschule Bremen, Fachbereich Elektrotechnik und Informatik,
28199 Bremen, Germany
jlovisca@informatik.hs-bremen.de, david.oswald@hs-bremen.de

Abstract. Music and mood carry a strong relationship, which is employed very effectively by classical music, Hollywood's soundtracks, and pop bands. Affective computing can provide support in selecting music that fits to a given mood. We describe a system that addresses a full range of functionality. It allows the user to semi-automatically tag music with mood descriptions, determines mood from sensors or from the state of a computer game, and plays appropriate music.

Keywords: Music information retrieval, playlists, MP3 tags.

1 Introduction

We present a system that supports a complete workflow from mood tagging to music selection and playback, see Fig. 1. We envision that the basic functions of such a system may become part of future operating systems in the same way as color management and force-feedback functionality have in the past:

- Request: Music can be requested through biosensors, from correspondingly instrumented games, or by manual selection.
- Play: Music from a repository is compiled into static or dynamic playlists.
- Tag: To guide music selection, mood tags are created and stored for a repository of audio files in MP3 format. These tags are partially set by the user, but can also be estimated from acoustic features.

This system combines and extends features that have been presented in isolation. Already in 1998, Healey, Picard and Dabek [1] used skin conductance in their "Affective DJ." The XPod of Dornbush et al. [2] employs the BodyMedia SenseWear armband plus other data such as time of day, genre, and musical tempo as input to a neural network that estimates whether the user will skip the current song. Chung's "Affective Remixer" [3] records the galvanic skin response and the foot tapping. It plays back prepared music clips, targeting a prescribed mood. Meyer's "mySoundTrack" [4] guesses the mood from a text snippet and then generates a playlist. In June 2007, Sony-Ericsson have introduced mobile phones with a "SenseMe" function that displays songs as dots in a

C. Peter and R. Beale (Eds.): Affect and Emotion in HCI, LNCS 4868, pp. 220–228, 2008.

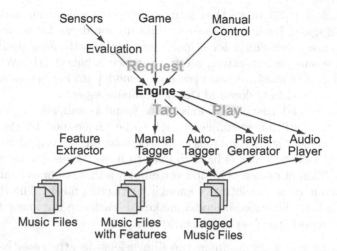

Fig. 1. The central engine of our system helps the user to tag the music files; it accepts queries concerning certain moods and controls a music player appropriately

2D space spanned by the poles happy, sad, fast and slow, based on an automated analysis.

Measuring physiological and motion data, Wijanda et al. [5] employ music as feedback for physical exercising, an idea that has also been picked up by Oliver and Flores-Mangas [6]. Reddy and Mascia [7] present a context engine that reacts to location, time, environment, and the user's motion; Corthaut et al. [8] employ a huge body of metadata to select music for a given atmosphere. Livingstone and Brown [9] propose rules to control music from game-state information. They map two-dimensional emotion descriptions to musical terms such as staccato or minor. On the side of emotion detection in music, Yang et al. [10] introduce fuzzy classifiers; Mandel et al. [11] employ active learning on a support vector machine. On top of that, novel ways to sort and select music have been described: Knees et al. [12] create playlists by placing similar songs next to each other; Andric and Xech [13] organize music in an imaginary 2D space according to rhythm, harmonics, and loudness.

2   Data Model

To process moods on a computer requires a data model. After researching into existing models we decided to develop a proprietary mood model for our needs. A good model balances expressivity and ease of use: It offers enough complexity to describe and tag music appropriately; at the same time it is comprehensible.

The concept of "basic emotions" is broadly discussed in psychology, see e. g. Ortonly and Turner [14]. However, we found it to be wanting for music. For instance, Kalinnen [15] shows that in most listener's ears music cannot depict surprise or disgust. Both are, however, typical candidates for basic emotions. Many works use a two-dimensional model of emotion with axes similar to negative/positive and passive/active, see for instance Schubert [16]. Whereas this has been applied to music, in our view such a model quickly deteriorates to the axes happy/sad and fast/slow and thus loses many aspects.

Models with an additional third axis can be found as well, offering the required complexity while still being simple enough to be understood by the user. The conventional choice for the third axis is "power/control," see e. g. Mehrabian [17]. But we found that this axis is hard to map to music. Thus, we developed and tested three different models. The first two employ a three-dimensional approach; both turned out to be not intuitive enough for tagging music. The third model is based on a high-dimensional model, making it easier to tag music but harder to visualize "mood space" as a geometric entity.

Model 1 is based on the common two dimensions negative/positive and passive/active; they are extended by a third axis specifying a time orientation: backward such as triumph or forward such as fear, see Fig. 2. This is independent of the first two axes, but employs a rather abstract concept. The basic idea seemed to be promising, but we could not find appropriate terms for a number of xyz triples in this 3D space. If there is no commonly agreed term for a position, it probably does not map to a meaningful mood.

Model 2 tries to overcome these shortcomings with four different z-axes. It comprises the same first two dimensions as the first model, but augments them by an additional dimension that depends on the first two dimensions. For instance,

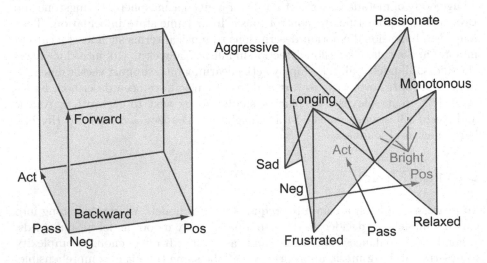

Fig. 2. Model 1 (left) is based on a standard three-dimensional approach with x denoting **neg**ative/**pos**itive and y denoting **pass**ive/**act**ive. Model 2, however, employs four different z-axes with soft transitions.

a passive negative mood can be either "frustrated" or "longing." Correspondingly, the z-axis changes depending on the user's selection on the first two axes. Nonetheless, this system can be mapped to 3D space as well, see Fig. 2. To form continuous transitions between the four regions in xy, the size of the z-axes shrinks to zero at the region borders. This, however, makes it harder to compute and understand geometric distances between songs.

The two models were tested to examine how well the geometric distances map to the listener's mental model of moods. Users were presented two songs with strongly different mood coordinates. Then a third song with mood coordinates located between the first two songs was presented. The user had to decide if the third song is closer to the first or the second. In our results we did not find any significant difference of the models in this respect. However, most of the users reported difficulties in finding representative music for some of the terms such as "pleasant anticipation": Even though model 2 does not contain large regions that lack a corresponding term in everyday language, it still seems to contain more points than can be represented by actual music.

Model 3 which was eventually implemented, employs a multidimensional model using antonymous pairs of terms. The idea leading to this model was the following: An optimal model would be one that allows describing music and moods with the same set of terms. This way, mapping musical parameters to moods would be easy and would feel natural to users.

We started by collecting terms to describe both music and mood, basing our discussion on a collection of terms used in the literature. After a process of adding, replacing and reorganizing, we ended up with the following pairs: lively/calm, happy/sad, peaceful/aggressive, light/heavy, funny/serious, emotional/sober, and diverse/monotonous. These span a seven-dimensional space, which may be presented to the user through a set of seven slider controls.

3   Tagging

To include a music file in the automatic selection process, the system requires a description of the mood that this file represents. Such a "tag" can be attached manually by setting seven sliders, see Fig. 3. After the user clicks on a slider or drags it, a diagram displays the overall distribution in the music repository's corresponding dimension. Every song is represented by a dot, with more data displayed on demand as a tooltip. To never overlap, the dots are stacked in the vertical direction.

Tagging every song by hand would be impractical. Thus, we implemented a system for automatic tagging based on feature-extraction methods from content-based music information retrieval. This automatic tagging serves as a starting point for the user's own adjustments: As previous studies [18] have shown, high granularity—as required by our seven-dimensional model—leads to only vague automatic detection results.

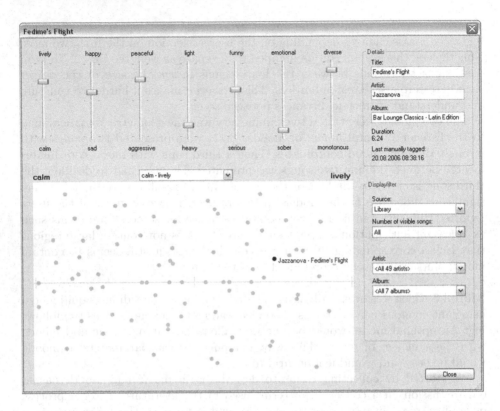

Fig. 3. To facilitate manual tagging, the data of other files are displayed as a reference

The feature extraction determines a set of eight typical spectral envelopes by first computing twelve mel-frequency cepstral coefficients (MFCCs, see [19]) per audio frame (23 ms duration) and then forming twelve clusters from these coefficients. Every one of the eight largest of these clusters (i. e., typical spectral envelopes) is represented by its twelve-dimensional centroid. To also capture rhythmic properties, an apparent beat-per-minute (BPM) number is computed from a power analysis in the range of 40 to 400 BPM.

To generate tags automatically, the system looks at the feature vectors of an untagged song and the feature vectors of all manually tagged songs. To compute the tag of the former song, the tags of the latter songs are blended using weights that decay with distance in feature space. The extracted features are stored in a proprietary ID3 tag inside the MP3 files. The mood tags, however, vary from user to user and need to be queried quickly. Thus, they are stored in a database.

4   Music Selection

The system offers four playback modes that use mood data in the player software: sensor, game, proximity, and chain.

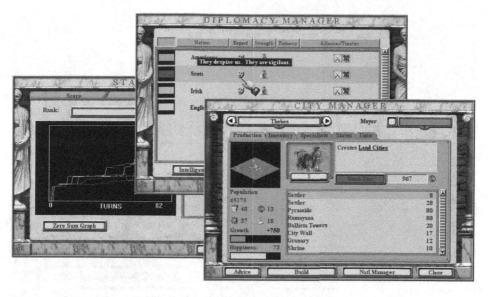

Fig. 4. The "game mode" is based on rules that translate the statistics of Activision Call to Power II into mood coordinates

Sensor mode. This mode selects music that corresponds to the user's current mood. To this end, we employ inexpensive, off-the-shelf hardware—a system that cannot match the sophistication of the one of Peter et al. [20]. Five physiological signals are measured:

- The galvanic skin response is recorded as the electrical conductance between the user's index and middle finger.
- The temperature of the skin is measured through a temperature-dependent resistor such as used in digital thermometers.
- The heart rate is captured by placing an infrared light-emitting diode and a photometer chip on either side of a finger to detect the oscillation in light absorption. Signal processing adapts to the strong temporal drift.
- The breath rate and volume are determined from the noise pattern the exhalation causes in a microphone mounted below the user's nose.

A microphone connected to the computer's audio input records the breath signal. The other sensors are attached to a standard computer mouse; their signals are fed into a low-cost USB-based analog-to-digital converter. The raw sensor data are converted to mood data by a neural network, which the user has to train in advance. At any time, the user may override the result of the automatic conversion of sensor data to mood data. The mood data will be taken into account to select the upcoming song; the user may skip the current song.

Game mode. A game on the same or another computer sends requests via Internet Protocol that control the mood of the music to be played. These are taken into account when the current song ends or may be enforced immediately

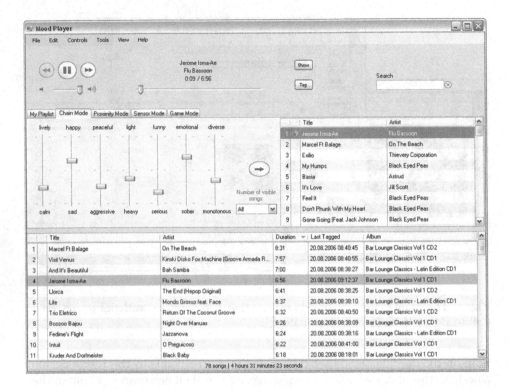

Fig. 5. The main user interface displays standard playback controls, mood controls (here in chain mode), the generated playlist, and the music repository

for an abrupt change, for instance to accompany a sudden threat. Nonetheless, we chose the round-based strategy game Activision Call to Power II, see Fig. 4, as opposed to, for instance, a first-person shooter to focus on gradual processes instead of quick changes. Converting the game's statistics to mood values was straightforward. For instance, the number of military units in action is mapped to the dimension lively/calm; the happiness of the citizens, a value directly available from the game, is mapped to the dimension happy/sad.

Proximity mode. The user selects a song or adjusts seven mood sliders to set a mood. This will form the "center" of the generated playlist. The songs that lie within a given similarity radius are sorted by their distance to the center. This way, the mood oscillates about the center, comparable to a spiral motion.

Chain mode. Te user selects a song or a mood to start with. The player software now looks for the song that is closest to the slider setting, see Fig. 5. The next song in the playlist will be the one which is closest to its predecessor and so on until all songs in the library have been played once. After some time the mood will have drifted away from the initial setting. If the user prefers a different mood, he or she can readjust the mood sliders at any time.

5   Conclusion and Outlook

We presented an integrated system for automatic music selection based on mood. Prototypes of the hardware and software have been created. Currently we are tuning the parameters for the feature extraction and for the evaluation of the sensors. As the work by Lichtenstein et al. [21] shows, valence and arousal can be determined to a good degree through sensors. Whether such data suffice to measure the parameters of our more fine-grained mood model is still an open question. Preliminary user tests have been conducted on the mood data models; further user tests of the complete system remain to be done.

Future extensions of the system include creating a playlist along a user-specified trajectory through mood space as well as a port to iPodLinux. On top of that, mood metadata may be learned from the sensor data during everyday music listening, in a spirit similar to the CUEBA approach [22]. We hope that not only strong "chill" events as examined by Nagel et al. [23] are detectable by the sensors. Other aspects yet to be explored in our system are mood control and the feedback loop formed by the sensors, the music selection and its effect on the user's mood, as has been proposed by Livingston et al. [24].

References

1. Healey, J., Picard, R., Dabek, F.: A new affect-perceiving interface and its application to personalized music selection. In: Proc. of PUI 1998 (1998)
2. Dornbush, S., Fisher, K., McKay, K., Prikhodko, A., Segall, Z.: Xpod – a human activity and emotion aware music player. In: Proc. of the International Conference on Mobile Technology, Applications and Systems, pp. 1–6 (2005)
3. Chung, J.-W., Vercoe, G.S.: The affective remixer: personalized music arranging. In: CHI 2006 Extended Abstracts, pp. 393–398 (2006)
4. Meyers, O.: mySoundTrack: A commonsense playlist generator (2005), http://web.media.mit.edu/~meyers/mysoundtrack.html
5. Wijnalda, G., Pauws, S., Vignoli, F., Stuckenschmidt, H.: A personalized music system for motivation in sport performance. IEEE Pervasive Computing 04(3), 26–32 (2005)
6. Oliver, N., Flores-Mangas, F.: MPTrain: a mobile, music and physiology-based personal trainer. In: Proc. of MobileHCI 2006, pp. 21–28 (2006)
7. Reddy, S., Mascia, J.: Lifetrak: Music in tune with your life. In: Proc. of HCM 2006, pp. 25–34 (2006)
8. Corthaut, N., Govaerts, S., Duval, E.: Moody tunes: The Rockanango project. In: Proc. of ISMIR 2006, pp. 308–313 (2006)
9. Livingstone, S.R., Brown, A.R.: Dynamic response: real-time adaptation for music emotion. In: Proc. of IE 2005, pp. 105–111 (2005)
10. Yang, Y.-H., Liu, C.-C., Chen, H.H.: Music emotion classification: a fuzzy approach. In: Proc. of MULTIMEDIA 2006, pp. 81–84 (2006)
11. Mandel, M.I., Poliner, G.E., Ellis, D.P.W.: Support vector machine active learning for music retrieval. Multimedia Systems 12(1), 3–13 (2006)
12. Knees, P., Pohle, T., Schedl, M., Widmer, G.: Combining audio-based similarity with web-based data to accelerate automatic music playlist generation. In: Proc. of MIR 2006, pp. 147–154 (2006)

13. Andric, A., Xech, P.L., Fantasia, A.: Music mood wheel: Improving browsing experience on digital content through an audio interface. In: Proc. of AXMEDIS 2006, pp. 251–257 (2006)
14. Ortony, A., Turner, T.J.: What's basic about basic emotions? Psychological Review 97, 315–331 (1990)
15. Kalinnen, K.: Emotional ratings of music excerpts in the Western art music repertoire and their self-organization in the Kohonen neural network. Psychology of Music 33(4), 373–379 (2005)
16. Schubert, E.: Measuring emotion continuously: validity and reliability of the two-dimensional emotion-space. Australian J. of Psychology 51(3), 154–156 (1999)
17. Mehrabian, A.: Pleasure–arousal–dominance: A general framework for describing and measuring individual differences in temperament. Current Psychology: Developmental, Learning, Personality, Social 14, 261–292 (1996)
18. Li, T., Ogihara, M.: Detecting emotion in music. In: Proc. of ISMIR 2003, pp. 239–240 (2003)
19. Pampalk, E., Dixon, S., Widmer, G.: On the evaluation of perceptual similarity measures for music. In: Proc. of DAFx 2003, pp. 7–12 (2003)
20. Peter, C., Ebert, E., Beikirch, H.: A wearable multi-sensor system for mobile acquisition of emotion-related physiological data. In: Tao, J., Tan, T., Picard, R.W. (eds.) ACII 2005. LNCS, vol. 3784, pp. 691–698. Springer, Heidelberg (2005)
21. Lichtenstein, A., Oehme, A., Kupschick, S., Jürgensohn, T.: Comparing Two Emotion Models for Deriving Affective States from Physiological Data. In: Peter, C., Beale, R. (eds.) Affect and Emotion in Human-Computer Interaction. LNCS, vol. 4868. Springer, Heidelberg (2008)
22. Money, A.G., Agius, H.: Automating the extraction of emotion-related multimedia semantics. In: Workshop on The Role of Emotion in Human-Computer Interaction (2005)
23. Nagel, F., Grewe, O., Kopiez, R., Altenmller, E.: The relationship of psychophysiological responses and self-reported emotions while listening to music. In: Proc. of the 30th Göttingen Neurobiology Conference (2005)
24. Livingstone, S.R., Brown, A.R., Muhlberger, R.: Influencing the perceived emotions of music with intent. In: Proc. of the 3rd International Conference on Generative Systems (2005)

Using Paralinguistic Cues in Speech to Recognise Emotions in Older Car Drivers

Christian Jones[1] and Ing-Marie Jonsson[2]

[1] University of the Sunshine Coast, Queensland, 4558 Australia
cmjones@usc.edu.au
[2] Department of Communication, Stanford University, California 94305, USA
ingmarie@csli.stanford.edu

Abstract. Interactive speech based systems are moving into the car since speech interactions are considered less detrimental to the driver than interactions with a display. The introduction of in-car speech-based interactions highlights the potential influence of linguistic and paralinguistic cues such as emotion. Emotions direct and focus people's attention on objects and situations, and affects performance, judgment and risk-taking. All of these properties are crucial for driving where the smallest slip-up can have grave repercussions. Emotional cues in a car-voice, paired with the emotional state of the driver, have been found to influence driving performance. This initiated the design of an in-car driver emotion detection and response system. Results show that the in-car system can recognise and track changes in the emotional state of the driver. This study considers older drivers who often feel both unsafe and insecure due to concerns about declining abilities and in particular vision.

Keywords: Automotive control, In-car systems, Paralinguistic cues, Affective computing, Emotion recognition, Speech interaction.

1   Introduction

Interactive information systems are rapidly finding their way into the car. Current research and attention theory both suggest that speech-based interactions would be less detrimental to the driver than would interactions with a visual display [1]. Introducing speech-based interaction and conversation into the car highlights the potential influence of linguistic and paralinguistic cues. These cues play a critical role in human—human interactions, manifesting among other things, personality and emotion [2]. The research literature offers a number of definitions of "Emotion", where two generally agreed-upon aspects of emotion stand out [3]: 1) Emotion is a reaction to events deemed relevant to the needs, goals, or concerns of an individual; and, 2) Emotion encompasses physiological, affective, behavioural, and cognitive components. Emotions can be relatively short lived, and when they are sustained they are called *moods*. Just as humans are built to process and produce speech [4], humans are built to process and produce emotion/mood [2].

Emotions direct and focus people's attention on objects and situations that have been appraised as important to current needs and goals. In a voice interface, this

C. Peter and R. Beale (Eds.): Affect and Emotion in HCI, LNCS 4868, pp. 229–240, 2008.

attention- function can be used to alert the user, as by a navigation system's "turn left right now", or it can be distracting, as when users are frustrated by poor voice recognition. Just as emotions can direct users to an interface, emotions can also drive attention *away* from the stimulus eliciting the emotion [5]. For example, if a person becomes angry with a voice recognition system, the user may turn off or actively avoid parts of an interface that rely on voice input. Emotions have been found to affect cognitive style and performance, where even mildly positive feelings can have a profound effect on the flexibility and efficiency of thinking and problem solving [6]. People in a good mood are significantly more successful at solving problems [2]. Emotion also influences judgment and decision making. This suggests, for example, that users in a good mood would likely judge both a voice interface itself, as well as what the interface says, more positively than if they were in a negative or neutral mood. It has also been shown that people in a positive emotional state also accept recommendations and take fewer risks than people in a negative emotional state [7].

Driving presents a context where emotion can have enormous consequences. Attention, performance, and judgment are of paramount importance in automobile operation, with even the smallest disturbance potentially having grave repercussions. There is overwhelming evidence suggesting that older adult drivers may have more difficulty in attending to the driving task than younger drivers, especially when required to make complex decisions [8]. The driving task places significant perceptual and cognitive demands on the driver and the normal aging process negatively affects many of the perceptual, cognitive and motor skills necessary for safe driving [9]. Older adults are also more easily distracted by irrelevant information than young adults, and thus may direct their attention to the wrong place and miss cues indicating potential hazardous situations [10].

Older drivers often feel both unsafe and insecure as drivers. This is to a large extent due to observations and concerns about declining abilities and in particular vision [11]. There is also a strong link between age, visual task load, stimulus location and reaction time to unexpected stimuli. Reaction times are longer for older drivers, and reaction times in general are longer for roadside stimuli than for stimuli in the middle of the road [12]. Common causes and dangerous risk factors for older adult drivers include:

- Failure to maintain proper speed.
- Improper left turns.
- Failure to yield right-of-way.
- Confusion in heavy traffic.
- Hesitation in responding to new traffic signs, signals, road markings.
- Hesitation in responding to different traffic patterns and roadway designs.

Previous studies show that alerting young drivers to hazards in the road results in a more cautious and safer driving [13]. An in-car voice system was used to give the drivers relevant and timely road information, and thereby providing extra time and distance for them to evaluate the driving situation. A similar in-car voice system designed for older adults with car-voice prompts that compensate for memory loss suggesting actions that have not been remembered i.e. speed limits; prompts that provided contextually relevant advice i.e. road conditions; and prompts that provided warnings in safety critical situations, showed the same benefits as for younger drivers, that is improved driving performance [13]. Emotion of the car-voice impacts driving performance, results from a study using a car-voice system where the emotion of the car-voice and the emotion of the driver were matched or miss-matched showed that matched emotions positively impacted driving performance [14]. These results make it interesting to investigate the feasibility of designing the emotionally responsive car.

2 The Emotionally Responsive Car

The development of an emotionally responsive car involves a number of technically demanding stages. In practise, the driver and car will converse two-way, where each will listen and respond to the others request for information and their emotional well-being. However for the purpose of outlining implementation stages of the emotionally intelligent car we present the conversation linearly and as two technical streams: informational response and emotional response.

Firstly the driver will make a verbal request to the car. The car must recognise what is said using automatic speech recognition (ASR). The car must possess facilities for natural language processing (NLP) in order to determine the message within the speech and then perform the instruction whether that be a satellite navigation request; mobile phone call; control of the in-car multimedia system; in-car climate control; or request for nearest petrol station, service station, hotel, car park etc. The car must then generate the required response using grammatical structure and vocalise the response using text to speech (TTS) synthesis.

Recognising, understanding, information retrieval, response generation and the verbal response are only one stream of the intelligent car. The emotional state of the driver has been shown to affect driving performance and incidence of accidents [13]. However as yet emotional intelligence is not built into the control and safety features of the car. Emotional empathy is key for human conversation and by omitting emotional information from any voice-control system prevents that system from achieving natural and social human-computer interaction.

The proposed emotionally responsive car will recognise the emotional state of the driver using automatic, acoustic emotion recognition (ER). The emotion recognition tracks acoustic features in the speech of the driver to determine and track their emotion. Having knowledge of the emotion of the driver enables the car to modify its response both in the words it uses but also the presentation of the message by stressing particular words in the message and speaking in an appropriate emotional state. By the car altering its 'standard' voice response, it will be able to empathise with the driver and ultimately improve the wellbeing and driving performance.

This paper is focused on the novel emotionally responsive part of the in-car system. In particular the paper reports on our research to develop the acoustic emotion recognition part of the project and test the technology within the car environment.

3 Recognising Driver Emotions

There is considerable research interest into detecting and recognising human emotions automatically [15]. Emotional information can be obtained from a car driver by tracking facial motion, gestures and body language using image capture and processing; monitoring physiological changes using biometric measurements of Galvanic Skin Response,

Blood Volume Pulse, Respiration and Electromyograms taken from the steering wheel and seat/seat-belt; and also analysing the acoustic cues contained in speech. Although it may only be a matter of time before video cameras and biometric sensors are fitted as standard in cars, speech controlled systems are already commonplace. Voice-controlled satellite navigation, voice-dial mobile phones and voice-controlled multimedia systems exist and drivers are more educated and comfortable with their use. Therefore the project can incorporate voice-based emotion recognition without any requirement of additional hardware or changes to the driver's environment.

The acoustic emotion recognition system used in this project has been trained to recognise a range of emotions including boredom, sadness, grief, frustration, extreme anger, happiness and surprise, from United Kingdom and North American native English speakers. The emotion recognition can track changes in emotional state over time, presenting emotion decisions numerically to represent the degree of emotional cues present in the speech. Details of the acoustic emotion recognition system and the emotive speech data on which it was trained and tested appear in the article 'Acoustic Emotion Recognition for Affective Computer Games'.

For the propose of diagrammatic clarity with the in-car emotion project, the acoustic emotion recognition system outputs a range of emotional faces, including 'not sure' when there is the possibility that the speech exhibits multiple emotions e.g. boredom and sadness, or happiness and surprise; and 'no decision' when no emotion has been detected e.g. neutral / natural emotion, Table 1.

Table 1. Visual representations for emotional categories

Emotional state	Visual representation	Emotional state	Visual representation
Boredom		Surprise	
Sadness and grief		Not sure	
Frustration and extreme anger		No decision	
Happiness			

4 The Emotive Driver Project

The experimental project sets out to test the feasibility of drivers conversing emotionally with the car, and the accuracy and validity of the automatic acoustic emotion recognition system in detecting, recognising and tracking these emotions.

The experiment consisted of a six day study at Oxford Brookes University, UK using 28 participants, 15 male and 13 female. All participants were informed that the experiment would take 45 minutes. All participants volunteered their time for their participation, gave informed consent and were debriefed at the end of the experiment.

The driving simulator consisted of software from STISim, Fig. 1, running on a windows 2000 desktop machine, wheel and pedals from Microsoft and a car seat mounted on a wooden box. All participants experienced the same pre-defined route and properties for both driving conditions and the car. The driving simulator was operated using an accelerator pedal, a brake pedal, and a force-feedback steering wheel, Fig. 2. The drive lasted approximately 30 minutes for each participant.

Fig. 1. Simulator driving software   **Fig. 2.** Simulator driving hardware

Car environment sound effects were played through stereo speakers. These sound effects included engine noise, brake screech, indicators, sirens etc. Verbal information from the car was also played through the speakers. The information present included:

- There is thick fog ahead.
- You are approaching an intersection.
- Warning there is a fallen tree in the road ahead.
- Beware of cyclists ahead.
- The current speed limit is 60 miles an hour.
- There are crosswinds in this area.
- Stop sign ahead.
- The police use radar here, you might need to slow down.
- There is heavy traffic ahead, turn left to avoid it.
- There is an accident ahead, turn right to avoid it.

Participants were not forced to converse with the car but instead told that they could talk back to the car if they wished.

Speech from the participants was recorded using multiple microphone and sampling configurations. These included an Andrea superbeam array microphone placed 40cm to the left of the steering wheel and directed towards the mouth of the driver and recorded directly onto a laptop; an AKG microphone co-located with the Andrea superbeam and recording onto Minidisk (MD); and an Andrea directional bean with 4 microphones placed in front and about 1.5 meters away from the driver and recorded on a Sony Handicam DVD201. All audio recordings were synchronized using an audio marker at the start of the drive. These microphones are typical of those used in the cars of today. Without including noise reduction and cancellation systems, the first two configurations were degraded by significant engine acceleration, brake, indicator, and other car noise. The final configuration of a directional beam Andrea to DVD

Handicam provided the cleanest acoustic recordings without overly sampling the car noise. Thus this final configuration was used by the acoustic emotion recognition system to detect and recognise the emotion of the drivers.

The driving sessions were also videotaped from the front left of the driver to show driver hands, arms, upper body, head and eye motion, and facial expressions. Although this study does not consider image processing as a means to recognise driver emotions the video is used to correlate results from the acoustic emotion recognition with the emotions displayed in the faces of the drivers.

Using the recorded speech the project aims to answer three questions:

- Do older drivers converse with the car when the car is providing information and instructions?
- Can acoustic emotion recognition detect and recognise the emotions of older drivers?
- Can acoustic emotion recognition track the older driver emotions so as to respond emotionally and with empathy?

5 Results

Of the 28 participants we consider a subset of 18 older drivers to perform the emotional older driver study. These drivers are both male and female and range in age from 57 to 73.

5.1 Do Older Drivers Converse with the Car When the Car Is Providing Information and Instructions?

The participants were not encouraged to converse with the car but were told that they could talk if they wished. The result was that around half of the participants spoke back to the car and the other half remained silent through the drive. Of those that spoke, some responded only when the car spoke to them and then only to say 'Thank you'. However 4 of the older participants conversed freely and extensively with the car and it is these 4 drivers which are considered in greater detail.

The in-car system was instructional rather than conversational, providing information rather than requesting it from the driver. Consequently the car does not provide significant opportunity for the driver to establish dialog. By considering alternative discursive messages from the car we will be able to provide more opportunities for the driver to respond, and respond more freely.

5.2 Can Acoustic Emotion Recognition Detect and Recognise the Emotions of Older Drivers?

To ascertain whether the emotion recognition system can detect and recognise older driver emotions, this paper considers the 4 older drivers who conversed freely with the car. The participants exhibit a range of emotions including boredom, sadness, anger, happiness and surprise, however for most of the drive the participants have a neutral/natural emotional state. When challenged in the drive by obstacles in the road, other drivers, difficult road conditions and pedestrians, we observe strong emotions from the drivers. During these emotional events the acoustic emotion recognition system must detect and recognise the emotional state of the driver.

By listening to the speech recording only, a human labeler transcribes the drive, including not only the words of the conversation but also the emotional state of the driver. The human labeler is not shown the video recording of the drive and is therefore not aware of the driving situations associated with the driver speech. Also the human labeler is unaware of the output classifications of the automatic emotion recognition system. The same driver speech recording was processed by the acoustic emotion recognition system and its output classification represented as emotive faces for each second of the drive. The performance of the automatic emotion recognition system was determined by comparing the human emotion transcript against the output from the recognition system. The comparative study is presented for each emotive segment from the 4 talkative older drivers. Only parts of the complete transcript and emotional classifications are included for conciseness.

Driver: Female, age 73
Speech recording: 29 minutes of speech, during which there is one crash. The driver is talkative, offering opinions and a commentary throughout the drive.

Emotive event 1: The driver is warned by the car of heavy traffic ahead and advised to turn left to avoid it. Carrying out this manoeuvre she has a problem with the steering wheel and becomes emotive. Whilst the passenger explains what has happened her emotion can be seen to be detected as frustration. There is also laughter during the conversation which is detected as happiness, Fig. 3.

T: Help the steering wheel work loose my left turn that crashed tree <laugh>

Fig. 3. Transcription (T), human emotion recognition (H) and automated emotion recog (A)

Emotive event 2: The driver has been warned of slow moving vehicles and is stuck behind one which is in the outside lane. She observers a near-miss and comments on the other cars undertaking the slow traffic, Fig. 4.

T: Something's coming the other way   Ooh   everybody else is going on the inside

Fig. 4. Transcription (T), human emotion recognition (H) and automated emotion recog (A)

Driver: Female, age 69
Speech recording: 28 minutes of speech, during which there are two crashes. The driver is talkative, responding to the car and offering opinions. She appears to be quite a nervous driver (of the simulator).

Emotive event 1: The driver has been warned of an accident ahead and is instructed to turn right to avoid it. In doing so she cuts in front of another car then complains that she can't see the other traffic and doesn't know how to work the simulator, Fig. 5.

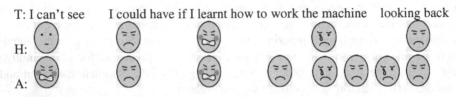

Fig. 5. Transcription (T), human emotion recognition (H) and automated emotion recog (A)

Driver: Male, age 58
Speech recording: 30 minutes of speech, during which there are no crashes. The driver is talkative and for much of the track his speech appears to be natural. The driver appears to be enjoying the simulation, and is confident both in his driving and in the use of the simulator.

Emotive event 1: The driver has been warned of heavy traffic and is advised to turn left to avoid it. In doing so, he becomes frustrated by other drivers shouting at them to hurry up and change, Fig. 6.

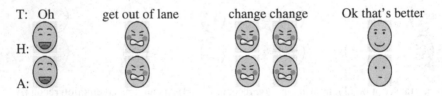

Fig. 6. Transcription (T), human emotion recognition (H) and automated emotion recog (A)

Emotive event 2: The driver starts to whistle. This is an 'upbeat' song and is detected as surprise. He then becomes genuinely surprised by something and brakes, Fig. 7.

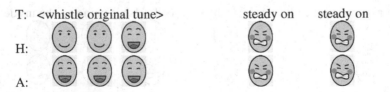

Fig. 7. Transcription (T), human emotion recognition (H) and automated emotion recog (A)

Emotive event 3: The driver was warned by the system that the road is very slippery. He agrees and encourages himself to keep calm, Fig. 8.

Fig. 8. Transcription (T), human emotion recognition (H) and automated emotion recog (A)

Emotive event 4: The driver is warned of a stop sign ahead, and while looking for it starts humming 'Strangers in the night'. This is detected by the acoustic emotion recognition system as sadness. The human listeners also considered the driver to be in a sad/negative mood whilst singing. The driver then notices actions of another driver and becomes frustrated by actions of some 'bloody kids!', Fig. 9.

Fig. 9. Transcription (T), human emotion recognition (H) and automated emotion recog (A)

There is a strong correlation between the emotional transcript created by the human listener and the emotion output returned automatically by the acoustic emotion recognition system. It is more difficult to objectively measure the performance of the emotion recognition system with driver speech as there are occasions where the speech is masked by car noise (such as engine, brakes etc) and times when the driver could be one of two emotions such bored or sad, happiness or surprised. In these cases it is inappropriate to say that the acoustic emotion recognition system is erroneous, rather the human listener could also be confused in classifying the emotion. Considering these limitations in the ability to objectively measure performance, we considered a second by second comparison between the human listener and the automated emotion recognition system for emotionally distinct events, and which provides a performance accuracy of greater than 70% for the 7 emotion categories.

The current range of emotions detected (boredom, sadness, grief, frustration, anger, happiness, and surprise) may not be the optimal range of emotions required for the emotionally responsive car. If the car doesn't need to recognise the difference between boredom and sadness and instead detect 'downbeat' (human listeners also have problems deciding between boredom and sadness) then the performance accuracy of the emotion recognition system can be further improved.

5.3 Can Acoustic Emotion Recognition Track the Older Driver Emotions So as to Respond Emotionally and with Empathy?

The automatic recognition system can recognise and classify emotion for every second of speech (seen in the emotion plots). This creates an emotion track showing the mood of the driver throughout their drive. Additionally, the emotion recognition system can output the emotion classification numerically showing the level of presence of emotion every second. In this way the granularity of recognition is appropriate for the car to be able to track and respond to the driver's emotion. In a driver-car conversation, the car would be able to follow the conversation, continuously monitoring the changing emotion of the driver and thus respond reflectively to the driver's mood. The car could modify its synthesized words for its response together with placements of stresses and emotional cues.

6 Discussion

Considerable amounts of time and money are spent by car manufacturers on improving car safety. These include installation of anti-locking brakes, adaptive steering system, air bags, parking sensors as well as many in-car warning indicators. All of these systems have required comprehensive, lengthy and costly design stages.

Although research into voice-based car interfacing is relatively immature by comparison, it has been shown that simple, inexpensive and fully controllable aspects of a car interface can also have a significant impact on driver safety. It is well known that upset drivers perform much worse on the road than happier drivers [7]. Changing the paralinguistic characteristics of the in-car voice is sufficient to have a dramatic impact on driving performance [14]. Furthermore, the number of accidents and the drivers' attention to the road can be strongly influenced by the voice of the car. However it has been found that there is not one effective voice for happy and sad drivers. Upset drivers benefit from a subdued in-car voice while happy drivers benefit from an energetic in-car voice. This suggests that the car must adapt its voice to the driver.

In order for the car to modify its voice so as to respond to the emotion of the driver and thus improve their driving, the car must first be able to assess the driver's mood. Emotion recognition could be achieved from tracking facial expressions using in-car cameras and image processing, monitoring driver physiological changes from sensors in the steering wheel, and voice analysis from driver-car conversations. As the car industry already uses voice-controlled systems in their cars it is sensible to consider voice emotion recognition as an inexpensive addition to safety.

The project has reported on the application of an in-house acoustic emotion recognition system for the recognition and tracking of driver emotion for older participants using a driving simulator. We have been able to conclude that there is sufficient accuracy and granularity of emotion recognition to enable an emotionally intelligent in-car voice to adapt to the mood of the driver.

7 Extensions of the Research

In the current research the in-car system provided instructions and did not encourage conversation. A number of the participants did not converse with the car and thus we were unable to ascertain their emotional state acoustically. We envisage the in-car system to not only provide information but also request information from the driver as to their desired course of action. This will encourage conversation and enable the acoustic emotion recognition to gain insight into the mood of the driver.

Once the car knows the emotional state of the driver how should it adapt? Previous studies have considered varying the paralinguistic cues only [7], however should the content of the response also change, and how? Should the car become less or more talkative depending on the mood of the driver? Should the car alter the telematics, climate, music in the car in response the mood of the driver?

Further research should consider the affect of altering the car response and car environment to driver emotion. One strategy is to exhibit empathy by changing the emotion of the car-voice to match the user. Empathy fosters relationship development, as it communicates support, caring, and concern for the welfare of another. A voice which expresses happiness in situations where the user is happy and sounds subdued or sad in situations where the user is upset would strongly increase the connection between the user and the voice [16].

How fast should the emotion of voice change? Although rapid response to predicted emotion of the user can be effective, there are a number of dangers in this approach. Emotions can change in seconds in the human brain and body [17]. A sad person may momentarily be happy if someone tells a joke, but will fall back into their sad state relatively quickly. Conversely, happy drivers may become frustrated as they must slam on the brakes for a yellow light, but their emotion may quickly switch back to feeling positively. If the voice in the car immediately adapted to the user's emotions, drivers would experience occurrences such as the car-voice changing its emotion in mid-sentence. This would dramatically increase cognitive load [18], constantly activate new emotions in the driver and be perceived as psychotic. This might be entertaining when performed by manic comedians like Robin William, but an in-car voice would quickly be marked as manic-depressive instead of empathetic!

Mood must be taken into account to make the car-voice an effective interaction partner. Moods tend to bias feelings and cognition over longer terms, and while moods can be influenced by emotions, they are more stable and effectively filter events. A person in a good mood tends to view everything in a positive light, while a person in a bad mood does the opposite. Drivers that are in a good mood when entering a car are more likely to experience positive emotion during an interaction with a car-voice than drivers in a bad mood. It would therefore seem that emotion in technology-based voices must balance responsiveness and inertia by orienting to both emotion and mood.

Humans are what they feel: Performance, knowledge, beliefs, and feelings are to a large extent determined by emotions. People are also influences by voice interactions with people and interfaces. This makes it important for designers of speech based systems to work with linguistic and para-linguistic cues, especially emotional cues, to create the desired effect when people interact with the system.

References

1. Lunenfeld, H.: Human Factor Considerations of Motorist Navigation and Information Systems. In: Proc. of Vehicle Navigation and Information Systems, pp. 35–42 (1989)
2. Strayer, D., Johnston, W.: Driven to Distraction: Dual-Task Studies of Simulated Driving and Conversing on a Cellular Telephone. Psychological Science 12, 462–466 (2001)

3. Brave, S., Nass, C.: Emotion in Human-Computer Interaction. In: Jacko, J., Sears, A. (eds.) Handbook of Human-Computer Interaction, pp. 251–271. Lawrence Erlbaum Associates, Mahwah (2002)
4. Pinker, S.: The Language Instinct. W. Morrow and Company, New York (1994)
5. Gross, J.J.: Antecedent- and Response-Focused Emotion Regulation: Divergent Consequences for Experience, Expression, and Physiology. Journal of Personality and Social Psychology 74, 224–237 (1998)
6. Hirt, E.R., Melton, R.J., McDonald, H.E., Harackiewicz, J.M.: Processing Goals, Task Interest, and the Mood-Performance Relationship: A Mediational Analysis. Journal of Personality and Social Psychology 71, 245–261 (1996)
7. Isen, A.M.: Positive Affect and Decision Making. In: Lewis, M., Haviland-Jones, J.M. (eds.) Handbook of Emotions, pp. 417–435. The Guilford Press, New York (2000)
8. McGehee, D., Lee, J., Rizzo, M., Bateman, K.: Examination of Older Driver Steering Adaptation on a High Performance Driving Simulator. In: Proceedings of International Driving Symposium on Human Factors in Driver Assessment, Training, and Vehicle Design (2001)
9. Nemoto, H., Yanagishima, T., Taguchi, M.: Effect of Physical Changes in Aging on Driving Performance, Nissan Research Center, Vehicle Research Laboratory. In: Proceeding of First International Driving Symposium on Human Factors in Driver Assessment, Training and Vehicle Design, pp. 131–136 (2001)
10. Ponds, R., Brouwer, W., van Wolffelaar, P.: Age Differences in Divided Attention in a Simulated Driving Task. Journal of Gerontology 43, 151–156 (1988)
11. Johansson, K.: Older Automobile Drivers: Medical Aspects, Doctoral Dissertation, Karolinska Institutet, Stockholm (1997)
12. Owens, J., Lehman., R.: The Effects of Age and Distraction on Reaction Time in a Driving Simulator. Journal of Vision 2(7), 632a (2002)
13. Nass, C., Jonsson, I.-M., Harris, H., Reaves, B., Endo, J., Brave, S., Takayama, L.: Improving Automotive Safety by Pairing Driver Emotion and Car Voice Emotion. In: CHI 2005 Extended Abstracts on Human factors in Computing Systems, Portland, USA, pp. 1973–1976 (2005)
14. Jones, C.M., Jonsson, I.-M.: Performance Analysis of Acoustic Emotion Recognition for In-Car Conversational Interfaces. In: Proceedings of HCI International, Beijing, China (2007)
15. Cowie, R., Douglas-Cowie, E., Tsapatsoulis, N., Votsis, G., Kollias, S., Fellenz, W., Taylor, J.: Emotion Recognition in Human-Computer Interaction. IEEE Signal Processing Magazine, 32–80 (January 2001)
16. Brave, S.: Agents that Care: Investigating the Effects of Orientation of Emotion Exhibited by an Embodied Computer Agent. Doctoral Dissertation. Communication. Stanford University, Stanford, CA (2003)
17. Picard, R.W.: Affective Computing. MIT Press, Cambridge (1997)
18. Mullennix, J.W., Bihon, T., Bricklemyer, J., Gaston, J., Keener, J.M.: Effects of Variation in Emotional Tone of Voice on Speech Perception. Language and Speech 45, 228–255 (2002)

Author Index

Printed in the United States
By Bookmasters

Printed in the United States
By Bookmasters